T0214681

Communications
in Computer and Information Science 987

Commenced Publication in 2007
Founding and Former Series Editors:
Phoebe Chen, Alfredo Cuzzocrea, Xiaoyong Du, Orhun Kara, Ting Liu,
Dominik Ślęzak, and Xiaokang Yang

Editorial Board

More information about this series at http://www.springer.com/series/7899

Ignazio Mauro Mirto · Mario Monteleone
Max Silberztein (Eds.)

Formalizing Natural Languages with NooJ 2018 and Its Natural Language Processing Applications

12th International Conference, NooJ 2018
Palermo, Italy, June 20–22, 2018
Revised Selected Papers

 Springer

Editors
Ignazio Mauro Mirto
University of Palermo
Palermo, Italy

Max Silberztein
Université de Franche-Comté
Besancon, France

Mario Monteleone
University of Salerno
Fisciano, Italy

ISSN 1865-0929 ISSN 1865-0937 (electronic)
Communications in Computer and Information Science
ISBN 978-3-030-10867-0 ISBN 978-3-030-10868-7 (eBook)
https://doi.org/10.1007/978-3-030-10868-7

Library of Congress Control Number: 2018965614

This Springer imprint is published by the registered company Springer Nature Switzerland AG
The registered company address is: Gewerbestrasse 11, 6330 Cham, Switzerland

Preface

NooJ is a linguistic development environment that provides tools for linguists to construct linguistic resources that formalize a large gamut of linguistic phenomena: typography, orthography, lexicons for simple words, multiword units and discontinuous expressions, inflectional, derivational and agglutinative morphology, local, phrase-structure and dependency grammars, as well as transformational and semantic grammars. For each linguistic phenomenon to be described, NooJ proposes a set of computational formalisms, the power of which ranges from very efficient finite-state automata (that process regular grammars) to very powerful Turing machines (that process unrestricted grammars). NooJ also contains a rich toolbox that allows linguists to construct, maintain, test, debug, accumulate, and share linguistic resources. This makes the approach of NooJ different from most other computational linguistic tools that typically offer a unique formalism to their users, and are not compatible with each other.

NooJ provides parsers that can apply any set of linguistic resources to any corpus of texts, to extract examples or counter-examples, annotate matching sequences, perform statistical analyses, and so on. Because NooJ linguistic resources are neutral, they can also be used by NooJ generators to produce texts. By combining NooJ parsers and generators, one can construct sophisticated NLP (natural language processing) applications such as MT (machine translation) systems, abstracts, and paraphrases generators, etc.

Since its first release in 2002, NooJ has been enhanced with new features to respond to the needs of researchers who need to analyze texts in various domains of human and social sciences (history, literature and political studies, psychology, sociology, etc.), and more generally of all the professionals who analyze texts. In 2013, a new version for NooJ was released, based on the JAVA technology and was made available to all as an open source GPL project and distributed by the European Metashare platform. Several private companies are using the NooJ engine to construct business applications in several domains, from business intelligence to opinion analysis. To date, there are NooJ modules available for over 50 languages; more than 140,000 copies of NooJ have been downloaded.

During this year's conference held in Palermo, all members of the NooJ community paid tribute to the late Morris Salkoff, who, at the LADL Laboratory (Paris), has worked on natural language automatic parsing and on machine translation. By its exhausitivity and its accuracy, Morris Salkoff's French string grammar has been an inspiration for all the researchers who tried to figure out how to use the linguistic resources accumulated by linguists of the LADL laboratory in order to construct NLP software.

This volume contains 20 articles selected from the papers and posters presented at the International NooJ 2018 conference at the Palazzo Comitini in Palermo, Sicily.

In her article "Morris Salkoff: A Life Dedicated to Automatic Syntactic Analysis," Mireille Piot explains how Morris Salkoff came to work on String grammars and other projects in computational linguistics, which have been influencial to the design of the INTEX and thereafter the NooJ software.

The following articles are organized in three parts: "Vocabulary and Morphology" containing seven articles, "Syntax and Semantics" containing six articles, and "Natural Language Processing Applications" containing six articles.

The seven articles in the first part involve the construction of electronic dictionaries and the description of morphological phenomena:

- In his article "An automated French–Quechua Conjugator," Maximiliano Duran presents a bilingual French–Quechua system that aligns conjugations of French and Quechua.
- In "Implementation of Arabic Phonological Rules in NooJ," Rafik Kassmi, Mohammed Mourchid, Abdelaziz Mouloudi, and Samir Mbarki present two implementations for the Arabic phonological system: one by adding a specific module to the NooJ software, the other by formalizing the rules with NooJ's own local grammars.
- In "Arabic Broken Plural Generation Using the Extracted Linguistic Conditions Based on Root and Pattern Approach in the NooJ Platform," Ilham Blanchete, Mohammed Mourchid, Samir Mbarki, and Abdelaziz Mouloudi present an Arabic morphological set of inflectional and derivation rules that can be used to describe Broken Plural for adjectives and gerunds.
- In "Detecting Latin-Based Medical Terminology in Croatian Texts," Kristina Kocijan, Maria Pia di Buono, and Linda Mikić present a set of linguistic resources in the form of dictionaries and morphological grammars that can recognize Latin-based medical terms, even when they are inflected in Croatian.
- In "Processing Croatian Aspectual Derivatives," Krešimir Šojat, Kristina Kocijan, and Matea Filko present a system that can detect unknown verbal forms and connect them to the verbs they are derived from. This system can be used as a teaching tool, and is feeding a database that represents aspectual derivatives of Croatian verbs.
- In "Construction of Morphological Grammars for the Tunisian Dialect," Roua Torjmen and Kais Haddar present the development of a new dictionary and morphological grammars for the Tunisian Arabic dialect.
- In "A Chinese Electronic Dictionary and Its Application in NooJ," Zhen Cai presents the result of over four years of work: a full-coverage Chinese dictionary that contains about 63,000 entries, along with a test corpus of 45,000 characters covering many domains. Finally, Zhen Cai presents a system that can automatically segment any Chinese text.

The six articles in the second part describe the construction of sophisticated syntactic and semantic grammars:

- In "Automatic Extraction of Verbal Phrasemes in the Culinary Field with NooJ," Tong Yang shows how to use NooJ to automatically detect verbal phrasemes of the culinary vocabulary, and its application for language teaching.

– In "Some Considerations Regarding the Adverb in Spanish and Its Automatic Treatment: A Pedagogical Application of the NooJ Platform," Andrea Rodrigo, Silvia Reyes, and Paula Alonso construct a grammar that describes the syntax of Spanish adverbs.

– In "Expansive Simple Arabic Sentence Parsing Using the NooJ Platform," Said Bourahma, Mohammed Mourchid, Samir Mbarki, and Abdelaziz Mouloudi show how they merged grammars for Arabic verbal and nominal sentences in order to cover all Arabic simple sentences, the main difficulty being how to represent syntactic and semantic agreement constraints.

– In "A Construction Grammar Approach in the NooJ Framework: Semantic Analysis of Lexemes Describing Emotions in Croatian," Dario Karl, Božo Bekavac, and Ida Raffaelli show how they could implement a Construction Grammar (CxG) by using new NooJ annotations. They applied the grammar to automatically distinguish the various uses of the Croatian word *strah* (fear).

– In "The lexicon-Grammar of Predicate Nouns with ser de in Port4NooJ," Cristina Mota, Jorge Baptista, and Anabela Barreiro describe the development of the automatic paraphrasing Port4NooJ system by using syntactic and distributional constraints described in lexicon-grammar tables.

– In "Unary Transformations for French Transitive Sentences," Max Silberztein describes the construction of a grammar for French that contains over 100 transformational operations that can be applied to simple direct transitive sentences, either to compute paraphrases automatically, or, reciprocally, to parse a complex sentence and produce its analysis.

The six articles in the last part involve the construction of four software applications: a consistency checker for clinical encoding, an Arabic-to-French machine translation software, a detector of hate speech, and an original use of NooJ in forensic sciences. The last two articles show the NooJ software can be enhanced: one article shows how to improve its parser's efficiency, whereas the last article uses an abstract model to describe NooJ functionalities, which can be used to enhance NooJ in the future.

– In "A Set of NooJ Grammars to Verify Laboratory Data Correctness," Francesca Parisi and Maria Teresa Chiaravalloti present a system that can automatically check the semantic correctness of the encoding of clinical texts.

– In "A Semantico-Syntactic Disambiguation System of Arabic Movement and Speech Verbs and Their Automatic Translation to French Using NooJ," Mariem Essid and Hela Fehri describe an Arabic-to-French Translation system for Arabic movement and speech verbs.

– In "NooJ Grammars and Ethical Algorithms: Tackling On-Line Hate Speech," Mario Monteleone presents an automatic hate-speech recognizer built with specifically developed NooJ dictionaries and grammars.

– In "Pastries or Soaps? A Stylometric Analysis of Leonarda Cianciulli's Manuscript and Other Procedural Documents, with NooJ," Sonia Lay shows an application for NooJ in Forensic Sciences, where it is used to investigate judicial and jurisprudential contexts.

– In "Improvement of the Arabic NooJ Parser Through Disambiguation Rules," Nadia Ghezaiel Hammouda and Kais Haddar show how they spectacularly improved the efficiency of their Arabic syntactic parser, by applying specially designed disambiguation techniques in cascade.

- In "NooJ App Optimization," Zineb Gotti, Samir Mbarki, Naziha Laaz, and Sara Gotti develop a model-driven methodology to analyze NooJ platform's functionalities, using the abstract knowledge discovery model (KDM) that would allow the platform to evolve while gaining efficiency.

This volume should be of interest to all users of the NooJ software because it presents the latest development of its linguistic resources as well as its future enhancements.

Linguists as well as computational linguists who work in Arabic, Chinese, Croatian, French, Italian, Portuguese, Quechua, or Spanish will find advanced, up-to-the-minute linguistic studies for these languages.

We think that the reader will appreciate the importance of this volume, both for the intrinsic value of each linguistic formalization and the underlying methodology, as well as for the potential for developing NLP applications along with linguistic-based corpus processors in the social sciences.

December 2018

Ignazio Mauro Mirto
Mario Monteleone
Max Silberztein

Organization

Organizing Committee

Ignazio Mauro Mirto	University of Palermo, Italy
Luisa Brucale	University of Palermo, Italy
Max Silberztein	Université de Bourgogne Franche-Comté, France
Mario Monteleone	University of Salerno, Italy

Scientific Committee

Max Silberztein (Chair)	Université de Bourgogne Franche-Comté, France
Xavier Blanco	Autonomous University of Barcelona, Spain
Mohammed El Hannach	Sidi Mohammed Ben Abdellah University, Morocco
Héla Fehri	University of Gabes, Tunisia
Yuras Hetsevich	National Academy of Sciences, Belarus
Kristina Kocijan	University of Zagreb, Croatia
Philippe Lambert	Université de Lorraine, France
Denis Le Pesant	Université Paris 10, France
Peter Machonis	Florida International University, USA
Elisabeth Méthais	Conservatoire National des Arts et Métiers, France
Samir Mbarki	Ibn Tofail University, Morocco
Ignazio Mauro Mirto	University of Palermo, Italy
Mario Monteleone	University of Salerno, Italy
Slim Mesfar	University of Manouba, Tunisia
Johanna Monti	University of Naples, Italy
Jan Radimský	University of South Bohemia, Czech Republic
Andrea Rodrigo	University of Rosario, Argentina
François Trouilleux	Université Blaise-Pascal, France

In Memoriam

Morris Salkoff: A Life Dedicated to Automatic Syntactic Analysis

Mireille Piot

Université Grenoble Alpes
piot.canoe@gmail.com

Abstract. Morris Salkoff was a research scientist, first in Physics, and then he collaborated with Naomi Sager at the Linguistic String Project on English in New York University. At the same time and during his entire professional life he worked at the French Institute National Center for Scientific Research in Paris (1958–2012). He elaborated the Linguistic String Project on French at the Ladl (Cnrs) before his works on Harris' transformational Grammar about some English verbal classes, and later his contrastive French English Grammar.

Keywords: Computational linguistics · Automatic syntactic analysis
String grammar · Machine translation

Introduction: About Morris Salkoff

Morris Salkoff was an American linguist, born on April 10, 1928 in New-York City (USA) and died on August 29, 1917 in Paris (France). He spent most of his life working in France in Computational Linguistics. As for his scientific life and activities, we can distinguish six different phases.

Research in Physics

The first phase concerns the domain of Physics and Salkoff's early life and education. In 1951 he obtained a Master of Science (1951), and a PhD in Physics (1958) from the New York University (NYU). Subsequently, he published several papers in The Journal of Chemical Physics [1–4] with Ernest Bauer, who worked at AA (Aeronutronic), a Division of Ford Motor Company, based in Newport Beach, California. From June 2015, the last two papers [3, 4] are now available in a scholar edition, meaning that they are still relevant and studied.

Research in Computer Science

A second phase concerns Computer Science. From 1952 to 1958, Morris Salkoff worked as a Programmer, for NYU and IBM, at the Atomic Energy Commission,

Computing Center New York University, New York City. Besides, from 1954 to 1958, he worked as a as research programmer at the CNRS (Institute National Center for Scientific Research, Institut Blaise Pascal, Paris, France). Subsequently, from 1958 to 1968, he was a research scientist (chargé de recherché) for the same CNRS.

AS for his experience in Paris, it is worth noting that Morris Salkoff was recruited by the director of the Institut Blaise Pascal, the brilliant mathematician René de Possel, for both positions of research programmer and research scientist. René de Possel was one of the founders of the Bourbaki group, the famous group of French mathematicians, and actively developed computer facilities, computer science teaching and research. Furthermore, he worked to the achievement of a universal optical character recognition system (Mounier-Kuhn, 1989). The Institut Blaise-Pascal was divided into several independent teams, involved in developing research in computer sciences. One of these teams was the Department of Automatic Documentation, founded by the archaeologist Jean-Claude Gardin, before 1969, therefore before the creation of the LADL (Laboratoire d'Automatique Documentaire et Linguistique) by Maurice Gross.

Research in Computational Linguistics

During those years, Morris Salkoff also developed a genuine interest in human language. This led him to the University of Pennsylvania, where he became one of Zelig Harris's students, among many others, like Naomi Sager, Richard Kittredge, Lila Gleitman, Carlotta Smith, Hadj Ross, Noam Chomsky, and so on. There, at the University of Philadelphia, in 1946, Harris founded the first USA department of Linguistics, and trained generations of young linguists.

Shortly after, Morris Salkoff worked as a research scientist at the New York University (1963–1967), joining Naomi Sager and James Morris in the "Linguistic String Project". This project was under Sager's leadership, and Naomi Sager herself had set up the team of linguists. It was officially launched by the NYU in 1965, but it lasted from 1963 to 1970. It was intended to develop a natural language parsing software, or better, a set of computer methods usable to access information in the scientific and technical literature, based on linguistic principles. In particular, the team drew on Zellig Harris's discourse analysis methodology to develop a system for computer analysis of the natural language. Several papers written by Morris Salkoff with Naomi Sager [5–7] describe the aim, scope and results of this project as it was applied to the English language.

At any rate, even during this period, Morris Salkof never abandoned his work in Paris as a research scientist at the Institute Blaise Pascal.

La grammaire en chaîne du français (1968–1980)

Subsequently, Morris Salkoff joined Maurice Gross' team at the LADL. However, he did not take part in the research for the creation of the French Lexicon-Grammar, but he started working on his own project, which was: *La grammaire en chaîne du français*, the String Grammar of French, based on the same linguistic principles and methodology as those developed by the NYU team on English. He worked on this project first with the young French linguists Anne Zribi Hertz, André Valli and Jean-Marie Marandin. Subsequently, after a technical report [8], he published two books [9, 10]. In 1975, he also wrote his *Thèse d'Etat dès Lettres* and in 1976 he became Directeur de recherches of the CNRS.

His first book [9] presents the beginnings of the distributional analysis and the major constituents of the sentences in French, in order to analyze scientific discourse. His second book [10] extends this analysis of French to some more complicated problems as sentential conjunction, and so on.

Later, on the same theme, he supervised the thesis of a young computer linguist [11] who had been focusing idioms automatic processing.

Syntax Ambiguity and Linguistic Productivity in Verbal Constructions (1980–2004)

He further developed his expertise and capacities in other issues such as linguistic productivity and syntactic ambiguity. Many of his various papers were actually dedicated to investigate verbal classes and the resulting definition and classification problems.

The first one [12] described the so-called phrase-internal argument alternations for verbs of the locative type (the swarm group). A second one [13] focused on sentences like "Max elbowed his way through the crowd", which had not been yet studied in detail. In this book, Morris Salkoff undertook a systematic investigation to show that the verbs governing such sentences have a large lexical extension.

Besides, a paper written in 1990 [14] concerns the automatic translation of English support verbs. Another paper [15] is a summary of a longer investigation of the so-called psychological verbs, which had been studied thoroughly in the literature. Morris Salkoff defined that a psych verb is a verb that selects a subject complement clause of the kind "That S", and a human noun (Nh) as its object.

Finally, other two papers [16, 17] described syntactic and semantic problems solved without elaborating an independent semantic component.

The English Darwin Project (Cora-Sinequa, 1988–2005)

He at the same time worked as consultant in field for two IT French Companies: Cora and then Sinequa, which elaborated The DARWIN Project, establishing automatic indexing of lexical entries on newspapers, based on linguistic principles, first for French, and then for English, the version of which was elaborated by Morris Salkoff.

A French English Machine Translation Project (1999–2012)

Subsequently, his research path led him to tackle problems regarding translation, especially those occurring between English and French. During his last years of activity, he wrote three books to expose his main interest, based on the results he achieved in the context of a machine translation project. This project is presented in [18], as follows:

> *"M. S. adopts a rule-based MT approach in which rules are written in the form of a string grammar, as defined by Harris (1962). The RBMT system developed by Salkoff relies on two linguistic modules: a French string grammar which contains a list of structures of the French language; a translation module which contains the list of comparative schema in English".*

In [19] Morris Salkoff exemplifies this project: the comparisons between French structures and their English equivalents are formulated as rules that associate a French schema (of a particular grammatical structure) with its translation into an equivalent English schema. This grammar contains all the rules which produce the English equivalents under translation of the principal grammatical structures of French: the verb phrase, the noun phrase and the adjuncts (modifiers). In addition to its intrinsic linguistic interest, this comparative grammar represents a useful application for translation technique teaching. Furthermore, such a comparative grammar represents a necessary preliminary phase to any program of machine translation. Another but unavailable book [20] describes the same principles.

Morris Salkoff's last book [21] is devoted to the important French verb *pouvoir* (can, may, have to) and to the difficulties of translating its multiple uses into English. It focuses on the explanations of how its translation depends both on the subject and on the object occurring in the source sentences. Besides, the variation of its tenses, when occurring, will also be useful in the translation of new sentences in which *pouvoir* selects other different subjects and objects. This book also represents a valuable tool for languages teaching and learning

Another example of translation difficulties and solutions appears in [22], a book in which Morris Salkoff presents several fascinating cases arising from his systematic study of French-English translation patterns. For instance, there are cases in which the two languages present a semantic contrast that is in rough correspondence, such as the French *être en train de* and the English progressive be V-ing. If *Max est en train de comprendre le problème* (Max is beginning to understand the problem) is an acceptable and grammatical French sentence, the same cannot be said for the English equivalent *?Max is understanding the problem. A similar case happens with the English sentence I am loving it, which cannot be translated in French as *?Je suis en train de l'aimer.*

LEXVALF

His last work [23] was written in collaboration with André Valli, a former PhD student of his [24]. The topic coped with is the creation of a French verbal database, that is LEXVALF, available at the Aix-Marseille University, in France, and at [25]. As showed in [23], for several years Morris Salkoff and André Valli had been constructing a complete dictionary of French verbal complementation, using the already available dictionaries, the tables of verbal constructions made at LADL, and in a large measure, the database available at Google.fr. The LEXVALF issue of November 2011 contains one thousand verbs together, which at present have become many more, as André Valli is still working on.

Conclusion

As a scholar and a researcher, Morris Salkoff's life has been longly and an entirely devoted to natural language processing and the many different aspects it brings along. However, his main research concerns focused both on the teaching of translation to human speakers of different languages (he also had these concerns of transmission, which went beyond simple research) and on the improvement of machine translation performance. In this fields, the contribution given by Morris Salkoff has been very important, both qualitatively and quantitatively. Still it remains in many ways unexplored. The wish that we can make to the computational linguists and translators of the future is to deepen it thoroughly, and use it as a starting point for the goals yet to achieve.

References

1. Kraemer, U.A.F., van Overveld, C.W.A.M., Peterson, M.B.: Is there an ethics of algorithms? Ethics Inf. Technol. **13**(3), 251–260 (2011). http://dx.doi.org/10.1007/s10676-010-9233-7
2. Salkoff, M., Bauer, E.J.: Chem. Phys. 29, 26, (also Research Rept. CX-31 (1957)). Institute of Mathematical Sciences, New York University, Scitation, CAS (1958). https://doi.org/JCPSA6
3. Salkoff, M., Bauer, E.J.: Chem. Phys. **30**, 1614, Scitation, CAS (1959). https://doi.org/JCPSA6
4. Salkoff, M., Bauer, E.J.: Three-body recombination of oxygen atoms. J. Chem. Phys. **33**, 1202 (1960). http://doi.org/10.1063/1.1731357
5. Salkoff, M., Bauer, E.J.: Excitation of molecular vibration by collision. Res. Rept. CX-31 Institute of Mathematical Sciences, New York University (1960)
6. Sager, N., Salkoff, M., Morris, J., Raze, F.C.: Report on the String Analysis Programs. Introductory Volume. String Program Reports (SPR), no. 1. Linguistic String Project, New York University & University of Pennsylvania (1966)
7. Salkoff, M., Sager, N.: The elimination of grammatical restrictions in a string grammar of English. In: 2ème Conférence Internationale sur le Traitement Automatique des Langues, August 1967, Grenoble, Theoretical paper: Relation of string analysis to context-free grammar (1967)
8. Salkoff, M., Sager, N.: Grammatical Restrictions in the IPL V and FAP String Programs, New York University Linguistic String Project, New York University (1969)
9. Salkoff, M., Zribi-Hertz, A.: La lexicographie pour une grammaire en chaînes du français, Université de Paris-7 : L.A.D.L. (ERA n° 247 du CNRS) (1974)
10. Salkoff, M.: Une grammaire en chaine du français: analyse distributionnelle. Monographies de Linguistique Mathématique (1973)
11. Salkoff, M.: Analyse syntaxique du Français: Grammaire en chaîne. Lingvisticae Investigationes Supplementa (1980)
12. Pellegrini, P.: Ecriture d'un analyseur syntaxique du français basé sur une grammaire en chaine. Ph.D. thesis, University of Paris 7 (1994)
13. Salkoff, M.: Bees are swarming in the garden. Language **59**(1983), 288–346 (1980)
14. Salkoff, M.: Analysis by Fusion, Lingvisticae Investigationes, 12 (1988)
15. Salkoff, M.: Automatic translation of support verb constructions. In: COLING 1990, pp. 243–246 (1990)

16. Salkoff, M.: Verbs of mental states. In: Leclère, Ch., Laporte, É., Piot, M., Silberztein, M. (eds.) Lexique, Syntaxe et Lexique-Grammaire. Papers in Honour of Maurice Gross, Amsterdam/Philadelphia: Benjamins, vol. 24, pp. 561–571. Lingvisticae Investigationes Supplementa (2004)

17. Salkoff, M.: Syntactic analysis and semantic processing. Revue Québécoise de Linguistique, **14**(2), 49–63 (1985)

18. Salkoff, M.: A study of ambiguity using INTEX. Linguisticae Investigationes, **22** (1998/1999)

19. Monti, J.: Multi-word Unit Processing in Machine Translation, Ph.D. thesis, University of Salerno, Italy (2012)

20. Salkoff, M.: A French English Grammar: A contrastive grammar on translational principles. Linguisticae Investigationes Supplementa (1999)

21. Salkoff, M.: Loquatur! A program for LOw QUality Automatic Translation of Unrestricted Range, EME (2007)

22. Salkoff, M.: Pouvoir and his Pitfalls. In: Berlinski, D. (ed.) Copyright M. Salkoff. Printed in the USA (2012)

23. Salkoff, M.: Some new results on transfer grammar. In: Nevin, Br., (Ed.) The Legacy of Zellig Harris: Language and information into the 21st century, vol. 1, Philosophy of science, syntax and semantics, Philadelphia, John Benjamins (2002)

24. Salkoff, M., Valli, A.: A dictionary of french verbal complementation. In: 22nd Language & Technology Conference (LTC 05), In Memory of Maurice Gross and Antonio Zampolli (2005)

25. Valli, A.: Etablissement d'un lexique automatique de verbes français. Ph.D., Université Paris 7 (1980)

26. LexValf. http://lexvalf.lif.univ-mrs.fr/LEXVALF.html

Contents

Natural Language Processing Applications

Vocabulary and Morphology

An Automated French-Quechua Conjugator

Maximiliano Duran(⊠)

UFC Université de Franche-Comté, Besançon, France
duran_maximiliano@yahoo.fr

Abstract. This paper presents the first version of an automated French-Quechua conjugation system of verbs. Using the key structure of Quechua Undefined Tense conjugation and the transformations induced by Interposed suffix IPS sets, I built a complete system of paradigms. I used NooJ linguistic platform to formalize the morpho-syntactic grammar and this serves to automatically obtain the entire set of conjugated forms of transitive, intransitive and impersonal verbs in all tenses, moods, aspects and voices.

Keywords: Quechua · NooJ · Automated conjugator
French-Quechua conjugator · Undefined tense · Simple verbs · Derived verbs
LVF and LVQ dictionaries

1 Introduction

This paper presents the first version of an automated French-Quechua conjugation system of verbs.

This system is expected to play an important role in the different linguistic resources that the research laboratory is developing in the context of the Machine Translation project (MT) for Quechua.

Using the detailed verb grammar described in my PhD thesis [6], I present the key structure of the conjugation of the Undefined Tense in Quechua. In section two, I then describe details of the construction of the formalized morpho-syntactic paradigms and grammar[1] that were built using the NooJ[2] linguistic platform. These paradigms correspond to the different aspects of tenses and moods that constitute the monolingual part of the conjugator and they cover 1,400 Quechua simple verbs [4]. I then present a user interface that shows in detail the entire table of conjugation for all of these verbs.

The second part of the work consisted of obtaining the detailed French conjugated forms of all the corresponding sets of French equivalents contained in our laboratory's enlarged Quechua verb dictionary (FR_QU_V). These derived verbs were taken from the bilingual LVQ French-Quechua dictionary, obtained by Duran [6]. In this manner I was able to isolate 8,735 French verbs. All the verbs can be found in the LVF (Dubois Dubois-Charlier [2] French Verb dictionary[3]).

The LVF dictionary was adapted to NooJ by Silberztein [8] and is now integrated into the NooJ library. Among the ten properties of each entry in LVF_NooJ, we find

---

[1] See (Duran 2013, 2014).
[2] See (Silberztein 2003, 2015).
[3] See (https://modyco.fr/fr/base-documentaire/760-dubois-les-verbes-fran%C3%A7ais-le-livre.html).

© Springer Nature Switzerland AG 2019
I. Mauro Mirto et al. (Eds.): NooJ 2018, CCIS 987, pp. 3–15, 2019.
https://doi.org/10.1007/978-3-030-10868-7_1

the entry's conjugation paradigm. For instance, for the verb 'abaisser', its paradigm is 'CHANTER' and appears as follows:

```
abaisser,V +FLX=CHANTER+AUX=AVOIR+...
```

The inflection of this (FR_QU_V) dictionary, gives us a text file of inflected and annotated verbal forms, including the conjugated forms of any verb. Each entry appears as follows:

```
abaisseras,abaisser,V +QU= "wichqarinki"+Emploi=06
+AUX=AVOIR+FLX=AIMER+T1108+P1000+DERIV=ANT+DERIV=MENT
+DOM=PSYt+CLASS=R2a+OPER="m.e.état mvs qn abs"+BASE=
"baisse" +LEXI=5+N+s+2+s+F
```

The last step consisted of the development of a user interface of the conjugator for the enhanced French-Quechua dictionary of verbs. This conjugator will display a sequence of windows, corresponding to the Quechua conjugated forms of a French verb.

1.1   The Essential Structure of Endings of the Undefined Tense

The structure of endings of the conjugation of the undefined tense[4] plays a fundamental role in the generation of all derived and inflected forms of verbs. It constitutes the basic structure for the generation of the respective sets of endings of all grammatical tenses, moods and aspects[5].

The conjugation of a verb in the undefined tense is detailed in Table 1 which gives the ending structure of the unmarked tense (UT) in the column «Personal ending».

Table 1. Unmarked Tense conjugation

Subject (PRO)	Fr	V lemma	Personal ending
ñuqa	je	lemma	*ni*
qam	tu	lemma	*nki*
pay	il, elle	lemma	*n*
ñuqanchik	nous	lemma	*nchik*

(*continued*)

---

[4] "It is a conjugation where time is not expressed, only the person is" Itier 1997, p. 68. We call it undefined tense because it can simultaneously indicate: **the present**, *rimani* /je parle (I speak); **the accomplished past** *rimani ñaqa*/ j'ai parlé tout à l'heure (I spoke earlier) or **the habitual aspect** *rimani sapa punchaw*/ je parle tous les jours (I speak every day).

[5] For a detailed definition of tense, moods, and aspects in Quechua, see Duran (2017).

Table 1. (*continued*)

Subject (PRO)	Fr	V lemma	Personal ending
ñuqayku	nous excl.	lemma	*niku* (**)
qamkuna	vous	lemma	*nkichik* (*)
paykuna	ils, elles	lemma	*nku*

(*) In the Quechua variant of Cuzco, the suffix "*chik*"
becomes systematically "*chis*" for the first person plural
and for the second person plural: *Ñuqanchis
kanchis* «nous sommes» (we are); *qamkuna
kankichis* «vous êtes» (you are).
(**) In the Quechua variety of Cuzco, the suffix "niku"
corresponds systematically to "yku" for the first exclusive
plural person: *Ñuqayku ka-yku* "nous autres sommes" (we
are).

UT_s (TI-s in French) symbolize the set of these personal endings: UT_s = {*ni,
nki, n, nchik, niku, nkichik, nku*}.

The corresponding NooJ[6] grammar of this conjugation is:

UT = <B>(*ni*/TI+1+s|*nki*/TI+2+s |*n*/TI+3+s |*nchik*/TI+1+pin |*nkichik*/TI+2+p
|*nku*/TI+3+p |*niku*/TI+1+pex);

Or when represented graphically (Fig. 1):

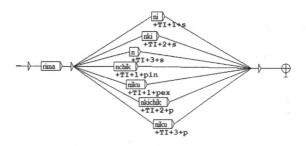

Fig. 1. Conjugation of the verb rima_ in the undefined tense UT.

---

[6] See (Silberztein 2003, 2015).

Applying this paradigm, we obtain the conjugation of the undefined tense of any verb. For instance, for *rimay/*parler (to talk), whose lemma is *rima-*, we will have the following result (Table 2):

Table 2. UT generation of rimay/to talk

Pronoun	UT conjugation	French conjugation
ñuqa	*rimani*	je parle
qam	*rimanki*	tu parles
pay	*riman*	il, elle parle

2   The Monolingual Automated Quechua Conjugator

In order to automatically generate an exhaustive set of conjugated forms of a verb, we need to construct the corresponding paradigms of all the conjugations of a Quechua verb. In order to do this and using the detailed verb grammar described in my PhD thesis [6], I first programmed all the paradigms of the possible conjugations of any transitive, intransitive and impersonal verb. I then attached the corresponding paradigm (as a NooJ grammar) to each of the 1,400 simple verbs of Quechua[7] as a inflexion property. The ". flx" file generated when we inflect this dictionary allows us to obtain a data base, which constitutes the source set for the monolingual automated conjugator we are looking for.

I will now present some detailed algebraic expressions of these formalized morpho-syntactic grammars[8] corresponding to several grammatical tenses.

2.1   Conjugation of the Future Tense

The following grammar describes the conjugation of the future tense for a transitive Quechua verb:

$$F = <B>(saq/F+s+1 \mid nki/F+s+2 \mid nqa/F+s+3 \mid sunchik/F+pin+1 \mid saqku/F+pex +1 \mid nkichik/F+p+2 \mid nqaku/F+p+3;\ (2.1.1)$$

[Conjugation of the future tense]

This paradigm tells us that if we input the infinitive form of a verb e.g. *rimay/*parler (to talk), the operator <B> erases the character that lies before the pointer, producing the verbal lemma *rima-*. To this lemma we can successively add the suffixes *saq, nki, nqa, sunchik, saqku, nkichik* and *nqaku*, annotating, at the same time, the future tense F

---

[7] See *Dictionnaire Quechua-Français-Quechua* (2009)

[8] See (Duran 2013, 2014)

and the person. As a result, this operation will produce the following forms: *rima-saq, rima-nki, rima-sun, rima-sunchik*, etc. and their annotations as follows:

```
rimanki,rimay,V+FR="parler"+FLX=F+F+s+2
rimanqa,rimay,V+FR="parler"+FLX=F+F+s+3
rimasaqku,rimay,V+FR="parler"+FLX=F+F+pex+1
```

[Excerpt from the conjugation of the verb rimay/parler (to talk)]

2.2 Conjugation of the Past-Preterit Tense

To describe the conjugation of the past-preterit tense of a transitive Quechua verb, symbolized as PPR, we use the following grammar:

PPR = <B>rqani/PPR+1+s| <B>rqanki/ PPR+2+s | <B>rqan/ PPR+3+s | <B>rqanchik/ PPR+1+pin | <B>rqaniku/ PPR+1+pex | <B>rqankichik/ PPR+2+p | <B>rqanku/ PPR+3+p; (2.2.1)

[Past-preterit tense conjugator PPR]

As the previous example, this paradigm tells us that if we input a verb in the infinitive form, e.g. rimay/parler (to talk), once the operator <B> has erased the infinitive suffix "*y*" that lies before the pointer, the lemma *rima-* is produced. To this lemma we add the suffix *rqa* to all the endings appearing in the UT_s set to obtain, *rqani, rqanki, rqan, rqanchik, rqaniku, rqankichik, rqanku,* annotating the past-preterit tense PPR and the person. Applying this grammar, NooJ will produce the following forms: *rima-rqani, rima-rqanki, rima-rqan, rima-rqanchik, rima-rqaniku, rima-rqan-kichik, rima-rqanku (the annotations are not shown)*.

2.3 The Past-Perfect Tense

For the past-perfect tense (marked as PPAS[9]) and whose paradigm is symbolized by SQA_TI, we have the following formula:

SQA_TI = <B>(:SQA_TI_V |:SQA_TI_C); (2.3.1)

---

[9] In Quechua, this tense expresses established facts when the speaker is not aware of them or when the speaker does not witness them.

Where we have:

> $SQA\_TI\_V = sqani/\ PPAS+s+1\ |\ sqanki/\ PPAS+s+2\ |sqaniku/\ PPAS+pex+1\ |$
> $sqanku/\ PPAS+p+3;$
> $SQA\_TI\_C = sqan/\ PPAS+s+3\ |sqanchik/\ PPAS+Pin+1\ |\ sqankichik/\ PPAS+p$
> $+2;$

The symbols used bear the following properties:

SQA_TI_V stands for the set of past-participle endings corresponding to the four Quechua pronouns (*ñuqa, qam, ñuqaiku, paykuna*) whose composed endings finish in a vowel (*sqani, sqanki, sqaniku, sqanku*). SQA_TI_C corresponds to the three Quechua pronouns (*pay, ñuqanchik, qamkuna*) whose composed endings *sqan, sqanchik, sqankichik* finish in a consonant.

For example, for the verb to sing/*takiy* the application of the paradigm (2.3.1) will produce:

```
takisqani/PPAS+s+1
takisqanki/PPAS+s+2
takisqaniku/PPAS+pex+1
takisqanku/PPAS+p+3;
```

2.4   The Paradigm of the Past-Participle

The past-participle is symbolized as PP. To obtain it, we begin with the structure of the TIM2 conjugation. Between the lemma and the personal endings of TIM2, we interpose the SIP suffix -sqa and we achieve the following expression (corresponding to the second meaning of -sqa):

> $SQA\_TI2 = <B>sqai/PP+1+s|\ <B>sqaiki/\ PP+2+s\ |\ <B>sqan/\ PP+3+s\ |$
> $<B>sqanchik/\ PP+1+pin\ |\ <B>sqaiku/\ PP+1+pex\ |\ <B>sqaikichik/\ PP+2+p\ |$
> $<B>sqanku/\ PP+3+p;\ (2.4.1)$

[The past-participle conjugator]

For instance, for the verb *takiy/chanter* (to sing), the application of the paradigm (2.4.1) will produce the conjugation:

```
takisqai/PP+s+1
takisqaiki/PP+s+2
takisqan/PP+s+3
```

2.5   The Present Progressive

The present progressive, symbolized as CHKA, in Quechua and marked as PROG, has the following NooJ grammar:

CHKA = <B>(chkani/PROG+1+s| chkanki/PROG+2+s | chkan/PROG+3+s | chkanchik/PROG+1+pin | chkankichik/PROG+2+p| chkanku/PROG+3+p | chkaniku/PROG+1+pex); (2.5.1)

For the verb to talk/*rimay* the application of the grammar (2.5.1) will give us the conjugation:

```
rimachkani/PROG+1+s
rimachkanki/PROG+2+s
rimachkankichik/PROG+2+p
rimachkanku/PROG+3+p
```

3   Transformations of the Undefined Tense

To describe the preceding conjugations and the remaining tenses, aspects (perfective and imperfective), as well as all moods (indicative, imperative, subjunctive, conditional and gerund), we must introduce the notion of modified structures of the Undefined Tense (MUT).

Using UT as the basic set of endings, we have described, in Sect. 2.2, the Past-Preterit as the grammar 2.2.1., the Past-Perfect as the grammar 2.3.1, the Progressive in Sect. 2.5 as the grammar 2.5.1., but for the Past-Participle, described in Sect. 2.4, for the grammar in 2.4.1 we have used the set of endings MUT2 = {*i, iki, n, nchik, iku, ikichik, nku*}, which—as we will see—is in fact a modified form of UT. The operator TIM2 produces the following modifications:

TIM2(ni) > *y;* TIM2(*nki) > yki;* TIM2(*inkichik) > ykichik*

That is to say TIM2(UT) = MUT2. And, in general TIMi(UT) = PUTi, where i = 1...n. In the following Table 3 we show these transformations of UT (MUT1... MUT6).

For example, the operator TIM1 produces the modified form MUT1 = (i, *nki, n, nchik, iku, nkichik, nku*) which allows us to automatically obtain the conjugation in the conditional or potential mood by agglutinating at the end of them the suffix *man*.

Table 3. *Ending structure for the UT transformations*

UT ending	MUT1	MUT2	MUT3	MUT5	MUT6
ni	*i*	*i*	_	_	*iki*
nki	*nki*	*iki*	*nki*	*i*	_
n	*n*	*n*	*n*	*chun*	*sunki*
For all inter-posed suffixes	For SPP *man*	*For na, pti, spa, sqa*	*-wa translates on object s + 1 from subject 2 + s et 3 + s*	For the imperative, and translator on 1 + s with *wa*	For the translative on 2 + s

Its NooJ grammar is:

> *TIM1 = <B>(i/COND+s+1| nki/ COND+2+s | n/ COND+3+s | nchik/ COND +1+pin | iku/ COND+1+pex | nkichik/ COND+2+p | nku/ COND+3+p);*

[Conditional or potential mood conjugator]

When applied to the verb *rimay*/parler (to talk) it produces the following annotated forms:

> *rimaiman,rimay,V+FR="parler"+FLX=TIM1_man+COND_man+s+1*
> *rimankiman,rimay,V+FR="parler"+FLX=TIM1_man+COND_man+s+2*
> *rimanman,rimay,V+FR="parler"+FLX=TIM1_man+COND_man+s+3*

The aspects of obligation and potential are obtained using the TIM2 operator combined with the suffix *na*.

> *TIM2_na = <B>(nai/OBL+1+s|nayki/OBL+2+s |nan/OBL+3+s |nanchik/OBL +1+pin |naiku/OBL+1+pex |naikichik/OBL+2+p |nku/OBL+3+p);*

Here are two examples:

> *rimanaiki,rimay,V+FR="parler"+FLX=SIP1_TR_TIM+OBL+s+2*
> *rimanaiku,rimay,V+FR="parler"+FLX=SIP1_TR_TIM+OBL+pex+1*

This same operator is used to obtain the conjugation of the two gerund moods when we combine them respectively with the suffixes *spa* and *pti*. The subjunctive mood is obtained with the suffix *sqa*. For taht we have the general grammar SIP1_TR_TIM:

SIP1_TR_TIM = <B>(i/ SIP1_TR_TIM+1+s|naiki/ SIP1_TR_TIM+2+s |
nan/OBL+3+s |nanchik/ SIP1_TR_TIM+1+pin |naiku/ SIP1_TR_TIM+1+pex |
naikichik/OBL+2+p |nku/ SIP1_TR_TIM+3+p);

A sample of the generated conjugations of this grammar is given below:

```
rimaptiiki,V+FR="parler"+FLX=SIP1_TR_TIM+GER2+s+2
rimaptiiku,V+FR="parler"+FLX=SIP1_TR_TIM+GER2+pex+1
rimaptinku,V+FR="parler"+FLX=SIP1_TR_TIM+GER2+p+3
```

In order to obtain the conjugation of the imperative mood we use the TIM5 operator:

TIM5 = <B>(i/I+2+s |chun/I+3+s |sun/I+1+pin |sun/I+1+pex |ichik/I+2+p | chunku/I+3+p);

When combined with the suffix *wa,* the same operator will give the transfer mood in the first singular person:

```
TIM5_wa = <B>(wai/I_wa+s+1|wachun/I_wa+s+3 |waichik/I_wa
+p+2|wachunku/I_wa+p+3)
```

It generates the following conjugations:

```
rimawai,rimay,V+FR="parler"+FLX=TIM5_wa+I_wa+s+1
rimawachun,rimay,V+FR="parler"+FLX=TIM5_wa+I_wa+s+3
rimawaichik,rimay,V+FR="parler"+FLX=TIM5_wa+I_wa+p+2
```

When we assemble all of these paradigms, along with those we have described here, and follow similar steps, we obtain a comprehensive NooJ grammar, symbolized by V_TR_CONJ0, which allows us to automatically generate all the conjugated forms of a transitive Quechua verb.

V_TR_CONJ0=:TI |:F |:I |:RQA_TI |:TIM1_man |:RQU_TI |:SPA_TIM2|: RU_TI |:RA_TI |:RQU_F |:SQA_TI | :SQA_TIM2 |:RQUSQA_TI | :SQA_TIM2 | : RUTIM1MAN | :RQUTIM1MAN | :PTITIM1QA | :F_ÑA | :PTI_TIM2 |:SQA_- TIM2_MAN |TIM5_wa;

In the following section, I will present a user interface that display these conjugations as a table:

3.1   Conjugation in the Enhanced Quechua Verb Lexicon

When we refer to a printed Quechua dictionary, we observe that many frequently used French verbs do not have a Quechua equivalent (e.g. abandonner, comprendre, sourire, raisonner, déménager, bivouaquer). However, when we look these verbs up in the corpus, we find Quechua equivalents as forms of derived verbs. In fact, it has been demonstrated that the lexicon of Quechua simple verbs can be enhanced by suffix derivation[10].

To formalize this phenomenon, I first gathered each suffix capable of generating such verbs. They exhibit a remarkable characteristic property; namely that they are positioned between the lemma of the simple verb and the suffix "y" of the infinitive. We use SIP-DRV to symbolize the set of these derivation suffixes:

SIP_DRV = {-*chaku, -chi,- chka, -kacha, -kamu, -kapu, -ku, -lla, -mpu, -mu, -naya, -pa, -paya, -pu, -raya, -ri, -rpari, -rqu, -ru, -tamu, -ykacha, -ykachi, -ykamu, ykapu, -ykari, -yku, -ysi*} (27)

I then constructed the corresponding NooJ grammar V_SIP1_INF, which generates all the derived forms that can be conjugated.

When we apply this grammar, we obtain 27 derived forms that can be conjugated. We can illustrate this with the following excerpt of the derived forms for the verb to turn/*muyuy*:

```
muyurquy,muyuy,V+ITR+EN="to turn"+FLX=V_SIP1_INF+PAPT+INF
muyurayay,muyuy,V+ITR+EN="to turn"+FLX=V_SIP1_INF+DUR+INF
muyupayay,muyuy,V+ITR+EN="to turn"+FLX=V_SIP1_INF+FREQ+INF
```

Thus, the paradigm, V_SIP1_INF, allows us to enlarge the original simple verb dictionary from 1,400 to over 37,000 new forms which can be conjugated. Many of them keep the same semantics but, as we have just seen, many others derive into different meanings, furnishing us with the desired new verbs. For instance, we show that when we apply:

− the suffix *rqu* to the simple verb *saqiy*/laisser (to leave)

we obtain the derived form *sagirquy* which stands for abandoner (to abandon)

− the suffix *ri* to the simple verb *yachay*/apprendre (to learn)

we obtain the derived form *yachariy* which stands for comprendre (to understand).

---

[10] Duran (2017).

In this manner and after verification, I was able to obtain over 8,700 derived verbs that have French equivalents. These derived verbs come from the bilingual LVQ French-Quechua dictionary obtained by Duran [6]. I name this LVF_QU and an excerpt appears in Fig. 2.

```
abaisser 08 (s'~)(descendre vers_ La route s'a~ vers la rivière.),V+VEH+QU="uraykuy"
abaisser 09 (s'~)(s'avilir_ tomber jusqu'à_ On s'a~ au niveau de cet escroc.),V+PSY+QU="uraykuy"
abalourdir (s'~)(abêtir_ abrutir_ On s'a~ avec un tel film_ On a~ P avec ce livre.),V+PSYt+QU="upayakuy"
abandonner 01(laisser_ léguer_ On a~ ses biens à ses enfants_ à une fondation.),V+DRO+QU="saqiykuy"
abandonner 02(laisser aller_ On a~ sa barque à un fort courant.),V+MAR+QU="saqiykuy"
abandonner 03(lâcher_ laisser aller_ On a~ les rênes de l'attelage.),V+EQU+QU="wayarichiy"
```

Fig. 2. The enhanced QU-FR dictionary of verbs

3.2   An Automated French-Quechua Conjugator

A remarkable feature of the Quechua grammar is that LVF_QU may be conjugated using the grammar V_ITR_CONJ0 and is the same grammar that I used for the simple verbs. For instance, for the verb *saqiykuy*/déposer (to drop someone or something with care) which was obtained by the derivation of the verb *saqiy*/laisser (to leave) using the suffix *ri*, this grammar will generate the same number of conjugated forms as *saqiriy*/ abandoner pour un petit moment (to lay down someone or something with care). An excerpt of the result is shown in the following sample:

```
saqiykuni,saqiykuy,V+FR="abandonner"+FLX=V_TR_CONJ0+TI+s
+1 (je l'ai déposé)
saqiykunqa,saqiykuy,V+FR="abandonner"+FLX=V_TR_CONJ0+F+s
+3 (il va le déposer)
saqiykusaqku,saqiykuy,V+FR="abandonner"+FLX=V_TR_CONJ0+F
+pex+1 (nous le déposerons)
```

3.3   A User Interface for the Fr-QU Conjugator

By using part of the interface module of www.lingwarium.org written by Berment [1], I have built a user interface for the Fr-QU conjugator that allows me to show the entire set of conjugations of a Quechua verb.

When the user enters a verb (in French) in this interface, he or she will obtain the entire table of conjugations (tenses, moods, aspects, voices) of the corresponding Quechua equivalent, as shown below in Fig. 3.

Conjugueur français-quechua de Maximiliano Duran

Français	Quéchua
raisonner	qamutay

[Et hop !]

Indicatif présent en français	Indicatif présent en quéchua
1ère personne du singulier	qamutani
2ème personne du singulier	qamutanki
3ème personne du singulier	qamutan
1ère personne du pluriel	qamutanchik
2ème personne du pluriel	qamutankichik
3ème personne du pluriel	qamutanku
Futur simple en français	Futur en quéchua

Fig. 3. Excerpt from the conjugation of *qamutay*/raisoner (to reason).

4   Conclusion and Future Work

In this paper I have shown some of the details of the construction of the paradigms that serve to obtain the conjugation of the undefined tense and of its transformations. I used then these paradigms to implement an automated monolingual Quechua conjugator of a French verb that has a simple Quechua equivalent.

I have also developed a user interface of a conjugator of an enlarged French-Quechua verb lexicon.

The first aim is to complete the user interface and to place it online where it would be available to the public.

The second goal is to develop some pedagogical applications and interactive tools for learning Quechua.

Thirdly, I plan to continue developing the project of aligning the two monolingual conjugations, in order to produce an electronic dictionary of equivalent conjugated French-Quechua verb forms for our MT project.

References

1. Berment, V.: http://www.lingwarium.org/
2. Dubois, J., Dubois-Charlier, F.: Les verbes français. Larousse, Paris (1997)
3. Duran, M.: Formalizing Quechua verbs Inflexion. In: Proceedings of the NooJ 2013 International Conference, Saarbrücken (2013)
4. Duran, M.: Dictionnaire Quechua-Français-Quechua. Editions HC, Paris (2009)
5. Duran, M.: Morphological and syntactic grammars for recognition of verbal lemmas in Quechua. In: Proceedings of the NooJ 2014 International Conference and Workshop, Sassari (2014)

6. Duran, M.: Dictionnaire électronique français-quechua des verbes pour le TAL. Thèse Doctorale. Université de Franche-Comté. Mars 2017 (2017)
7. Silberztein, M.: NooJ Manual (2003). http://www.nooj4nlp.net (220 pages updated regularly)
8. Silberztein, M.: La formalisation du dictionnaire LVF avec NooJ et ses applications pour l'analyse automatique de corpus. Langages 3/2010 (no. 179-180), pp. 221–241 (2010)
9. Silberztein M.: La formalisation des langues. L'approche de NooJ, ISTE edn. London (2015)

Implementation of Arabic Phonological Rules in NooJ

Rafik Kassmi[✉], Mohammed Mourchid[✉], Abdelaziz Mouloudi[✉],
and Samir Mbarki[✉]

MISC, Ibn Tofail University, Kénitra, Morocco
rafik.kassmi@gmail.com, mourchidm@hotmail.com,
mouloudi_aziz@hotmail.com, mbarkisamir@hotmail.com

Abstract. In this paper, we are going to implement Arabic phonological rules. We will present the speech organs apparatus with a description of Arabic sounds. Then, we will describe the phonological changes and provide a brief linguistic study of such changes. Finally, we will propose two solutions to implement Arabic phonological rules in NooJ. The first solution is a newly developed java module in NooJ platform which deals with phonological rules using an independent formatted file. The second solution uses local grammars within the NooJ platform, to locate anomalies in words and then give the appropriate transformations.

Keywords: Arabic language · Speech organs · Phonological change · Substitution · Local grammar · Transducer · NooJ

1 Introduction

In the first century of the Hijrah (A. H.), the Arabs began to study phonetics with other branches of linguistics such as grammar, lexicography and rhetoric. The basis of these studies was drawn from the Quran in order to preserve its text from corruption. It manifested itself at that time mainly in the science of tajwid, which is the correct recitation of the Quran [1]. Ibn jinni (392 A. H.) was the first Arab linguist interested in phonetics and his best work on the subject was entitled "Sirr ṣināʿat al-iʿrāb" [سِر صِنَاعَة الْإِعْرَاب the secret of grammatical cases industry] [2].

Arabic has 28 consonants and six vowels, three of which are short and three are long. The total number of Arabic sounds is 34. The Arabic writing system contains only 32 signs because [و – wa] and [ي – ya] have the same symbol as [و – ū] and [ي – ī] respectively. It is only from the second century A. H. that the short vowels, namely [´ / a / فَتْحَة], [ِ / i / كَسرَة] and [ُ / u / ضَمة], were written in Arabic orthography. But they still remain absent in most Arabic hand-written and printed documents.

© Springer Nature Switzerland AG 2019
I. Mauro Mirto et al. (Eds.): NooJ 2018, CCIS 987, pp. 16–26, 2019.
https://doi.org/10.1007/978-3-030-10868-7_2

2 Speech Organs

Speech organs or articulators produce the speech sounds of language. They are one of the most important subjects in the study of phonetics. The linguist David Crystal defines articulators as "any specific part of the vocal apparatus involved in the production of a sound" [3]. Speech organs can be divided into two kinds: active and passive articulators. Active articulators are the movable parts of the vocal apparatus relative to passive articulators, such as the lips, tongue and lower jaw. It produces various speech sounds, in particular manners of articulation [4]. Passive articulators are organs that make little or no movement during a speech gesture. It includes the upper lip, the upper teeth, the various parts of the upper surface of the oral cavity, and the back wall of the pharynx (see Fig. 1).

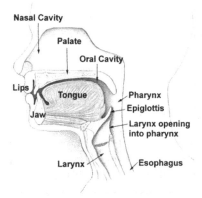

Fig. 1. Speech organs apparatus.

There are three main functions for speech organs to produce sounds. Breathing: the lung and the diaphragm are considered as the source of energy. Phonation: The vocal folds are responsible for vibration and can produce voiced sounds (majhūr/مَجْهُور) or voiceless sounds (mahmūs/مَهْمُوس). Resonation: mouth cavity, nasal cavity, pharynx and larynx alter the resonating effects to sounds. These functions help a person to produce the consonants and vowels in a right way.

The Arabs have described Arabic sounds in relation to both point of articulation (makhraj/مَخْرَج) and manner of articulation (ṣifah / صِفة) [1]. Arabic sounds are divided into three groups: the first group is made of plosives or stops (šadīda/شَدِيدَة) consisting of eight consonants. The second includes fricatives (riḫwa/رِخْوَة) and consists of 14 consonants. The third group, between plosive and fricative, contains resonants (rannāna/رَنَّانَة) and includes nasal, lateral, trill and glide sounds (see Fig. 2).

Point of articulation / Manner of articulation		bilabial	labiodental	interdental n.e.	interdental em.	alveolar n.e.	alveolar em.	alveopalatal	palatal	velar	uvular	pharyngeal	glottal
Plosive	voiceless					ت t				ك k			ء ʔ
	voiced	ب b				د d	ط ṭ		ج ǧ		ق q		
Fricative	voiceless		ف f	ث ṯ		س s	ص ṣ	ش š			خ ḫ	ح ḥ	ه h
	voiced			ذ ḏ	ظ ẓ	ز z	ض ḍ				غ ġ	ع ʕ	
Resonant	nasals	م m				ن n							
	lateral					ل l							
	trill					ر r							
	glides	و w							ي y				

n.e. : non emphatic em. : emphatic

Fig. 2. Chart of Arabic consonants

3   Phonological Changes

In Arabic, the phonological change is a transformation of a word from one base form to another derived form in order to ease the pronunciation. We can distinguish three main categories:

3.1   ʾIdġām

ʾidġām (إِدْغَام) is the assimilation of one letter with another. It is defined as the gemination in pronunciation of two identical sounds and may be written as one letter with the brief vowel šadda (ó) above it. For example, let's consider the verb *abata* (أَبَتَ – heat up) in the 1st person of the past tense (pattern [فَعَلْتُ - faʿaltu]). According to the phonological rule, for verbs ending with t [ت], if the 1st t is vowelless followed by a vowelled t, we keep only one t carrying šadda (تُ ← تْ + تُ) (see Table 1[1].)

Table 1.   ʾidġām (إِدْغَام)

Root	Pattern	Underlying structure	Phonological rule	Surface structure
أبت	فَعَلْتُ	أَبَتْتُ	تُ ← تْ + تُ	أَبَتَّ
ʾBT [Heat up]	faʿaltu	ʾabat-tu	1st t vowelless + 2nd vowelled → t carrying šadda	ʾabattu [I heat up]

3.2   ʾIbdāl

ʾibdāl (إِبْدَال) is the substitution. It consists of removing a letter and replacing it by another. Only nine consonants are concerned: [ا - ā], [ي - y], [و - w], [ء - ʾ], [ط - ṭ], [م - m], [ت - t], [د - d], [ه - h]. For example, let's consider the derived form [إِفْتَعَلَ - ʾiftaʿala] of the root [صحب - ṣḥb]. According to the phonological rule, the prefix ʾišta (إِشْتَ) is replaced by ʾišṭa (إِشْطَ) (see Table 2).

---

[1] The table is designed according to the phonological process suggested by Spencer [5].

Let us further consider now the root baya'a [بَيَعَ – to sell] with the pattern fā'ilu [فَاعِل]. The underlying structure is bāyi'u [بَايِع]. The [ي – ya] changes to hamza (glottal stop) [ء – '] in any subject of name of trilateral hollow verb with ya as second radical. It is known in Arabic as glide metathesis ['i'lāl bil-qalb - إِعْلَال بِالقَلْب]. The derivation is based on the principles of prosodic morphology, proposed by McCarthy [9], is shown in Figs. 3 and 4 below:

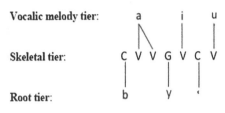

Fig. 3. The underlying structure bāyi'u

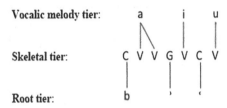

Fig. 4. The surface structure bā'i'u

6 Contribution

In this study, we have managed to implement Arabic phonological rules in NooJ by providing two solutions.

6.1 Development of a New Java Module

As a first solution, we have created a new java module in NooJ, like a toolbox, which deals with phonological rules. Fifty rules until now have been grouped by a line in an independent formatted file. A rule is composed of the triplet anomaly, correction and condition.

We can feed easily this file by adding, replacing and suppressing rules. This module can be used in all generative operations including inflections and derivations. In fact, Fig. 5 shows that we use our new transformation process module after the NooJ inflectional process.

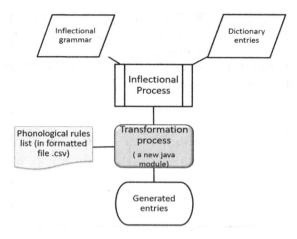

Fig. 5. Our inflectional process in NooJ

Figure 6 shows some entries of our dictionary, which is based on the root and pattern approach, the used inflectional paradigm, and a part of the resulting inflected forms. Notice that all transformations were automatically applied to the inflected forms.

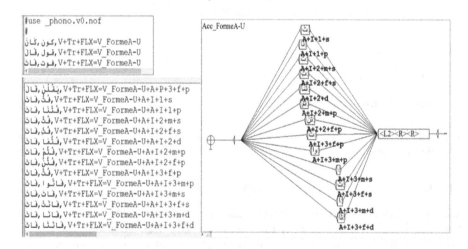

Fig. 6. Example of used resources

Then, we have created and added a new box dialog in NooJ Labs (Fig. 7). This application provides to users a tool to perform phonological corrections to the input words and displays all applied rules.

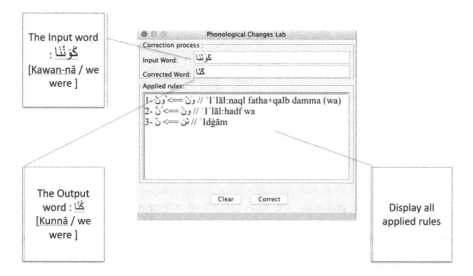

Fig. 7. The created Box dialog: Phonological Changes Lab

6.2 Using Local Grammars in NooJ

As a second solution, we have used local grammars within the NooJ platform [10], to locate anomalies in words and then give the appropriate transformations. To perform those local grammars, we have created two types of NooJ transducers:

- Morphological grammars: allows us to verify the presence of the anomaly and if the condition is verified, it adds a lexical trait that will also include the correction (Fig. 8).

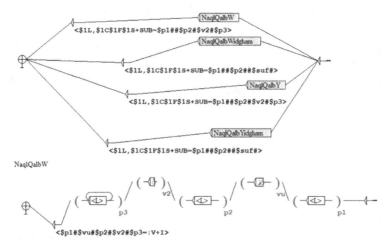

Fig. 8. Two sub graphs of our morphological grammar

- Syntactic grammars: allows us to apply the transformations and add them to annotations for output (Fig. 9).

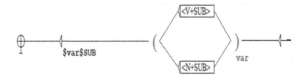

Fig. 9. Syntactic grammar

To test our local grammar, we have used two different functions allowed in NooJ. Manually by using the concordance functionality [11] (Fig. 10). So, for each word in which we have detected the anomaly, we generated the correction as an output. Note that a word can undergo several transformations.

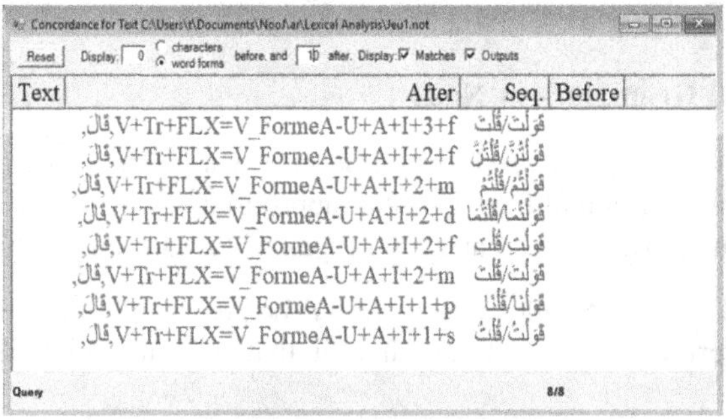

Fig. 10. Example of using concordance

We have also tested our local grammar by adding all grammars in NooJ preferences. Then, by launching the command TEXT > Linguistic Analysis, NooJ's engine apply all selected resources [11]. Figure 11 shows an example of the transformations applied to the verb 'aman-nā; the correction is 'amannā.

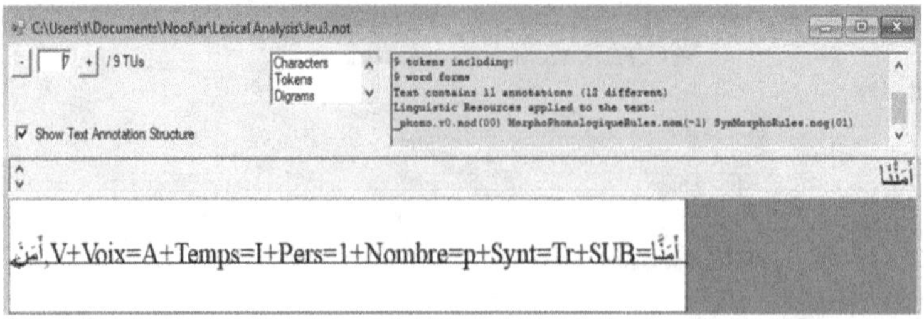

Fig. 11. Example of linguistic analysis of the verb 'aman-nā

We have to mention that for words that contain several anomalies, our local grammar displays all the possibilities (all the possible paths in the graphs). For example, the word kawan-nā gives three possibilities (Fig. 12).

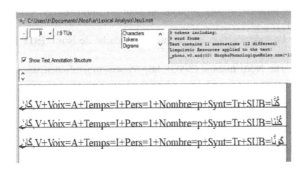

Fig. 12. Example of linguistic analysis of the verb kawan-nā

7   Conclusion and Perspectives

In this paper, we have presented a speech organs apparatus with a description of Arabic sounds. Then, we have described the phonological changes. After that, we have presented a brief linguistic study. Finally, we have proposed two solutions to implement Arabic phonological rules in NooJ. Ti begin with, we have developed a new java module in NooJ platform which deals with phonological rules using an independent formatted file. We have also created a new dialog box in NooJ for processing and displaying all phonological transformations applied to entries. Second, we have used local grammars within the NooJ platform in order to locate anomalies in words and to give the appropriate transformations.

As for perspectives, we aim to add other rules in order to process all morphological changes. Furthermore, we want to improve our local grammar to give more precision in the processing of words with multiple anomalies.

References

1. Affozan, A.I.: Assimilation in Classical Arabic, a phonological study, Ph.d. Thesis, University of Glasgow, Scotland (1989)
2. Ibn jinni: "Sirr ṣināʿat al-iʿrāb/الإعْرَاب صِنَاعَة سِر ," الحلبي البابي مطبعة, Cairo (1954)
3. Crystal, D.: A Dictionary of Linguistics and Phonetics, 6th edn. Blackwell (2008). ISBN: 978-1-405-15296-9
4. https://en.wikipedia.org/wiki/Speech_organ
5. Spencer, A.: Phonology: Theory and Description, 9th edn. Wiley-Blackwell, Oxford (1996)
6. Zemirli, Z., Sellami, M., Vigouroux, N.: Modélisation des règles phonologiques dans un système de génération automatique de la langue arabe, pp: 361–368. JST FRANCIL, Avignon, France (1997)

7. Mesfar, S.: Analyse morpho-syntaxique automatique et reconnaissance des entités nommées en arabe standard. Ph.d Thesis, Franche-Comte University, France (2008)
8. Bohas, G.: Contribution à l'étude de la méthode des grammairiens arabes en morphologie et en phonologie, d'après certains grammairiens arabes tardifs en morphologie et en phonologie. Atelier de reproduction des thèses, University of Lille 3 (1982)
9. McCarthy, J.: A prosodic theory of nonconcatenative morphology. Linguist. Inquiry **12**, 373–418 (1981)
10. Silberztein, M.: La formalisation des langues: l'approche de NooJ. ISTE Editions, Londres (2015)
11. Silberztein, M.: The NooJ manual (2003). http://www.nooj4nlp.net/pages/references.html

Arabic Broken Plural Generation Using the Extracted Linguistic Conditions Based on Root and Pattern Approach in the NooJ Platform

Ilham Blanchete[(✉)], Mohammed Mourchid, Samir Mbarki,
and Abdelaziz Mouloudi

MIC Research Team, Laboratory MISC,
Ibn Tofail University Kenitra, Kenitra, Morocco
ilham.blanchete@gmail.com, mourchidm@hotmail.com,
mbarkisamir@hotmail.com, mouloudi_aziz@hotmail.com

Abstract. This paper presents a linguistic study of number's morphological feature that affects nouns, verbs, adjectives and gerunds (verbal nouns) by giving a special attention to the Arabic Broken Plurals (BPs). The difficulty lies on specifying the candidate Broken plural Pattern/Patterns (BPP/BPPs) to find the BP Form/Forms (BPF/BPFs) of a given Singular Form (SF). The Arabic BP is not automatically generated as other grammatical categories, e.g. verbs. The BP generation depends on SF's morphological, phonological and semantic features. We have extracted from a deep linguistic study 108 sets of morphological, phonological and semantic conditions, which serve to restrict the generation process of the BPF from its SF. The extracted conditions may give one or more BPP for a given SF. We take into account the exceptions that permeate the extracted conditions. We have implemented inflectional and derivational grammars that generate the BPF using the Root-Pattern approach. This requires building a dictionary that considers not only the root and pattern of the SF as its entries, but also the SF's morphological, phonological and semantic features using NooJ platform.

Keywords: ANLP · Arabic Broken Plural · Arabic morphology
NooJ platform · Root-Pattern approach · Inflections and derivations

1 Introduction

Plural is a number morphological feature applied to nouns, adjectives, gerunds, pronouns and verbs [1]. Plural in Arabic is formed by two different procedures: Non-linear root and pattern affixation, referred as the 'broken plural', and linear suffixation by either a feminine or a masculine suffix, termed 'sound plural' [2].

This article presents a linguistic study of Arabic BP that constitutes 10% of Arabic texts content [3]. We have extracted conditions that restrict the generation process of the BPF from its SF. SFs are also linked to all their possible generated BPFs through the use of a dictionary, inflectional and derivational grammars. Our dictionary

I. Mauro Mirto et al. (Eds.): NooJ 2018, CCIS 987, pp. 27–37, 2019.
https://doi.org/10.1007/978-3-030-10868-7_3

considers the SF, its root and pattern as well as other morphological, phonological and semantic features. We use a linguistic platform that allows us to link our dictionary to our inflectional and derivational grammars called NooJ platform.

"Traditional grammarians of Arabic distinguish between two modes of plural formation, sound plurals or suffixed plurals and the broken plural (BP). Sound plurals take certain suffixes to form plural nouns" [1]. They are automatically generated from their SF by adding specific suffixes. For instance, the singular noun (طَاوِلَة-TTaAWiLa/table) takes the sound plural (طَاوِلَات-TTaAWiLaAT/tables). Similarly the same thing for the adjective like (جَمِيلَة-JaMiLaaa- beautiful) takes the sound plural (جَميلَات-JaMiILaAT-beautifuls). In other words, the generation of the sound plural necessitates adding (وُنَ-WuNa) to the singular masculine and (ات-aAT) to the singular feminine nouns, adjectives and gerunds.

Unlike the sound plural, the BP involves internal modification of its SF. It is also divided into two kinds: (1), the plural of multitude and, (2) the plural of paucity. This article discusses these kinds in detail in the next section.

In Arabic the SF may take one or more BP forms, e.g. the SF (نَفَس-NaFoS/soul) that has the root (NFS-نفس) and the singular pattern (فَعَل-FaEoL) takes two BP forms: (نُفُوس-NuFuOS/souls) and (أَنْفُس-AaNofuS/souls). Their BPPs are (فُعُول-FoEuL) and (أَفْعُل-AFoEuL) respectively. These two BP forms refer to the same meaning "souls", but they have been generated using different rules. The first BP (نُفُوس-NuFuOS/souls) is assigned to the BP that refers to the plural of multitude (جَمْع الْكَثْرَة-JaMoEo AaLo-KaToRaP) while the second one (أَنْفُس-AaNofuS/souls) refers to the plural of paucity (جَمْعُ الْقِلَّة-JaMoEo AaLoKiLa). A second example clarifies the irregularity of BP generation from its SF: (جَمَل-JaMaL/camel) takes 11 BPFs. "Camels" in Arabic takes the following forms that are formed respectively (SF/its pattern):

- (جِمَال-JiMaAL/فِعَال-FiEaAL).
- (أَجْمُل-AaJoMuL/أَفْعُل-AaFoEuL).
- (أَجْمَال-AaJoMaAL/أَفْعَال-AaFoEaAL).
- (جَمَالَة-JaMaALa/فَعَالَة-FaEaALa).
- (جِمَالَة-JiMaALa/فِعَالَة-FiEaALa).
- (جُمَالَة-JuMaALa/فُعَالَة-FoEaALa).
- (جُمُل-JuMoL/فُعُل-FuEoL).
- (جِمَالَات-JiMaALaAT/فِعَالَات-FiEaALaAT).
- (جَمَالَات-JaMaALaAT/فَعَالَات-FaEaALaAT).
- (جُمَالَات-JuMaALaAT/فُعَالَات-FuEaALaAT).
- (جَمَائِل-JaMaAXiL/فَعَائِل-FaEaAXiL).

These irregularities that affect the SF make the process of BP generation difficult and hard to implement. We are also going to enumerate the main obstacles challenging the BP generation, which may fall into some ambiguities:

- When both of the BP and SF share the same pattern, this may increase the complexity of the search process within a text. For instance, a search process using the pattern (فِعَال-FiEaAL) in a text that contains these two words: the SF (ذِرَاع-DiRaAE-arm) and the BPF (جِمال-JiMaAL-camels) will retrieve both of them because they share the same pattern. This will cause an ambiguity if the SF is the desired result.
- Another obstacle affects BP generation is the root alternations or orthographical variations [4], e.g. the SF (طَعَام-TTaEaAM/food) has the root (TEM-طعم). The interlock between this root, which is free of long vowels, with the pattern (أَفْعِلَة-AFoEiLaP) gives the BPF (أَطْعِمَة-AaTToEiMaP/foods) and the SF (قَبو-KaBuW/cave) that takes the root (KBW-قبو) and the pattern (أَفْعِلَة-AFoEiLaP) gives the BPF (أَقْبِية-AaKoBiIaP/caves). As the root (KBW-قبو) contains a long vowel, an alternation occurs on this long vowel during the process of the BP generation. In fact, roots with long vowel require a root alternation using morph-phonologic rules. The same thing applies to BPs that their roots contain glottal stop, they undergo orthographical alternations [4].
- As previously mentioned, a SF may take more than one BP form. For instance, the noun (مَكَان-place-MaKaAN) takes (أَمْكِنَة-AaMoKiNaP-places) and (أَمَاكِن-places-AaMaAKiN). The question here is: how can we examine the number of the BPF of a given SF?
- Two different singular nouns with different concepts give two different BP forms even if they share the same root and pattern. E.g. SF1: (أَمْر-AaMoR-issue), SF2: (أَمْر-AaMoR-order), both of them have the same root (AMR-أمر) and the same pattern (فَعْل-FaEoL), but its BPFs are different: (أُمُور-AuMuOR- issues) and (أَوَامِر-AWMiR- issues), which its patterns respectively are (فُعُول-FuEuOL) and (فَاعِلَة-AaFaAEiL). As can be seen in this example, even if SF1 and SF2 share the same root and pattern, they, however, have different concepts, BPFs and BPP.

After enumerating the Above-Mentioned problems, the root and pattern approach [5] has been adopted to solve them and generate a comprehensive model of Arabic BPs. In fact, it is impossible to extract conditions that generate BPs without specifying the root, the singular pattern and other morphological, phonological and semantic features. These features have been adopted to our dictionary entries to solve the problems in question. This will be clarified in the next section. Inflectional and derivational grammars have been implemented to generate BPF from their SF. As previously mentioned, these grammars link each generated BPF with its SF, singular pattern, BPP and the root. Our work has been implemented using NooJ platform [6].

First, section two of this paper is concerned with previous works. Second, the focus of the next paragraph will be on the approaches that deal with the generation process of the Arabic PB. Third, a linguistic study will be detailed in Sect. 3. Forth, our contribution will be also presented in this section. Fifth, section four will give the implementation of the linguistic study. Finally, a conclusion and perspective will be presented in section five.

2 Previous Works

Many works have been achieved on Arabic BP. These works stand on two different methods [7]. The first method generates the BPF from its SF or its root [8, 9]; and the second one extracts the SF from the BPF [10]. In this paper, we are going to mention works that deal with the first method.

2.1 The Broken Plural Pattern Classification Approach

In this work [8] assume that only 31 BPPs are mostly used in Arabic texts. These patterns are then divided into four categories: Iambic, Trochaic, Monosyllabic and others. According to [11], each one of these categories has its own properties [8]:

- The Iambic has been allocated for BP that starts with a fix part (letter-diacritic), e.g. the SF (نَفْس-NaFoS-soul) takes the BPF (نُفُوس-AaNoFuS-souls). As they assume that this is the most used category.
- The Trochaic has been allocated for BP that starts with the part (letter-diacritic, letter-diacritic, letter), e.g. the SF (رُكْبَة-RuKoBaa-knee) takes the BPF (رُكَب-RuKaB-knees).
- Monosyllabic has been allocated for BP that starts with the part (letter-diacritic, letter, letter), e.g. takes the BPF (حُمْر-HuMoR-reds) takes the BPF (خُضْر-KHuDoR-greens).
- Others contain the rest of the words [7].

After this classification [8] suggest an algorithm that extracts the BPF from its SF. The algorithm divides the SF into parts. Then it detects which category the SF belongs to. Finally, changes are required to achieve the BPF. As has been observed, the problem with McCarthy & Prince's approach is that they consider only the most used patterns, and they ignored the rest.

2.2 The Root and Pattern-Based Approach

Pattern and Root Inflectional Morphology (PRIM), as defined by [4] is "an implemented model of description of the inflectional morphology of Arabic nouns, the model includes BPs i.e. plurals formed by modifying the stem" [4]. The shortcoming of PRIM is that each entry of the SF accepts only one BPF, even if this SF has more than one BPF. For instance, the entry (جَمَل-JaMaL/camel) that has 11 BPFs, the PRIM will insert 11 entries for the same SF. This will cause a redundancy of Morph-syntactic features in 11 lines that refer to the same SF.

3 Theoretical Study

3.1 The Linguistic Study of Arabic BP

Grammarians recognize three number categories for Arabic nouns (including adjectives): singular (مُفْرَد-MuFoRaD), dual (مُثَنّى-MuTaNa), and plural (جَمْع-JaMoE).

They also divide the plural into sound plural (الجَمع السَّالِم-AaLoJaMoEo AaLoSaLiM) and broken plural (جَمْعُ التَّكسِير-JaMoEo AaLoTaKoSiR). BPs are then divided into two plurals: the first one is the plural of paucity (جَمْعُ القِلَّة-JaMoEo AaLoKiLa), which denotes from three to ten items. The second one is the plural of multitude (جَمْع الكَثْرَة-JaMoEo AaLoKaToRa), which denotes more than ten items [1]. The BP primarily involves internal modification of the singular stem [4]. We have studied and analyzed the generation process of the BPF from its SF by extracting 108 conditions from a deep linguistic study. Then, we have inserted features, which form these conditions, to our dictionary to take them into consideration during the implementation of grammars, which generate the BPs forms. The following table presents two examples of the extracted rules, SP: Singular Pattern.

Table 1. Example of the extracted conditions.

SP	Root	SF	Conditions	BPP	BPF
فَعَل FaEaL	خشب-KHCHB	خَشَب/ KHaCHaB/wood	Noun 2nd letter is sound	فُعْلان FuEoLaAN	خُشْبَان/Woods KHuCHoBaAN
	توج-TWG	1- تَاج/ TaAG/Crown	Noun 2nd letter is (ا/A)	فِعْلان FiEoLaAN	تِيجَان/Crowns TiIoGaAN
	جور-JWR	2- جَار/ JaAR/Neighbor	2nd root letter is (و/ W)	فِعْلان FiEoLaAN	جِيران/ Neighbors JiIoRaAN
فَاعِل FaEiL	شعر-CHER	شَاعِر/ CHAER/poet	Adjective Masculine Rational	فُعَلَاء FuEaALaAX	شُعَرَاء/Poets CHuEaRaAX عُلَماء/Scientists EuLaAMaAX

The previous table can be read as follows:

- If the SP is (فَعَل/FaEaL) and it is a noun and its second root letter is sound, then its BPP must be (فُعْلان/FuEoLaAN).
- If the SP is (فَعَل/FaEaL) and it is a noun, its second letter is (ا/A) and its second root letter is (و/W), then its BP form is (فُعْلان/FuEoLaAN).
- If the singular pattern is (فَاعِل/FaEiL) and it is an adjective and masculine and rational, then its BP form is (فُعَلَاء/FuEaALaAX). Exceptions may, of course, permeate these conditions, and all of them have been covered during the generation process. The following section will concentrate on some of the remaining conditions.

3.2   The Extracted Conditions

Conditions have been extracted to restrict the generation process as have previously been explained. At least one of these conditions must be realized to extract one or more of the BPP. Finally, we use our inflectional grammars to make an interlock between the obtained BPP/BPPs and the SF root to get the desired BPF/BPFs. It is Worth-mentioning that if one SF realizes more than one set of conditions, then this SF has more than one BPF. In a point of fact, the pervious extracted conditions have been formed from the FS morphological, phonological and semantic features.

In this paper, we have extracted 108 conditions from a deep linguistic study using several Arabic books [12–16]. Two of them have been presented in Table 1. Now, some of the remaining conditions will be explained: The singular pattern (فَعَل-FaEaL) may take one of the following BPPs: {(فِعَال-FiEaAL), (فِعْلَان-FiEoLaAN), (فُعْلَان-FuEoLaAN), (أَفْعَال-AaFoEaAL) and (فُعُول-FuEuOL)} according to the following sets of conditions:

- The singular pattern (فَعَل-FaEaL or فَعْلَة-FaEoLaP) takes the BPP (فِعَال-FiEaAL) if, and only if, the singular is a noun, and not duplicated, means that the second root letter is different from the third one, and its third letter must be sound, which means that its third letter is not a long vowel letter. E.g. (جَمَل-JaMaL-camel)-(جِمَال-JiMaL-camels) and (رَقَبَة-RaKaBaP)-(رِقَاب-RiKaAB).
- The SF that its pattern is (فَعَل-FaEaL) takes the BPP (فِعْلَان-FiEoLaAN) if, and only if, it is a noun and its second letter is (أ-A), which belongs to (و-O) in its root letters. To explain this point, the letter (و-O) has been changed to (أ-A) according to Arabic morphophonemic phenomena. For instance, (تَاج-TaAJ-crown)-(تِيجَان-TIJAN-crowns) and (جَار-JaAR-Neighbor)-(جِيرَان-JiRaARaN-Neighbors). The letter (ي-YaE) is the result of appling Arabic morphophonemic phenomena.
- The SF that its pattern is (فَعَل-FaEaL) takes the BPP (فُعْلَان-FuEoLaAN) if, and only if, it is a noun and its second root letter is sound. E.g. The SF (بَلَد-BaLaD-country) takes the BPF (بُلْدَان-BuLoDaAN-countries) and the SF (شَبَخ-KHCHB-timber) takes BPF (شُبْنَان-KHuCHoBaAN- timbers).
- The SF that its pattern is (فَعَل-FaEaL) takes the BPP (أَفْعَال-AaFoEaAL) if, and only if, it is a noun. In fact, the pattern (أَفْعَال-AaFoEaAL) is a BPP of any Three-Letter noun else nouns that their singular pattern is (فُعَل-FuEaL) or nouns that their singular pattern is (فُعَل-FuEaL) and both of its first and second letters are sound and not a duplicated noun. E.g. (قَلَم-KaLaM- pen)- (أَقْلَام-AaKoLaAM-pens).
- The SF that its pattern is (فَعَل-FaEaL) takes the BPP (فُعُول-FuEuOL) if, and only if, it is a noun E.g. (أَسَد-AaSaD-lion) - (أُسُود-AuSuOD-lions).

The second pattern (فَعْل-FaEoL) takes {(أَفْعُل-AaFoEuL), (أَفْعَال-AaFoEaAL), (فُعُول-FuEuOL), (فِعَلَة-FiEaLaP) and (فِعَال-FiEaAL)} according to the following sets of conditions:

- The SF's that its pattern is (فَعْل-FaEoL) takes the BPP (أَفْعُل-AaFoEuL) if, and only if, it is a noun and it is not a duplicated noun, and its first and second root letters are sound. E.g. (بَحْر-BaHoR-see) - (أَبْحُر-AaBoHuR-sees) and (نَفْس-NaFoS-soul) - (أَنْفُس-AaNoFuS-souls).
- The SF that its pattern is (فَعْل-FaEoL) takes the BPP (أَفْعُل-AaFoEuL) if, and only if, it is a noun and its third letter is (و-O) or (ي-I); in other words, if it is a

defective noun. E.g. (دَلْو-DaLuO-buket) - (دِلاء-AaDoLin-bukets) and (صَاعَ-AaSaA-stick), its root letter (عصو-ESO), takes the PB (أُعْصِياء-AaSaX -stiks). As have been observed in these two cases the BP forms (أَدْل-AaDoLin-bukets) and (عُصِياء-AaSaX-stiks) that take the BPP (فِعُلا-AaFoEuL) change their form according to morphophonemic phenomena.

- The SF that its pattern is (فَعَل-FaEoL) takes the BPP (فُعُول-FuEuOuL) if, and only if, it is a noun and its second root letters must be different than the letter (O-و). E.g. the SF (بَيْت-BaYiT-hous) takes the BPF (بُيُوت-BuYouT-houses). The rest of the conditions have been extracted in the same manner.

3.3 Our Contribution

The previous linguistic study has been adopted to cover all BPPs. Then, we list all SFs' morphological, phonological and semantic features, which restrict the BP generation process. Each set of conditions gives a specific BPP. If one SF meets this set of conditions, then the result should be a BPP. An interlock between this BPP and the root will be executed using the grammar. This approach is based on traditional morphology. During the analysis, a stem is analyzed into a root and a pattern [4]. The Root-Pattern approach has been adopted to build our dictionary entries. The dictionary is linked to our inflectional and derivational grammars that generate BPFs.

4 Practical Study

4.1 Dictionary Structure

Our dictionary entries are formed as Fig. 1 Shows, (نَفْس-NaFoS-soul) is a SF, (نفس-nfs): its root, which is a N: Noun, m: masculine, its singular pattern (فَعَل, FaEoL), FLX: its inflectional paradigm, Flx-nfs: the name of the inflectional paradigm; DRV: its derivational paradigm. The same thing applies to the rest of entries: (ذِراع-DiRaE-arme) - (جَمَل-JaMaL-camel), each entry contains its morphological, phonological and semantic features. All entries that share the same root are linked to each other using this root, even if they don't share the same concept.

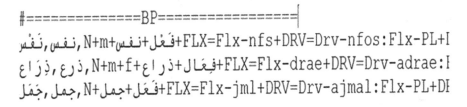

Fig. 1. Dictionary structure in NooJ platform.

The structure of the adopted dictionary allows to make advanced search in a text. Thus, we can extract both of singular's and BP's pattern/form.

4.2 Grammar Structure

The grammar contains two main Sub-grammars: the "FLX" and "DRV". The first one contains the inflectional forms of each dictionary entry. For example, "Flx-kabir" is the inflectional paradigm of the singular adjective (كَبِير-KaBiR/big). It reflects the interlock between the root of the entry (كَبِير-KaBiR/big), which is (KBR-كبر) and the singular pattern "فَعِيل-FaEiL" that is also stocked in the entry as we mentioned in the previous section. The grammar "DRV" generates the BPF. Linguistically, while the BP inflection doesn't change the grammatical category of the noun, adjective and grounds, it will be considered as an inflection of the SF not a derivation, to facilitate and distinguish between singular and BP graphs, we have considered it as derivational paradigm. Figure 2 Shows several derivational paradigms of certain BPPs, E.g. (Drv-3wasif) is a derivational paradigm, that generates the BPF of the SF (عَاصِفَة-EaSiFaP/storm) that has the root (ESF-عصف) and pattern (فَوَاعِل-FaWaAEiL).

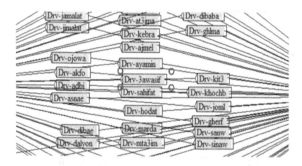

Fig. 2. A capture of derivational paradigms in NooJ Platform.

4.3 Text Analysis and Annotation

The analysis phase that relies on the dictionary and grammars detailed above, detects all BPFs in a given text. Figure 3 Shows a sentence that we are going to analyze: "I saw a sheep, camels, deers, whales, bears and lamps." The text contains:

- (خَرُوف - KHaRuF - sheep): SF that has the pattern: (فَعُول - FaEuOL), (جَمَل - JaMoL - camel): SF that has the pattern (فَعَل - FaEaL).
- (غِزْلَان - GHiZoLaAN - deers): BPF that has the pattern: (فِعْلَان - FiEoLAN).
- (حِيتَان - hitan - whales) BPF that has the pattern (فِعْلَان - FiEoLAN).
- (دِبَبَة - DiBaBa - bears) BPF that has the pattern: (فِعَلَة - FiEoLaP).
- (خَمَال - AaHoMaAL-lamps) BPF that has the pattern: (أَفْعَال - AFoEaAL).

The annotation in Fig. 3 shows the detailed features of the entry. The analyzed text contains several BPFs and SFs as shown in Fig. 4: (أنفُسٌ-أنفسَ-أنفساً-أنفسٌ-نُفوس-نُفوسٌ) are the inflections of the BPF (أنفُس-AaNoFuS-souls) and (نفَس-) are the inflections of the SF (نفَس-NaFoS-soul). The SF (حَمَل-HaMoL-lamp) takes the BPF (حُملانُ-HuMoLaANu-lamps)/(أحمال-AaHoMaAL-lamps). The analyzed text returns all features of each SF/BPF in a text.

Fig. 3. Text to be analyzed in NooJ platform.

Fig. 4. Annotation form in NooJ platform.

(نفَس-NaFoS-soul) refers to the SF of the analyzed BPF (أنفُس-anfes-souls) where the cursor is placed on. N: noun, Nb: number (singular, dual or plural). BP: means that the analyzed word is a BP, (فَعَل-FaEoL): the singular pattern of the analyzed BPF, (أفْعُل-AFoEuL) the BPP of the analyzed SF, (نفس-nfs): the root of the analyzed word. As we can observe that the dictionary stricter links each BPF with its SF.

4.4 Search Option Using Our Structure

As has previously mentioned, the dictionary structure allows us to make advanced searches in a text. We can extract any BPF using its SF. We can also extract all BPs using a specific root. In broad terms, we can make Root-Pattern search in an Arabic corp using the previous dictionary structure. Figure 5 refers to a search operation that

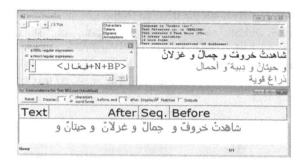

Fig. 5. An example of a Search using the pattern "FiEaAL", within a text using NooJ platform.

allows the extraction of all BPFs, which have the pattern (فِعَال-FiEaAL). As previously cited, this pattern may occur as a singular pattern or a BPP. This search will retrieve only BPFs that have (فِعَال-FiEaAL) as their patterns. Figure 5 Contains three merged wizards: text, search and annotation.

The sentence "strong arm" has been added to the previous text. The SF (ذراع-DiRaAE-arm) takes the pattern (فِعَال-FiEaAL). This pattern also occurs in the same text as BPP of (جمال-JiMaAL-camels). A search using the BPP (فِعَال-FiEaAL) wouldn't retrieve the SF "arm" even if its singular pattern is (فِعَال-FiEaAL), and reciproquely. A search of the singular pattern (فِعَال-FiEaAL) will not retrieve the BPF (جمال-JiMaAL-camels), even if this BPF has pattern is (فِعَال-FiEaAL) as its pattern. Thanks to NooJ's Text Annotation Structure (TAS), we have been able to annotate our text using this structure [6]. Our text annotation takes the form shown in Fig. 4.

5   Conclusion and Perspectives

This paper has presented a comprehensive BP model of Arabic HuMoR, adjectives and gerunds. We have generated BPFs using a Root-Pattern approach. We have also extracted 108 conditions that restrict this generation process. We have enumerated several obstacles that face the BP generation. We have presented our dictionary and grammar structure that allows to attach each generated BP to its SF. As it allows us to make advanced searches in Arabic corpora. Our model generates all inflectional and derivational paradigms of given nouns, adjectives and gerunds with their possible BP forms using NooJ platform.

Our perspective is concerned with covering other plural kinds like the ultimate plural (الجُمُوع مُنْتَهى-MuNoTaHaQ AaLoJuMuOE) that is considered as a kind of plural of multitude and plural of the plural (جَمْع الجُمُوع-JaMoEo AaLoJuMuOE) that is formed by pluralizing the BP using sound plural suffixes.

References

1. Majdi, S.S.S.: Open-source Resources and standards for Arabic Word Structure Analysis: Fine Grained Morphological Analysis of Arabic Text Corpora. Ph.D. School of Computing, the University of LEEDS, London (2011). http://etheses.whiterose.ac.uk/2165/
2. Dorit, R., Lubna, H.: Learning about different ways of expressing number in the development of palestinian Arabic. First Lang. 23, 41–63 (2003). https://doi.org/10.1177/0142723703023001003
3. El-Beltagy, S.R., Rafea, A.: A corpus based approach for the automatic creation of Arabic broken plural dictionaries. In: Gelbukh, A. (ed.) CICLing 2013, Part I. LNCS, vol. 7816, pp. 89–97. Springer, Heidelberg (2013). https://doi.org/10.1007/978-3-642-37247-6_8
4. Alexis, A.N., Eric, L.: Pattern-and-root inflectional morphology: the Arabic broken plural. Lang. Sci. 40, 221–250 (2013). https://doi.org/10.1016/j.langsci.2013.06.002
5. Blanchete, I., Mourchid, M., Mbarki, S., Mouloudi, A.: Formalizing Arabic inflectional and derivational verbs based on root and pattern approach using NooJ platform. In: Mbarki, S., Mourchid, M., Silberztein, M. (eds.) NooJ 2017. CCIS, vol. 811, pp. 52–65. Springer, Cham (2018). https://doi.org/10.1007/978-3-319-73420-0_5
6. Nooj association hom page. http://www.nooj-association.org/index.php?option=com_k2&view=item&id=2:arabic-resource&Itemid=611
7. Ellouze, S.: Etude ET Analyse du Pluriel Brisé Arabe avec la Platform NooJ. Master memory, faculty of economic sciences and management, Sfax, Tunisia (2010)
8. McCarthy, J.J., Prince, A.: Foot and word in prosodic morphology: the Arabic broken plural. Nat. Lang. Linguist. Theory 11 (1990). https://doi.org/10.1007/bf00208524
9. Beesley, K., Buckwalter, T., Newton, S.: Two-level finite- state analysis of Arabic morphology‖. In: Proceedings of the Seminar on Bilingual Computing in Arabic and English (1989)
10. Goweder, A., Poesio, M., De Roeck, A., Reynolds, J.: Identifying broken plural in unvowelised Arabic text. In: Proceedings of EMNLP, Barcelona, Spain, pp. 246–253 (2004)
11. Wright, W.: A Grammar of the Arabic Language. Cambridge University Press, Cambridge (1971)
12. Emeil, B.Y.: "الجُمُوع", first edition published by "AL-KOTOB AL-ILMIYAH", Beirut Lebanon. (2004)
13. ELSAMARAEI, F.: "مَعَاني الأبْنِيَة في اللُغَة العَرَبِيَة", second edition published by "DAR AMAR", aman Jordan, (2007)
14. Echbili, I.O.: "ألصَرْف في المُمْتِع", First Part published by " DAR EL-MAERIFAH", Beirut, Lebanon, (1987)
15. NEIMA, F.: "مُلخَص قَوَاعِد اللغة العَرَبِيَة", eighteenth edition published by " NAHDAT MASER" Deposit Num 3175
16. Ratcliffe, R.R.: The Broken " Plural Problem In Arabic and Comparative Semantic: Allomorphy and analogy in non-concatinative morphology". Jhone Benjamines Published Company, Amsterdam (1998)

Detecting Latin-Based Medical Terminology in Croatian Texts

Kristina Kocijan[1]([✉]) [ID], Maria Pia di Buono[2] [ID], and Linda Mijić[3] [ID]

[1] Department of Information and Communication Sciences,
Faculty of Humanities and Social Sciences, University of Zagreb, Zagreb, Croatia
krkocijan@ffzg.hr
[2] TakeLab ZEMRIS, Faculty of Electrical Engineering and Computing,
University of Zagreb, Zagreb, Croatia
mariapia.dibuono@fer.hr
[3] Department of Classical Philology, University of Zadar, Zadar, Croatia
lmijic@unidz.hr

Abstract. No matter what the main language of texts in the medical domain is, there is always an evidence of the usage of Latin-derived words and formative elements in terminology development. Generally speaking, this usage presents language-specific morpho-semantic behaviors in forming both technical-scientific and common-usage words. Nevertheless, this usage of Latin in Croatian medical texts does not seem consistent due to the fact that different mechanisms of word formation may be applied to the same term. In our pursuit to map all the different occurrences of the same concept to only one, we propose a model designed within NooJ and based on dictionaries and morphological grammars. Starting from the manual detection of nouns and their variations, we recognize some word formation mechanisms and develop grammars suitable to recognize Latinisms and Croatinized Latin medical terminology.

Keywords: Medical terminology · Morphological grammars
Latin terms · Latinisms · Croatian · Latin · NooJ

1 Introduction

Health data produced in today's world can easily be classified as big data: it has volume, it has variety and it has velocity. But the main problem we face is that it mostly comes in an unstructured format. NLP can help bring structure to it and with that structure enable learning. This paper will present the first step of a quest in bringing understanding that lies behind unstructured Croatian medical texts.

Before any NLP research on medical data can be started, it is presumed that it exists in the digital format, or as some like to call it the EHR (*Electronic Health Records*). Not all physicians have been eager to transfer to such format, nor happy when it is prescribed to them regardless the benefits such format of

© Springer Nature Switzerland AG 2019
I. Mauro Mirto et al. (Eds.): NooJ 2018, CCIS 987, pp. 38–49, 2019.
https://doi.org/10.1007/978-3-030-10868-7_4

data enables [1] like easily shared data among physicians but also hospitals and pharmaceutical industry that can help each other learn faster about different treatment results, or why is some drug working in some cases and not in others. This kind of data is usually found in an unstructured format in physicians' and nurses' notes, or CAT scans and MRI readings, that according to research, make up from 50% [2] up to 80% [3] of clinical records. In order to learn from such data and use it to improve patient's care, we need to understand it. Performance of such tools has been demonstrated in [3] and is reported to have more than 90% accuracy in detecting diseases.

There are also other health related data found in the digital format. More and more medical devices are Internet-enabled and are generating our biometric data. There is also metadata about the health terms we search for on the internet.

Still, we are mostly talking about 'privacy regulations' of health data that is present in medical institutions and not as much about how we can learn from this data faster to better suit the needs of each patient. One of the ways is to use the power of NLP to give some structure to the unstructured text and to find the paths to hidden knowledge that lies in it. The importance of morphological processing of biomedical text is seen in more advanced NLP tasks like information extraction [4] and question answering.

One of the potential problems in mining medical texts is diversity of terminology used [5]. The main characteristic of any (English, German, French, etc.) medical language is presence of Latin and Greek. However, in Croatian medical texts, these languages are not solemnly used in its pure original form [6,7]. We have found four types of notations that refer to the same concept: (1) **pure Latin terms** (lat. *diabetes mellitus*); (2) **Croatian translations** (hr. *šećerna bolest*); (3) **Latinisms or Croatian terms** with visible Latin root (hr. *dijabetes melitus*) and (4) **Croatinised Latin words** (Latin root with Croatian case ending) (lat_hr. *diabetes melitusom*). Still, when we search for cases of medicines prescribed, or diagnostics used for *diabetes mellitus*, we would like our results to include the remaining notations as well. Thus, it is important to find a way to link all notations i.e. to normalize them.

In the remaining sections, we will describe our learning corpus, dictionaries of pure Latin [Category 1] and pure Croatian terms [Category 2], and two morphological grammars that recognize the remaining two notations [Categories 3 and 4]. Before we conclude, we will show and explain the results we obtained on our learning corpus.

2   Related Work

The use of neo-classical compounds and morphemes in word formation has been widely analyzed, due to their intense use, especially in some domains with a very long tradition, like medicine. This phenomenon has been studied with regard to different languages [8–11].

The common finding is that a relatively short number of Greek and Latin forms (stems, prefixes and affixes) yields a high number of specialized terms. Further studies aim at extracting semantic information referring to medical entities from raw texts and the identification of the semantic categories that describe the located entities [12].

As regards the first task, many medical lexical databases (e.g., Medical Subject Headings (MeSH), RxNorm, Logical Observation Identifiers Names and Codes (LOINC), Systematized Nomenclature of Medicine (SNOMED), and Unified Medical Language System (UMLS), which includes all the other sources) can be used as knowledge base for the location of the medical entities. Anyway, the quick evolution of entity naming and the slowness of the manual development and updating of the resources often make it necessary to exploit some word formation strategies, that can be truly helpful in the automatic population of technical-scientific databases. Such strategies concern the morpho-semantic approach and have been successfully applied to the medical domain by [13] on terminal morphemes into an English medical dictionary; by [14] on medical formative elements of Latin and Greek origin; by [15] on the suffix *-itis*; by [16] on suffixes *-ectomy* or *-stomy* and by [17] on the suffix *-osis*. Among the most used tools for the Medical Entity Recognition (MER), we mention MetaMap [18], a reference tool which recognizes and categorizes medical terms by matching noun phrases in free texts to the corresponding UMLS Metathesaurus and Semantic Network, and MEDSYNDIKATE [19], a natural language processor able to automatically acquire data from medical findings reports.

With reference to the second task, we can find in literature rule-based, statistical and hybrid approaches. As regards the contributions that exploit statistical methods for the identification and classification of medical entities, we mention [20], that uses decision trees or SVMs; [21], that uses Hidden Markov Models or CRFs; [22], that presents a machine learning system which makes use of both local and syntactic features of the texts and external resources (gazetteers, web-querying, etc.); and [23], that obtains the nouns of disease, medical condition, treatment and symptom types, by using MQL queries and the Medlineplus Health Topics ontology. Rule-based methods are the ones proposed by [24], who identifies, with a set of graphical patterns, cause-effect information from medical abstracts in the Medline database, and [25], that manages to extract clinical entities disorders, symptoms and body structures from unstructured text in health records, using a rule-based algorithm.

Hybrid approaches have been proposed by [26] for the extraction of gene symbols and names; by [27] for protein name recognition and by [28], which combines terminology resources and statistical methods with sensible improvements in terms of Precision.

3   Corpus

For the preliminary learning phase, we chose two, relatively, small corpora that we have used for the purposes of terminology categorization. The first corpora (**MedNotes**) consists of 100 medical notes regarding the doctor's readings of MR, CT, X-ray and ultrasound images (total of 20.831 tokens). These documents were accessed with great difficulties taking all the necessary steps in protecting the patient's privacy and confidentiality of data (and General Data Protection Regulation (GDPR) as applied in May this year). Thus, the corpora has no mentions of any patient's name or any other personal information except for the gender inferred from the gender of word selections (feminine verbs, nouns and pronouns for female patients and masculine verbs, nouns and pronouns for male patients).

A second corpora (**MedInstruct**) consists of 100 randomly chosen instructions for the use of medicines (total of 213.275 tokens). These documents are not physician's notes but are written for the medical personal. Documents are published by the Agency for Medicines and Medical Products HALMED. Each instruction is written after the more-or-less same pattern and is much longer in length than the medical notes which explains the more numerous tokens then in the first corpora.

Our first assignment was to detect Latin-based nouns in both corpora and define their variations. Our data showed that terminology usage in Croatian medical texts is not consistent. So far, we have been able to detect 4 categories that needed somewhat different approaches for our NLP project:

1. Latin terms (usually written in italics in MedInstruct corpora),
2. Croatian terms,
3. Latinisms or Croatian terms with visible Latin root,
4. Croatinised Latin words (Latin word with Croatian case ending).

Some terms have been found in only two variations, e.g. Category 1 and Category 2: *vertigo* vs. *vrtoglavica*; or Category 1 and Category 3: *urticaria* vs. *urtikarija*; or Category 3 and Category 2: *agitacija* vs. *nemir* and *edem* vs. *otok*. There are also those terms that are found in all four categories. The best example is the term *diabetes mellitus* for which multiple versions are used inconsistently: *diabetes mellitus* (Category 1), *šećerna bolest* (Category 2), *dijabetes* (*melitus*) (Category 3), *diabetes melitusom* (Category 4).

The analysis shows that terminology from Category 1 have been used the least, usually for the names of microorganisms and common expressions like *in vitro*, *in vivo* etc. Some words used in nominative proved to be quite difficult to categorize since they can easily be found in Categories 1 and 4, like *fetus*, *agens*, *gastrosoma*, *lumen*, *tumor*, *uterus* or *retroperitoneum*. The only way to distinguish them was the usage of italics in the MedInstruct corpora. The reason for this ambiguity is that nominative form in both categories is the same.

Category 3 is the most numerous one. The words found in this category are loanwords adapted to the Croatian language by graphic system and appropriate declension. The rules of graphic changes are shown in Table 1.

As the examples from the table show, there are some words that have only one change of either vocal, diphthong or consonant, (sometimes, depending on the position) but there are also words with more changes, e.g. *erythema* to *eritem* and *resistentia* to *rezistencija* that have three changes each.

Some exceptions to these rules are represented by (i) the presence in Latin of two vowels that do not combine into a diphthong, e.g., ae in *aerob* and *aerobilija* and oe in *angioedem*, which in Croatian remain respectively ae and oe; (ii) the

Table 1. Change characteristics for Category 3

Letter	Condition	Latin	Croatian
æ > e	-	gangraena	gangrena
œ > e	-	œdem	edem
y > i	-	syncopa	sinkopa
ia > ija	except in words on *a-* w/prefix *anti-*	urticaria	urtikarija
ea > eja	-	diarrhoea	dijareja
c > k	w/o *-i*, *-e* behind *c*	syncopa	sinkopa
c = c	w/*i-*, *e-* behind *c*	faeces	feces
ph > f	-	sphincter	sfinkter
th > t	-	erythema	eritem
ch > k	-	chromaturia	kromaturia
rrh > r	-	diarrhoea	dijareja
ti > cij	w/vowels or diphthong	resistentia	rezistencija
ti = ti	w/*s*, *t*, *x* behind *ti*	*congestio	kongestija
s > z	between vowels	hyperhydrosis	hiperhidroza
x > ks	w/o a vowel behind *x*	radix	radiks
x > gz	w/a vowel behind *x*	exanthema	egzantem
dbl cons. > sgl cons.	-	tinnitus	tinitus

sequence *ea* in Latin, which is usually transposed in Croatian like *eja*, in some cases does not undergo any change, e.g., *urea* (and complexes with that word), *kreat(in)in, pankreas* (and complexes with that word), *proteaza, reapsorpcija* (hence all the words on *a-* with prefix *re-*); (iii) the transformation of double consonant into a single consonant is not applied to all words on *r-* with prefix *hiper-*. e.g., *hiperrefleksija*.

A noun of 2nd declension on *-ium* changes ending to *-ij*, e.g. *delirium* to *delirij, cranium* to *kranij* etc. A female noun of 3rd declension on *-tio* changes ending to *-cija*, e.g. *exacerbatio* to *egzacerbacija*. A 3rd declension neuter noun on *-ma* changes ending to *-m* e.g. *oedema, atis, n* to *edem; erythema, atis, n* to *eritem; *carcinoma* to *karcinom*. Terms with suffix *-oma*, meaning a swelling or tumor, always change *-ma* to *-m*. However, there are more examples where such a noun switches gender in Croatian to become a female noun on *-a* e.g. *coma > koma; asthma > astma; plasma > plazma; stroma > stroma;* etc. A 3rd declension female noun ending in *-osis* changes the ending to *-oza*, e.g. *hyperhydrosis > hiperhidroza.*

Croatinised Latin words are Latin words with Croatian case endings (Category 4): 2nd declension male nouns on *-us* (e.g. *cryptococcus, bacillus*) and 2nd declension male nouns on *-um* (e.g. *sputum*) receive set of case endings characteristic for the Croatian word *stol* (en. table) (a – Gen; u – Dat; / – Acc; e – Voc; u – Loc; om – Inst), and 2nd declension female nouns on *-a* (e.g. *Candida*) receive set of case endings typical of the word *kuća* (en. house) (e – Gen; i – Dat; u – Acc; o – Voc; i – Loc; om – Inst).

Our goal is to observe the words from different categories as morphological variants that are mapped into the single term. The normalization mapping rules that we use for each category are explained in the following sections.

4   Designing the Dictionary

For the purposes of this project, we have designed two separate dictionaries depending on the language the term belongs to: Latin and Croatian. We found it important to keep these two language data separate for both maintenance and cross-language usability purposes. As the new, to us 'UNKNOWN' terms are detected in corpora, they are processed, annotated and added to the main dictionary, either *Lat_MedicalTerms.dic* or *Hr_MedicalTerms.dic*.

4.1   Medical Latin Terminology

Medical Latin terms contain Greek terms that have been Latinized, original Latin terms and artificially created terms, according to the rules of word compilation which combine Latin and Greek stems, prefixes, and suffixes. The development of medicine also develops medical terminology so medical terminology needs to be standardized and taught at the medical faculties. The standardization in medical terminology is a necessity both for the successful work of physicians and for the development of medical informatics (by using computer software to increase the quality of diagnosis and treatment of patients).

Medical Latin encompasses anatomical, clinical and pharmacological nomenclature and is continually revised. The first anatomical nomenclature Basle Nomina Anatomica (BNA), published in 1895, is repetitively revised. The last version of anatomical terminology from 1998 Terminologia anatomica (TA98) is still developing and new terms are introduced every year. It seems that medical terminology now has about one million terms. The development of medicine nomenclature implies medical Latin is not a "dead language", but is still living and developing.

At present, our dictionary of Latin terminology consists of 583 nouns. Each term is marked for word category (N), gender (m—f—n), flective paradigm (FLX = paradigm). Additional semantic annotations are added, where appropriate, describing the language of the term (LAT), the main domain the term belongs to (Domena = MED), one or multiple subdomains where the term is used (DomenaType = ANAT—BACTERIA—DISEASE—DRUG—FUNGUS—KEM—PLANT—PROC—TOOL), Croatian translation of the term (HR = *translation*). Example of an entry *abdomen* [marked with letter A] is visualized in Fig. 1. The word is annotated as a noun [B], neutral in gender [D] using paradigm 3 to build remaining cases for Latin in both singular and plural forms [E] and using LAT as a language marker [F]. Sections marked with letters [G] and [H] show that the word belongs to the medical domain and anatomy as its subdomain field respectfully. The last letter [I] marks Croatian translation that is also provided and further annotated in the Croatian dictionary (Fig. 2).

Fig. 1. Example of a dictionary entry for Latin terms used in Lat_MedicalTerms.dic dictionary

We refer to terms found in this dictionary as Category 1 medical terms. It is to be expected that this dictionary can be used by any other language projects since, except for the last section [Fig. 1.: I], annotations used remain unchanged regardless the language. Thus, sharing this resource with others remains one of our priorities in this project since we believe that it will help us learn faster and be more productive if the similar projects across the globe do not have to start their work from the scratch.

4.2   Medical Croatian Terminology

The medical Latin terms are introduced and adapted to Croatian language or translated to Croatian. This type of terminology is found in the second dictionary, Hr_MedicalTerms.dic, since it is more language specific than is the case with the previously described dictionary. Still, the logic in annotation remains the same.

All the words found in the Latin dictionary, have their partner words (i.e. Croatian translations) in the Croatian dictionary. The opposite is not supported which is evident from the number of terms found in this dictionary (2373). Thus, continuing with our Latin example (Fig. 1) we have *trbuh* in Croatian dictionary (Fig. 2). The term [A] is annotated as a noun [B], of common type [C], masculine in gender [D] using paradigm PROPUH to build remaining 7 cases for Croatian in both singular and plural forms [E]. Sections marked with letters [G] and [H] show that the term belongs to the same domain and subdomain as in the Latin dictionary. Letters [F] and [I] found in the Latin example, are not used for Croatian terms.

Terms found in this dictionary are referred to as Category 2 medical terms. The remaining two categories are words that are produced following certain morphological rules. Thus, we decided to recognize them via grammars and link

Fig. 2. Example of a dictionary entry for Croatian terms used in Hr_MedicalTerms.dic dictionary

them to Category 1 medical term as their super-lemma [29]. We will explain this in more details in the following section.

5   Grammars

In order to recognize terms belonging to Categories 3 and 4, we have built two separate morphological grammars. We will explain each and discuss the problems we have encountered.

5.1   Grammar for Latinisms

Latinisms are Croatian terms with visible Latin root like *dijabetes melitus* that we recognize from Latin *diabetes mellitus*. These terms are classified as Category 3 and they all use specific morphological rules (see Table 1) to map Latin terms to Latinisms. These rules are consistent with rules for reading Latin. Grammar for recognizing and annotating described patterns (Fig. 3) requires the Latin term, from which Latinism is derived from, to exist in the dictionary. The rules make up a close set of IF-THEN statements such as *if (ae) in Latin **then** (e) in Latinism*. Building a grammar for these possibilities is quite straightforward in NooJ.

If each word could have only one change, our grammar would run much faster. However, there are words that undergo more than one change. Let us take the word *syncope* that comes from Latin *syncopa*. It's Latinism is *sinkopa*. In order to recognize it, we need to change *y* to *i* but also *c* to *k*. Another example is the Latin word *hyperhydrosis* that needs to change *y* to *i* twice and *s* to *z* to recognize Latinism *hiperhidroza*.

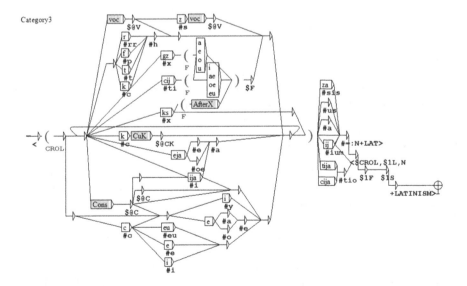

Fig. 3. Grammar for recognizing Latinisms in Category 3

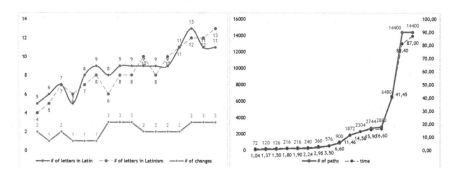

Fig. 4. Correlation of Latin vs Latinism word length vs number of expected changes (left graph) and number of paths vs run-time (right graph)

We have tested 16 example words from Table 1 to check what influences the time required for the grammar to check against all the possible varieties. As the graphs in Fig. 4 show, there is no clear correlation between the number of letters for either Latin words or Latinisms (in most cases, Latin words are longer) and the run time. The same is true for the number of expected changes, as well. There are six 9 letter words in our examples, with 2 or 3 expected changes, and each is taking different time to run, ranging from 2.24 s up to 15.90 s. But, what is correlated with longer run time, is the number of possible paths the grammar can take. This is best seen on a path for double consonants that are present in Latin words, but are not found in Latinisms. However, not all consonants are always doubled. But, since our grammar does not provide the context in which double consonants can occur, it assumes that there are no constraints for this rule and thus, every time it founds a consonant, it checks if it can pass the test that such a word exists in the Latin dictionary.

If we, for example, take the word *tinitus* that the grammar recognizes in the text, it will check for: *ttinitus, ttinnitus, ttinnittus, tinitus, tinnittus, tinittus* although only *tinnitus* will pass the constraint that it exists as a noun marked with +LAT in the main dictionary. To resolve this problem, we need to find more specific context for such paths in our graph.

5.2   Grammar for Croatinised Latin

Words that are placed in the Category 4 have kept the original Latin spelling in Nominative case. However, all the other case endings belong to the case markers characteristic of Croatian (and not Latin). Thus, instead of finding Latin ablative *diabete mellito* we have *diabetes mellitusom*.

The grammar for recognizing such Croatinised Latin words uses two variables **$LAT** and **$S** that hold any number of characters that, as such, exist in the Latin dictionary, and Croatian suffix, respectfully. The recognized string is also assigned Latin term as its super-lemma and a semantic label CROLAT (Fig. 5).

Fig. 5. Graph for recognizing Latinisms in Category 4

6   Results

Latin-based nouns detected by human annotators are distributed across categories in the following manner: Category 1 - 10%; Category 2 - 19%; Category 3 - 70%; Category 4 - 1%. This distribution is only in our test corpus and we expect it to change as the diversity of corpora gets larger.

After our preliminary tests failed to recognize all the terms from Categories 1 and 2, data quality was checked in both dictionaries to fix some erroneous data entries. Also, there were some multy word units that we have decided to deal with at the later stages of the project. Both grammars have correctly recognized and annotated all the tested terms.

Now, when we search for the Latin term *delirium* we recognize all the cases of this term belonging to categories 1 *delirium*, 3 *delirij* and 4 *deliriumom*. In order to recognize Croatian term as well, or all categories when Croatian term *bunilo* is given as a search term, additional grammars will have to be designed to manage such normalization mapping rules.

7   Conclusion

In this paper we present our preliminary work on the the usage of Latin-derived words and formative elements in the development of Croatian medical terminology. We identified four types of this usage: (1) pure Latin terms; (2) Croatian translations; (3) Latinisms or Croatian term with visible Latin root and (4) Croatinised Latin words (Latin root with Croatian case ending). The model we propose here for linking together Latin-Croatian combinations, can also be reused for other languages that are present in medical texts, like Greek, English, or French. Our results give an account of its usefulness and permit to foresee a future fields of work such as (a) establishment of further constraints regarding form combination and formation; (b) analysis in detail of the neoclassical suffixes and prefixes; (c) further study of the combination of a form with general language word, combining the current module with an ontology; (d) test these results in larger corpora.

We also plan to test the model on a bigger and more diverse texts and, if needed, expand the existing grammar with new nodes and rules. In later stages, we plan to expand the research with similar morphological grammars that will recognize other word types such as adjectives and verbs.

Acknowledgement. This research has been partly supported by the European Regional Development Fund under the grant KK.01.1.1.01.0009 (DATACROSS).

References

1. Schneier, B.: The Hidden Battles to Collect your Data and Control your World. Data and Goliath, London (2015)
2. Davenport, T.: Big Data at Work: Dispelling the Myths, Uncovering the Opportunities. Harvard Business Review Press, Boston (2014)
3. Simon, P.: Too Big to Ignore: The Business Case for Big Data, vol. 72. Wiley, Hoboken (2013)
4. Liu, H., Christiansen, T., Baumgartner, W.A., Verspoor, K.: Biolemmatizer: a lemmatization tool for morphological processing of biomedical text. J. Biomed. Semant. **3**(1), 3 (2012)
5. di Buono, M.P., Maisto, A., Pelosi, S.: From linguistic resources to medical entity recognition: a supervised morphosyntactic approach. ALLDATA **2015**, 82 (2015)
6. Poljak, Ž.: Quo vadis, Croatian medical terminology-should the diagnoses be written in Croatian, Latin or English? Acta Clinica Croatica **46**(1–Supplement 1), 121–126 (2007)
7. Gjuran-Coha, A., Bosnar-Valković, B.: Lingvistička analiza medicinskoga diskursa. JAHR **4**(7), 107–128 (2013)
8. Estopa, R., Vivaldi, J., Cabre, M.T.: Use of Greek and Latin forms for term detection. In: LREC (2000)
9. Herrero-Zorita, C., Moreno-Sandoval, A.: Medical term formation in English and Japanese. Rev. Cogn. Linguist. **13**(1), 81–105 (2015). Published under the auspices of the Spanish Cognitive Linguistics Association
10. Smith, G.L., Davis, P.E., Soltesz, S.E.: Quick Medical Terminology. In: Smith, G.L., Davis, P.E. (eds.) Consultation with Shirley Soltesz, E. Wiley, Hoboken (1972)
11. Piñero, J.M.L., Terrada, M.L.: Introducción a la terminología médica. Elsevier, España (2005)
12. Abacha, A.B., Zweigenbaum, P.: Medical entity recognition: a comparison of semantic and statistical methods. In: Proceedings of BioNLP 2011 Workshop, pp. 56–64. Association for Computational Linguistics (2011)
13. Pacak, M., Pratt, A.: Identification and transformation of terminal morphemes in medical English Part II. Methods Inf. Med. **17**(02), 95–100 (1978)
14. Wolff, S.: The use of morphosemantic regularities in the medical vocabulary for automatic lexical coding. Methods Inf. Med. **23**(04), 195–203 (1984)
15. Pacak, M.G., Norton, L., Dunham, G.S.: Morphosemantic analysis of-itis forms in medical language. Methods Inf. Med. **19**(02), 99–105 (1980)
16. Norton, L., Pacak, M.G.: Morphosemantic analysis of compound word forms denoting surgical procedures. Methods Inf. Med. **22**(01), 29–36 (1983)
17. Dujols, P., Aubas, P., Baylon, C., Grémy, F.: Morpho-semantic analysis and translation of medical compound terms. Methods Inf. Med. **30**(1), 30–35 (1991)
18. Aronson, A.R.: Effective mapping of biomedical text to the UMLS metathesaurus: the metamap program. In: Proceedings of the AMIA Symposium, p. 17. American Medical Informatics Association (2001)
19. Hahn, U., Romacker, M., Schulz, S.: Medsyndikate-a natural language system for the extraction of medical information from findings reports. Int. J. Med. Inform. **67**(1–3), 63–74 (2002)

20. Isozaki, H., Kazawa, H.: Efficient support vector classifiers for named entity recognition. In: Proceedings of the 19th international conference on Computational linguistics, vol. 1, pp. 1–7. Association for Computational Linguistics (2002)

21. He, Y., Kayaalp, M.: Biological entity recognition with conditional random fields. In: AMIA Annual Symposium Proceedings, vol. 2008, p. 293. American Medical Informatics Association (2008)

22. Finkel, J., Dingare, S., Nguyen, H., Nissim, M., Manning, C., Sinclair, G.: Exploiting context for biomedical entity recognition: from syntax to the web. In: Proceedings of the International Joint Workshop on Natural Language Processing in Biomedicine and its Applications, pp. 88–91. Association for Computational Linguistics (2004)

23. de la Villa, M., Aparicio, F., Maña, M.J., de Buenaga, M.: A learning support tool with clinical cases based on concept maps and medical entity recognition. In: Proceedings of the 2012 ACM international conference on Intelligent User Interfaces, pp. 61–70. ACM (2012)

24. Khoo, C.S., Chan, S., Niu, Y.: Extracting causal knowledge from a medical database using graphical patterns. In: Proceedings of the 38th Annual Meeting on Association for Computational Linguistics, pp. 336–343. Association for Computational Linguistics (2000)

25. Skeppstedt, M., Kvist, M., Dalianis, H.: Rule-based entity recognition and coverage of snomed ct in swedish clinical text. In: LREC, pp. 1250–1257 (2012)

26. Proux, D., Rechenmann, F., Julliard, L., Pillet, V., Jacq, B.: Detecting gene symbols and names in biological texts. Genome Inform. **9**, 72–80 (1998)

27. Liang, T., Shih, P.-K.: Empirical textual mining to protein entities recognition from PubMed corpus. In: Montoyo, A., Muñoz, R., Métais, E. (eds.) NLDB 2005. LNCS, vol. 3513, pp. 56–66. Springer, Heidelberg (2005). https://doi.org/10.1007/11428817_6

28. Roberts, A., Gaizauskas, R.J., Hepple, M., Guo, Y.: Combining terminology resources and statistical methods for entity recognition: an evaluation. In: LREC (2008)

29. Silberztein, M.: Formalizing Natural Languages: The NooJ Approach. Wiley, London (2016)

Processing Croatian Aspectual Derivatives

Krešimir Šojat[1], Kristina Kocijan[2]([⊠]) [iD], and Matea Filko[1]

[1] Department of Linguistics, University of Zagreb, Zagreb, Croatia
{ksojat,matea.filko}@ffzg.hr
[2] Department of Information and Communication Sciences,
Faculty of Humanities and Social Sciences, University of Zagreb,
Zagreb, Croatia
krkocijan@ffzg.hr

Abstract. The main objective of this paper is to detect and describe major derivational processes and affixes used in the derivation of aspectually connected Croatian verbs. This kind of analysis is enabled by previous detection of verbal derivational families, i.e. families of verbs with the same root as well as the derivational affixes they contain. Using NooJ, we automatically detect such derivational processes and assign the aspectual tag to derivatives. The procedure is based on the list of selected base forms and derivatives, on the list of derivational affixes and their allomorphs, and on the set of derivational rules. For this objective we selected 15 verbal derivational families comprising app. 250 derivatives in total. The output is being used for the development of a large on-line database of Croatian aspectual pairs, triples and quadruplets. Such a resource will be valuable for various research works in lexicology and lexicography.

Keywords: Derivationally connected verbs · Prefixation · Suffixation
Aspectual derivatives · Aspectual pairs · Aspectual triples
Aspectual quadruplets · Croatian · NooJ

1 Introduction

This paper deals with computational processing of Croatian derivational morphology. We focus on verbal derivation and aspect. Our objective is to present preliminary work done during the construction of the database of Croatian aspectually and derivationally connected verbs, i.e. **aspectual derivatives**.

Croatian is a South Slavic language with very rich inflectional and derivational morphology. Inflectional phenomena are extensively covered by two publicly available large lexica for Croatian – Croatian Morphological Lexicon (CML) (Tadić and Fulgosi 2003) and hrLex (Ljubešić et al. 2016). Each lexicon, used for various NLP tasks such as lemmatization, POS and MSD tagging, etc., contains complete inflectional data for more than 100 000 lemmas. The computational processing of Croatian derivation is on a much smaller scale compared to the size of these inflectional lexica.

© Springer Nature Switzerland AG 2019
I. Mauro Mirto et al. (Eds.): NooJ 2018, CCIS 987, pp. 50–61, 2019.
https://doi.org/10.1007/978-3-030-10868-7_5

CroDeriV (Šojat et al. 2013) is an on-line database that contains app. 14 500 Croatian verbs and provides information about their morphological structure and derivational relatedness. Derivational families consist of verbs that share the same lexical morpheme. Although CroDeriV enables the detection of all derivational affixes in lemmas, derivational processes, e.g. prefixation or suffixation, within derivational families are currently neither specified nor indicated to users. Still, CroDeriV is a valuable source of data for various research, including this one as well.

Here, we use linguistic data from CroDeriV for the detection of derivational processes and affixes within selected derivational families. By using NooJ (Silberztein 2016) as our NLP tool, we firstly aim to automatically detect processes such as prefixation or suffixation. Secondly, we want to automatically assign the aspectual tag to derivatives, i.e. to determine whether a verb is perfective or imperfective.

The paper is structured as follows: in Sect. 2 we briefly describe major derivational processes in Croatian and focus on the derivation of verbs from other verbs and aspectual changes that take place. Section 3 deals with analysis of data, whereas in Sect. 4 the NooJ dictionary of verbs is presented. In Sect. 5 we dissect the morphology to find the patterns that we can use for the NooJ grammar and provide an overview of underlying principles. In Sect. 6 the design and the structure of the web-based database of Croatian aspectual verbal pairs is briefly discussed. The paper concludes with an outline of the future work.

2 Derivational Processes and Aspectual Changes

Derivation and compounding are major word-formation processes used in Croatian. However, unlike in some other languages, e.g. German, compounding is not as productive as derivation. For the purposes of this project, we will deal only with derivation, which is in Croatian mainly based on affixation. Our main focus is the derivation of verbs from other verbs. Although there are some other processes, like conversion and back formation, they are not as prominent as for example prefixation and suffixation.

As far as derivationally connected verbs are concerned, i.e. those that share the lexical morpheme and therefore belong to the same derivational family, they are derived from other verbs via prefixation, suffixation, stem alternations or various combinations of these processes. We only briefly deal with stem alternations (cf. Sect. 3), since this area requires a different approach due to frequent allomorphy of roots or stems. Still, a complete list of variants is a prerequisite for an accurate description.

Full derivational spans of selected base forms in terms of verb-to-verb derivation used in this paper are extracted from CroDeriV. The derivational span refers to all derivatives that are connected to a particular base form. The base form refers to the simplest verb within a family regarding its morphological structure and is used for the derivation of other members. The size of verbal derivational families significantly varies: some of them consist of only one or two members, while others encompass more than 30 or 40 derivatives. For example, the derivational family based around the base form *pisati* 'to write' contains 31 verbal derivatives. Out of this number, more than 50% (16 in total) of verbs are derived via prefixation.

As in other Slavic languages, each verb in Croatian is always marked for aspect and classified as perfective, imperfective, or bi-aspectual. Generally, the perfective aspect is used to describe actions, processes and states as finished or completed, whereas the imperfective aspect refers to them as unfinished or ongoing, e.g.:

1. a. *Pisala je* [imperfective] članak jedan sat.   1b. She *was writing* an article for an hour.
2. a. *Napisala je* [perfective] članak za jedan sat.   2b. She *wrote* an article in an hour.

Verbs like *pisati* 'to write + imperfective' – *napisati* 'to write, to finish writing + perfective' are usually referred to as aspectual pairs. Verbs in aspectual pairs are closely related in meaning, except that one expresses perfective and the other imperfective aspect. Aspect in Croatian is inherent verbal category – it is morphologically marked in each verbal form and it affects inflectional properties of verbs to a certain degree (Kocijan et al. 2018). Furthermore, it is regarded as a word-formation process and members of aspectual pairs are treated as separate lexical entries in dictionaries.

Although the verbal aspect in Slavic languages is based on the opposition of only two aspects and it is overtly marked, numerous studies in the area of second language acquisition indicate that aspect is one of the most complicated category for learners of Slavic languages (Cvikić and Jelaska 2007).

In terms of derivation, perfectives are commonly derived from imperfectives by prefixation, while imperfectives can be formed from perfectives by suffixation or stem alternation. The presence of certain affixes indicates whether a verb is a perfective or an imperfective. A relatively small group of bi-aspectual verbs, mostly of foreign origin, can be used as perfectives and imperfectives in the same morphological form. Various factors can determine whether they will be used as perfectives or imperfectives (e.g. a context, the type of time adverbial used in a sentence, etc.).

As indicated, prefixation is the most productive process in the derivation of verbs from other verbs, although other affixes enable further derivation, either through multiple prefixation, suffixation or simultaneous prefixation and suffixation. Croatian verbs can thus be divided into simple imperfectives (*pisati* 'to write + imperfective') for on-going actions and prefixed perfectives (*na-pisati* 'to write + perfective') for completed actions. Such pairs are referred to as **primary aspectual pairs**. Further derivation of perfectives in primary aspectual pairs is not possible.

It is important to notice that other prefixes used for the derivation of perfectives in this derivational family can add different semantic features to the meaning of the base verb (e.g. *pisati* 'to write + imperfective' – *pre-pisati* 'to copy by writing + perfective' – *pot-pisati* 'to sign + perfective') as thoroughly discussed in Šojat et al. (2012). In such cases, further derivation of aspectual derivatives is possible, either through prefixation, suffixation or simultaneous prefixation and suffixation. Polančec (2018) explains how such perfectives can be derived into secondary imperfectives usually denoting iterative actions through suffixation (*potpis-iva-ti* 'to sign several/many times').

Simultaneous prefixation and suffixation yields derivatives usually denoting actions performed in a sufficient, abundant or excessive manner like in the following examples:

- *jesti* 'to eat + imperfective' – *najesti se* 'to eat one's fill + perfective';
- *raditi* 'to work + imperfective' – *naraditi se* 'to tire oneself out with work + perfective';

- *pisati* 'to write + _{imperfective}' – *napisati se* 'to be weary of writing + _{perfective}'.[1]

On the other hand, a set of suffixes is used for the derivation of diminutive verbs as is the case with

- *pisati* – *pis-kar-a-ti* 'to scribble + _{imperfective}'

or verbs expressing punctual actions

- *vikati* 'to shout + _{imperfective}' – *vik-nu-ti* 'to shout once + _{perfective}'.

Some secondary imperfectives are further derived via prefixation into perfectives denoting distributive actions as in

- *is-potpisivati* 'to sign each one + _{perfective}', e.g. each letter, every document, etc.

On top of that, aspectual distinctions are in some cases expressed by vowel variations or suppletive forms, like

- *doći* 'to come + _{perfective}' – *dolaziti* 'to come + _{imperfective}'.

To sum up, verbs in Croatian are derived from other verbs by prefixation and suffixation. Both processes can trigger a change in aspect and the addition of a new semantic component to the base form. Apart from aspectual change, semantic components brought by affixes can produce combinations that, in terms of meaning, can vary from compositional to completely idiosyncratic. Detailed account of such morphosemantic relations among Croatian verbal derivatives, frequently referred to also as Aktionsart, is found in Šojat et al. (2012).

In the following section, the analysis of selected derivational families is presented. This analysis should enable the automatic detection of derivational processes and aspectual changes as well as the development of morphological rules used by NooJ in the later stages of this research (cf. Sect. 5).

3 Data Analysis and Rules

In order to learn how we can automatically detect and annotate major derivational processes and affixes used in the derivation of aspectually connected verbs, a thorough analysis was performed. This analysis was facilitated by the extraction of derivational families, i.e. families of verbs with the same root, as well as the derivational affixes they contain. We started the analysis by selecting 15 verbal derivational families from CroDeriV comprising app. 250 derivatives in total. We manually analyzed all derivational processes in these families, marked derivational chains and inserted aspectual tags to derivatives.

---

[1] Although the element *se* is normally regarded as a reflexive particle and not treated as an affix in Croatian textbooks on this subject, for the sake of demonstration we treat it here as a suffix.

To demonstrate, we shall use the derivational family grouped around the base form *pisati* 'to write + ₍ₐ₎imperfective'. This family group consists of 32 members.[2] The analysis consisted of assigning tags for aspect (IPF – imperfective, PF – perfective, BI – bi-aspectual) and specifying the type of affixation (prefixation, suffixation, etc.):

- *pisati*   (IPF)   –   *napisati*   (PF)   –   [prefixation]
- *pisati*   (IPF)   –   *dopisati*   (PF)   –   [prefixation]
- *dopisati*   (PF)   –   *dopisivati*   (IPF)   –   [suffixation]
- *dopisivati* (IPF)   –   *dopisivati se* (IPF)   –   [suffixation + se]
- *pisati*   (IPF)   –   *potpisati*   (PF)   –   [prefixation]
- *potpisati*   (PF)   –   *potpisivati*   (IPF)   –   [suffixation]
- *potpisivati* (IPF)   –   *ispotpisivati* (PF)   –   [prefixation]
- *pisati*   (IPF)   –   *napisati se*   (PF)   –   [prefixation + se]

We manually marked 250 derivatives from 15 derivational families following the same procedure. On the basis of this analysis, we developed 10 general rules that can be used for automatic detection of particular derivational processes and possible change of aspect. The rules are designed for pairs of verbs, while the description of full derivational paths (e.g. *pisati – prepisati – prepisivati – isprepisivati*) is in the testing phase. Based on the analyzed data, we have formed the following set of ten IF-THEN rules:

1. **IF** base form is prefixed

   THEN simple imperfective →[3] prefixed perfective (*pisati – dopisati*)

2. **IF** prefixed perfective is suffixed

   THEN prefixed perfective → suffixed secondary imperfective (*dopisati – dopisivati*)

3. **IF** base form is suffixed

   THEN simple imperfective → suffixed (deminutive/pejorative) imperfective (*pisati – piskarati*)

4. **IF** base form is suffixed with *-nu-*

   THEN simple imperfective → suffixed (punctual) perfective (*vikati – viknuti*)

5. **IF** base form is simultaneously prefixed and suffixed

   THEN simple imperfective → prefixed/suffixed imperfective (*pisati – napisati se*)

---

[2] Complete data for this derivational family and other discussed in the paper can be retrieved from http://croderiv.ffzg.hr/.

[3] → stands for 'changes into'.

6. **IF** suffixed secondary imperfective is suffixed with *se*

   THEN suffixed secondary imperfective ➜ suffixed secondary imperfective + *se* (*dopisivati – dopisivati se* 'to correspond in writing')

7. **IF** prefixed perfective is prefixed

   THEN prefixed perfective ➜ multiple prefixed perfective (*dopisati – nadopisati*)

8. **IF** multiple prefixed perfective is suffixed

   THEN multiple prefixed perfective ➜ suffixed secondary imperfective (*nadopisati – nadopisivati*)

9. **IF** multiple prefixed secondary imperfective is prefixed

   THEN multiple prefixed secondary imperfective ➜ multiple prefixed (distributive) perfective (*potpisivati – ispootpisivati*).

10. **IF** simple perfective is prefixed

    THEN simple perfective ➜ prefixed perfective (*baciti – izbaciti*).
    For the derivation of aspectual pairs based on suffix alternation, e.g.:

- *bacati* 'to throw + $_{imperfective}$' – *baciti* 'to throw + $_{perfective}$' or
- *lupati* 'to hit + $_{imperfective}$' – *lupiti* 'to hit + $_{perfective}$',

an additional rule was introduced. Moreover, as mentioned in Sect. 2, these rules do not cover root or stem alternations used in verbal derivation. Such instances require a separate set of rules based on a list of detected allomorphs, as is the case in the following sets:

- *dovoditi* 'to bring + $_{imperfective}$' – *dovesti* 'to bring + $_{perfective}$',
- *gađati* 'to aim + $_{imperfective}$' – *pogoditi* 'to hit + $_{perfective}$'.

Due to frequently unpredictable derivational paths, the rules can also not tackle derivations of verbs like:

- *čekati* 'to wait + $_{perfective}$' – *očekivati* 'to await + $_{imperfective}$' or
- *raditi* 'to work + $_{perfective}$' – *surađivati* 'to cooperate + $_{imperfective}$'.

The problem is a missing link in a derivation from a simple imperfective to a prefixed secondary imperfective (prefixed perfectives like **suraditi* or **očekati* do not exist (Polančec 2018)). Thus, such examples have to be tagged manually.

In Sect. 5 we further discuss how the morphological structure of verbs affects aspectual tagging of lemmas and how this problem can be handled with NooJ. Before that, we briefly present how aspectual data was incorporated into NooJ dictionary of Croatian verbs and how it benefited in terms of its enlargement and enrichment.

4 Dictionary of Croatian Verbs

NooJ language resources for Croatian (Vučković 2009; Vučković et al. 2010; Kocijan et al. 2018) include a dictionary of verbs that holds 4 225 entries[4]. All the verbs have been marked for part of speech (V), paradigm responsible for generation of verbs' flective forms and recently for aspect (Kocijan et al. 2018) as well. Morphological grammar uses the aspect information in order to properly annotate derived forms. Thus, it was important to add information on aspect directly to the dictionary entries.

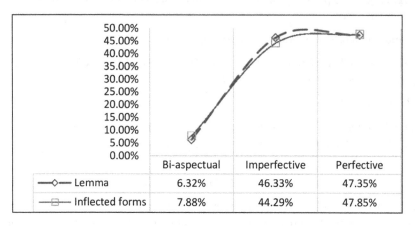

	Bi-aspectual	Imperfective	Perfective
◇ Lemma	6.32%	46.33%	47.35%
⊟ Inflected forms	7.88%	44.29%	47.85%

Fig. 1. Distribution of verbs by aspect in main (lemma) and flective dictionaries (inflected forms)

Aspect wise, there are 267 bi-aspectual verbs marked as [+Aspect = dual], 1 957 imperfective verbs [+Aspect = inf], and 2 000 perfective verbs [+Aspect = fin]. When linked to its paradigm rules, NooJ produces dictionary of 376 583 flective verb forms that holds 29 675 bi-aspectual, 166 753 imperfective and 180 155 flective entries. Distributions of Aspects in both dictionaries (main and flective) are almost identical (Fig. 1). The slight difference is due to the variation in number of tenses used in paradigm descriptions (Kocijan et al. 2018).

5 Dissecting Morphology

Croatian grammars (Babić 2002; Barić et al. 2003; Silić and Pranjković 2005) provided us with the list of prefixes and suffixes used for derivation of verbs. However, that was not enough for our project. We needed to make additional understanding of what

---

[4] The dictionary is continuously updated with new verbs. Thus, the number of main entries may vary from any previous and future references to this dictionary.

happens before and after the main verb, and in some cases, inside the word. For this purpose, as stated earlier, a list of 15 base verbs with all their verbal derivatives was prepared. The selected base verbs are:

pisati 'to write'	*raditi* 'to work'	*bacati* 'to throw'	*hraniti* 'to feed'
jesti 'to eat'	*piti* 'to drink'	*kuhati* 'to cook'	*čistiti* 'to clean'
čekati 'to wait'	*plakati* 'to cry'	*ljubiti* 'to kiss'	*reći* 'to say'
trčati 'to run'	*puzati* 'to crowl'	*plivati* 'to swim'.	

The selection of verbs was made mostly arbitrary trying to cover as much diversity as possible. The list was transferred to a sandbox area for thorough analysis that resulted with 8 distinguishable patterns that we will refer to as models 1 through 8.

The main difference between models is the number and position of affixes used for the derivation (Table 1). Prefixes are marked with letter P and a number 1 through 4 describing its position from the main root. Suffixes are marked with letter S and a number 1 through 3. In both cases, the larger the number, the farther away from the root affixes are found. Each model has at least one prefix (P1) and one suffix (S3). If there is a prefix in position four (P4), all the proceeding positions must be filled as well. The opposite is true for suffixes, i.e. if there is a suffix in position one (S1), all the following positions must be filled (in this case S2 and S3).

Table 1. Eight derivational models

Mod-el	Prefixes				Root	Suffixes		
	P4	P3	P2	P1	*root*	S1	S2	S3
M1	✻	✻	✻	✻	✻		✻	✻
M2		✻	✻	✻	✻		✻	✻
M3		✻	✻	✻	✻			✻
M4			✻	✻	✻	✻	✻	✻
M5			✻	✻	✻		✻	✻
M6			✻	✻	✻			✻
M7				✻	✻		✻	✻
M8				✻	✻			✻

Although the list of prefixes is a closed set, their selection depends on their position (P1, P2, P3 or P4). So far, we have detected only two paths for prefixes that fill all four positions[5] (Fig. 2 – Area 4). Each position is marked as global variable @P, @P2, @P3 and @P4 respectful of their position.

---

[5] In the present stage, we have treated the prefixes and their allomorphes as separate units in order to make the grammars in Nooj more simple and easier to process.

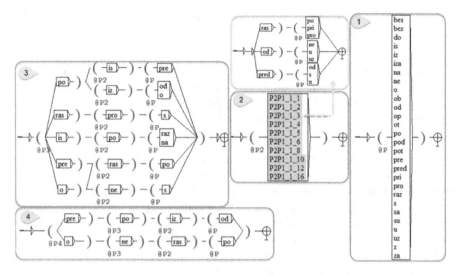

Fig. 2. Selection of prefixes depending on their number and position

Prefixes that fill three positions (Fig. 2 – Area 3) have 9 possible combinations (paths), and depending on the context, some prefixes may be found in any of three positions (e.g.: *po-*), but they are never doubled or tripled. The same is true for prefixes that fill two positions (Fig. 2 – Area 2). However, the number of their combinations (paths) is much higher. In order to keep the grammars as clean and readable as possible, these combinations have been categorized into ten sets, depending on the number of P prefixes that can be found after the prefix in P2 position. For example, there are 14 P2 prefixes that can have only 1 (not necessarily the same) P prefix, but there are only 2 P2 prefixes (*po-, pre-*) that can have 16 P prefixes.

The matrix in Table 2 is used to show detected pairs when only two prefix positions are filled. Most of the prefixes are found in both positions, while five are found only in the first position i.e. in position P (*bes-, bez-, op-, sa-, z-*)[6] and nine only in the second position i.e. in position P2 (*i-, poda-, pra-, pret-, raza-, re-, us-, ras-*).[7] This matrix served us as a reference point for constructing the paths for each of the models.

After the learning phase during which we worked on the grammar design, we tested it on 1 650 verbs to see how well it performs. The selected verbs were either base verbs or derivatives, and are presently in our NooJ dictionary. The system scored 87% on both precision and recall. As expected, we found a number of false positives. Our future work will include their thorough analyzes and categorization, so we can learn from them in order to enhance the existing grammar.

---

[6] Note that *bes-* and *bez-* are actually allomorphs of the prefix *bez-*, and that *sa-* and *z-* are allomorphs of the prefix *s-*. The prefix *i-* is actually an allomorph of the prefix *iz-*. Therefore, it would be correct to say that only three prefixes are found only in position P.

[7] In this case, the prefix *i-* is an allomorph of the prefix *iz-*, *raza-* and *ras-* are allomorphs of the prefix *raz-*, *pret-* is an allomorph of *pred-*, *poda-* is an allomorph of *pod-* and *us-* is an allomorph of *uz-*.

Table 2. Ten categories of pairs of prefixes found in positions P2 (rows) and P1 (columns)

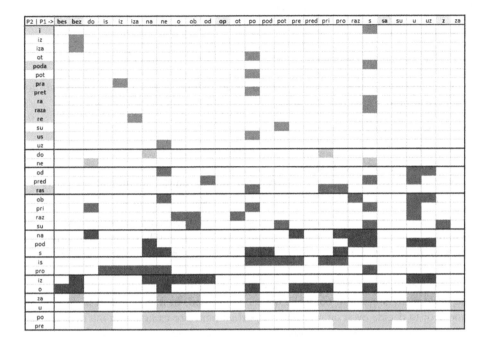

6 The Database of Aspectual Derivatives

Behind the main initiative for this project is the development of an on-line database of Croatian aspectual pairs. We used NooJ to detect derivational processes and automatically assign aspectual tags to derivatives in a database suitable format. The procedure was based on two separate lists and a set of morphological rules described earlier. The first list is a selection of base forms and derivatives and the second one of derivational affixes and their allomorphs. The morphological rules that were designed have to perform two tasks: recognize the derived form and the verb it is derived from, and annotate the derived verb appropriately. All the tagged verbs can subsequently be automatically imported to the web-based database and used in a web search as described in Kocijan et al. (2018).

In its present form, the database provides the information about the main verb (including its aspect), aspect of a derived verb and affixes used within derivational family. In future, we plan to upgrade the database entries taking into consideration lexical semantics of base forms and derivatives. As it is indicated in Sect. 2, apart from aspectual change, derivations produce combinations that, in terms of meaning, vary from compositional to completely idiosyncratic. For example:

a. compositional:

- *trčati* 'to run + _imperfective_' – *utrčati* 'to run into + _perfective_' – *utrčavati* 'to run into + _secondary imperfective_'
- *plivati* 'to swim + _imperfective_' – *uplivati* 'to swim into + _perfective_' – *uplivavati* 'to swim into + _secondary imperfective_'

b. (more or less) idiosyncratic:

- *zreti* 'to ripen + _imperfective_' – *prezreti* 'to scorn + _perfective_' – *prezirati* 'to scorn + _secondary imperfective_'
- *staviti* 'to put + _perfective_' – *predstaviti* 'to introduce, to present + _perfective_' – *predstavljati* 'to introduce, to present + _secondary imperfective_'.

Our aim is to group prefixed perfectives and secondary imperfectives, as in examples above, into single entries within derivational families. The same principle will be followed for the aspectual combinations covered by the morphological rules in Sect. 3 of this paper.

However, due to complex semantics of Slavic verbs, sometimes seemingly simple and basic matters can turn out to be quite complicated. In many cases it is difficult to choose or to decide even on a primary aspectual pair. For example, in the derivational family grouped around *raditi* 'to work + _imperfective_' there are two candidates (*uraditi* 'to make + _perfective_', *poraditi* 'to make an effort + _perfective_'). Since these derivatives cannot be further suffixed, their choice would be fully justified in terms of morphological rules. However, semantically, none of the candidates corresponds to the base form, the meaning of derivatives is not compositional and, consequently, the entries for these aspectual derivatives cannot be generated automatically. We plan to further experiment with this line of work in future. Since a large amount of manual work is expected, the design of the database will enable a collaboration of multiple editors.

7 Conclusion and Future Work

We have presented preliminary stages in the construction of the database of Croatian aspectually and derivationally connected verbs, i.e. aspectual derivatives. Detected derivational models and categories of prefix' combinations have been thoroughly described, visualized and exemplified to demonstrate the complexity of the project.

The morphological grammar proposed here lays down the fourfold basis for the following projects: (a) detection of unknown verbs in the text and connecting them to the main (root) verbs they were derived from; (b) automatic annotation of unknown verbs that will enlarge the existing NooJ dictionary of verbs (this should not be considered as the primary way of adding new verbs, but rather an auxiliary one and primary one being the regular dictionary input); (c) usage of derivational strings as a learning tool (either for learners of Croatian as the primary or secondary language); (d) export of annotated verbs to the web-based database. Such a database of Croatian aspectual derivatives is, to our knowledge, one of the first attempts to systematically present this area of Croatian derivational morphology. We believe that it will be a valuable resource for research not only in lexicology and lexicography, but in the domain of the second language acquisition, just the same.

References

Babić, S.: Tvorba riječi u hrvatskome književnome jeziku. HAZU, Nakladni zavod Globus, Zagreb (2002)

Barić, E., et al.: Hrvatska gramatika. Školska knjiga, Zagreb (2003)

Cvikić, L., Jelaska, Z.: Složenost ovladavanja glagolskim vidom u inojezičnome hrvatskome. Lahor **4**, 190–216 (2007)

Kocijan, K., Šojat, K., Poljak, D.: Designing a croatian aspectual derivatives dictionary: preliminary stages. In: Proceedings of the First Workshop on Linguistic Resources for Natural Language Processing, pp. 28–37. Association for Computational Linguistics, Santa Fe, New Mexico, USA (2018)

Ljubešić, N., Klubička, F., Agić, Ž., Jazbec, I.P.: New inflectional lexicons and training corpora for improved morphosyntactic annotation of Croatian and Serbian. In: Proceedings of the Tenth International Conference on Language Resources and Evaluation (LREC 2016), Portorož, pp. 4264–4270. ELRA (2016)

Polančec, J.: Osamostaljeni izvedeni nesvršeni glagoli u hrvatskom jeziku. Suvremena lingvistika **44**(85), 113–138 (2018)

Silberztein, M.: Formalizing Natural Languages: The NooJ Approach. Cognitive science series. Wiley-ISTE, London (2016)

Silić, J., Pranjković, I.: Gramatika hrvatskoga jezika za gimnazije i visoka učilišta. Školska knjiga, Zagreb (2005)

Šojat, K., Srebačić, M., Tadić, M.: Derivational and semantic relations of croatian verbs. J. Lang. Model. **0**(1), 111–142 (2012)

Šojat, K., Srebačić, M., Štefanec, V.: CroDeriV i morfološka raščlamba hrvatskoga glagola. Suvremena lingvistika **39**(75), 75–96 (2013)

Tadić, M., Fulgosi, S.: Building the croatian morphological lexicon. In: Proceedings of the EACL2003 Workshop on Morphological Processing of Slavic Languages (Budapest 2003), pp. 41–46. ACL (2003)

Vučković, K.: Model parsera za hrvatski jezik. PhD dissertation, Faculty of Humanities and Social Sciences. University of Zagreb, Zagreb (2009)

Vučković, K., Tadić, M., Bekavac, B.: Croatian language resources for NooJ. CIT J. Comput. Inf. Technol. **18**, 295–301 (2010)

Construction of Morphological Grammars for the Tunisian Dialect

Roua Torjmen[1]([envelope]) and Kais Haddar[2]

[1] Faculty of Economic Sciences and Management,
Miracl Laboratory, University of Sfax, Sfax, Tunisia
rouatorjmen@gmail.com
[2] Faculty of Sciences of Sfax, Miracl Laboratory,
University of Sfax, Sfax, Tunisia
kais.haddar@yahoo.fr

Abstract. The use of Tunisian dialect is growing rapidly in social networks. Also, the direct application of standard Arabic tools on Tunisian dialect corpora provides poor results. Thus, the construction of resources has become mandatory for this dialect. With the intention of developing inflected and derivational morphological grammars, we study many Tunisian corpora to elaborate different forms for grammatical categories. Our proposed method is based on four steps which start with the extraction of Tunisian dialect words and end with their morphological, lexical and syntactic enrichment. This method is established thanks to a set of morphological local grammars implemented in NooJ linguistic platform. In fact, the local morphological grammars are transformed into transducers using NooJ's new technologies. For the evaluation of our method, we apply our lexical resources to a Tunisian corpus with more than 18,000 words. The obtained results look promising.

Keywords: Tunisian dialect · Linguistic resources · Morphological grammars
Dictionaries

1 Introduction

Tunisian dialect (TD) is spoken in Tunisia. It is a variant of Arabic, but it is different from modern standard Arabic (MSA). Nowadays, TD is increasingly used in social media such as Facebook and Twitter. Therefore, it becomes necessary to construct morphological grammars for TD, especially with the poor results provided by the morphological grammars of MSA applied directly to the TD corpus. Moreover, these morphological grammars allow the recognition of words and their different parts. In addition, they can be integrated in many applications such as automatic annotation of Tunisian corpus, machine translation for TD and TD speech synthesis. Among the difficulties, Tunisian dialect does not have a standard spelling and its words are not only of Arab origin, but also of different origins (Amazigh, Maltese, Italian, Turkish and French).

In this paper, our main objective is the construction of morphological grammars for Tunisian dialect. To do this, some steps need to be taken. Firstly, we provide a

© Springer Nature Switzerland AG 2019
I. Mauro Mirto et al. (Eds.): NooJ 2018, CCIS 987, pp. 62–74, 2019.
https://doi.org/10.1007/978-3-030-10868-7_6

linguistic study for TD. Afterwards, we have to establish an appropriate TD dictionary and morphological grammars. Finally, we have to implement them in NooJ platform.

The paper is structured in six sections. In the second section, we present related works treating Magrebi and Tunisian lexical resources. In the third section, we carry out a linguistic study on specific grammatical categories of TD. In the fourth section, we display the proposed method. In the fifth section, we experiment and evaluate our morphological grammars on a TD test corpus. Finally, this paper is closed by a conclusion and some perspectives.

2 Related Work

Almost all papers are devoted to speech recognition. However, some works deal with morphological grammars for Magrebi dialect and particularly Tunisian dialect.

Among the works dealing with the construction of TD's resources, we quote [2]. The authors generated their own corpus from ATB corpus using the mapping rule. The main idea is the identification of the verbal concepts for the generation of an extensional lexicon. In addition, the creation of TD Translator enriches the corpus semiautomatically. Moreover, the authors of [9, 10] converted the MSA models to TD in order to build their morphological analyzer. To improve the performance of their analyzer, they resorted to Al-Khalil morphological analyzer and machine learning algorithms. This paper is a continuation of our previous work [8] which concerned the creation of a morphological analyzer for TD using NooJ linguistic platform.

Mentioning some Maghrebi works, the construction of resources for the Algerian dialect is the objective of [4]. The authors developed their morphological analyzer based on the BAMA and Al-Khalil analyzers. Moving on to the Moroccan dialect, we quote [1]. From the Moroccan corpus that is created and annotated, the authors developed a Moroccan morphological analyzer. In [7], the authors developed a MDED (Moroccan dialect electronic Dictionary). This dictionary is a bilingual one. It contained Moroccan dialect and MSA. Its entries are manually translated from Moroccan dialect to MSA and vice-versa.

Among the MSA works using NooJ, the authors [3, 5] constructed their lexical resources with 24732 nouns, 10375 verbs and 1234 particles and morphological grammars with 113 patterns of infected verbs, 10 patterns of broken plurals, and a pattern of agglutination.

TD's works do not have significant coverage, especially with words of non-Arabic origin. Also, rule systems are not well developed. Furthermore, we notice the absence of a lexical resource module for TD in NooJ linguistic platform.

3 Linguistic Study

The main purpose of this study is to identify grammatical categories such as prepositions, adverbs and verbs. We then study different forms of adjectives from verbs.

3.1 Prepositions

According to our study, there are some TD prepositions that resemble MSA preposi-tions as shown in Table 1.

Table 1. Same prepositions in TD and MSA

Preposition in TD	Preposition in MSA	Translation in English
مِنْ 'min'	مِنْ 'min'	from
عَنْدْ ''and'	عَنْدَ ''anda'	from
فِي 'fii'	فِي 'fii'	in
تَحْتْ 'taht'	تَحْتَ 'tahta'	under
قَبْلْ 'kbal' قَبْلْ 'gbal'	قَبْلْ 'kbal'	before
بَعْدْ 'ba'ad'	بَعْدَ 'ba'ada'	after
بِينْ 'biin'	بَيْنَ 'bayn'	between
عَلَى ''alaa'	عَلَى ''aalaa'	at
وَرَا 'wraa'	وَرَاءَ 'wraa'a'	behind
مْعَا 'm'aa'	مَعَ 'ma'aa'	with
إِلَّا ''illlaa'	إِلَّا ''illlaa'	except

However, there are other prepositions relatively far from the original word in MSA as presented in Table 2.

Table 2. Different prepositions in TD and MSA

Preposition in TD	Preposition in MSA	Translation in English
حْذَا 'hdhaa' حْذَى 'hdhaa'	حِذْوَ 'hithwa'	beside
بَحْذَا 'bahdhaa' بَحْذَى 'bahdhaa'	بِحِذْوٍ 'hithwa'	beside
جْنَبْ 'jnab'	جَانِبَ 'jaaniba'	beside
كِيفْ 'kiif'	كَ 'ka'	like
قُدَّامْ 'koddaam' قُدَّامْ 'goddaam'	أَمَامَ ''amaama'	in front

In Tunisian dialect prepositions, we notice that some of them have more than one form of writing.

3.2 Adverbs

Concerning TD adverbs, we notice the presence of the Amazigh soul especially in interrogative adverbs with the syllable "اش" 'ch'. The latter can exist at the beginning of the word, for example "اشْنُوّة" 'ichnuwwah' (what), or at the end, for example "مْنَاش" 'mnaach' (of what). In the first case, we can neglect the first letter and only keep the syllable "ش" and we just get the word "شْنُوّة" 'chnuwwah' (what). In the second case, the letter "ش" 'ch' can be replaced by the letter "ه" 'h'. Therefore, TD interrogative adverbs may have more than one written form.

Tunisian adverbs are of Arab origin but they are distorted. For example, the word "ديما" 'dimaa' (always) is the result of the deformation of the word "دَائِمًا" 'daa'iman'. In addition, we can quote the word "هَكَّة" 'hakkah' (like that) is the result of the deformation of the word "هَكَذَا" 'hakadhaa'. Adverbs can also have more than one form of writing. For example, the word "زَادَة" 'zaadah' (too) can be written as "زَادَه" 'zaadah', "زَادَا" 'zaadaa' and "زَادَ" 'zaada'.

3.3 Verbs

Tunisian verbs have different origins. Thereby, we can find Arabic verbs like كتب 'ktib' (to write), Amazigh verbs like "نَقِّز" 'naggiz' (to jump) and French verbs like "كُونِكْتَى" 'kuuniktaa' (to connect).

Like MSA, regular and irregular verbs do not have the same conjugation. For this raison, we classify Tunisian verbs under twelve different categories according to the nature of each verb. In what follows, we give an example for each category of verb, as shown in Table 3.

Table 3. Example of each category

Category	Verb in TD
1	قْتِل "ktil" (to die)
2	سَافِر "saafir" (to travel)
3	تْعَشَّى "t'achchaa" (to dine)
4	قْضَى "kdhaa" (to buy)
5	خَلَّى "khallaa" (to let)
6	رَى "raa" (to see)
7	خَان "khaan" (to betray)
8	صَار "saar" (to become)
9	خَاف "khaaf" (to fear)
10	كْلَى "klaa" (to eat)
11	وْلِد "wlid" (to give birth)
12	شَدّ "chadd" (to catch)

To show the difference between categories of verbs, we present in Table 4 an example of each category conjugated to the second person singular in past tense, present tense and imperative tense.

Table 4. Conjugation of each verb category

Category	Past	Present	Imperative
1	قُتِلْتْ	يَقْتِلْ	اقْتِلْ
2	سَافِرْتْ	تْسَافِرْ	سَافِرْ
3	تْعَشِّيتْ	تِتْعَشَّى	إتْعَشَّى
4	قْضِيتْ	تِقْضِي	إقْضِي
5	خَلِّيتْ	تْخَلِّي	خَلِّي
6	رِيتْ	تْرَى	أرَى
7	خِنْتْ	تْخُون	خُونْ
8	صِرْتْ	تْصِير	صِيرْ
9	خِفْتْ	تْخَاف	خَافْ
10	كْلِيتْ	يَاكِلْ	كُولْ
11	وْلِدْتْ	يُولِدْ	أوْلِدْ
12	شَدِّيتْ	يْشِدّْ	شِدّْ

The differences between verb categories appear in the diacritics of the verbs. For example, in the past tense, there are verbs, its conjugation begins with diacritics "ó" or "ô" or "ọ" or "ỏ". In addition, these differences exist in the transformation of the verb to present tense. For example, the difference between categories 7, 8 and 9 is the presence of vowels "و" 'uu', "ي" 'ii' and "ا" 'aa'.

3.4 Adjectives

Tunisian adjectives are derived from verbs. In fact, the formation of adjectives differs according to the category of verb. In Table 5, we present the appropriate adjectives to each verb category.

On the one hand, certain categories of Tunisian verbs undergo the same transformation of Tunisian adjectives as categories 7, 8 and 9 as well as categories 1 and 11. On the other hand, there are specific adjectives, such as category 12 which require redundancy of functions of the last letter.

In fact, the adjectives presented in Table 5 are masculine singular. In addition, they exist in singular feminine by adding the letter "ة" 'h' and in plural by adding the syllable "ين" 'iin'. For example in the second category, we obtain respectively "مْسَافْرَة" and "مْسَافْرِين" However, unlike MSA, adjectives do not exist in dual and there is no difference between masculine and feminine plural.

Table 5. Adjective of each verb category

Category	Verb in TD	Adjectives in TD
1	قْتِلْ "ktil" (to die)	مَقْتُولْ ,قَاتِلْ
2	سَافِرْ "saafir" (to travel)	مُسَافِرْ
3	تْعَشَّى "t'achchaa" (to dine)	مِتْعَشِّي
4	قْضَى "kdhaa" (to buy)	مِقْضِي ,قَاضِي
5	خَلَّى "khallaa" (to let)	مْخَلِّي
6	رَى "raa" (to see)	مْرِي
7	خَانْ "khaan" (to betray)	خَوَّانْ ,خَايِنْ
8	صَارْ "saar" (to become)	صَايِر
9	خَافْ "khaaf" (to fear)	خَايِفْ
10	كْلَى "klaa" (to eat)	مَاكِلْ
11	وْلِدْ "wlid" (to give birth)	مَوْلُودْ ,وَالِدْ
12	شَدّْ "chadd" (to catch)	شَادِدْ

This linguistic study helps us build TD's lexical resources and build the system of rules for recognizing the studied grammatical categories.

4   Proposed Method

Our proposed method is based on four phases. First, we start by extracting all non-repetitive words from the study corpus. This step is performed automatically. Secondly, we eliminate the same words written in different writing forms or transformed into other grammatical categories or into other genders or numbers. For this reason, we call this phase filtering. Afterward, we choose a single representative word for all these collected words. Finally, we enrich this representative word by morphological, lexical and syntactic features. The output of our proposed method is a text annotation structure (TAS). The process of this proposed method is illustrated in Fig. 1.

The representative words and their basic grammatical category are saved as an entry in our dictionary and the added traits are developed with morphological grammars as presented in Fig. 2.

Figure 3 presents the morphological grammar of adverbs. This transducer BARCHA containing four paths allows the recognition of four different writing forms. The used operator <B> permits the suppression of last letter and <E> designs the empty string and keeps the word in its initial form.

This way, to conjugate the Tunisian verbs we establish twelve finite transducers. In Fig. 4, we present the transducer VERBE7 which allows the conjugation of the verbs of the twelfth category by using the following operators: <E>, <B>, <LW> and <RW>. In this transducer, we propound different conjugation cases in all time tenses (past I and present P) and modes (imperative Y) with any person (first person 1, second person 2 and third person 3) and any number (singular s and plural p).

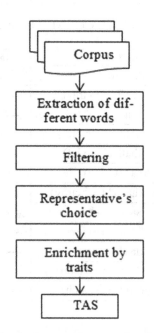

Fig. 1. Process of proposed method

شُوَيـَة, ADV+FLX=BARCHA
بَـرْشَة, ADV+FLX=BARCHA
زَاذَة, ADV+FLX=BARCHA
عِيـلَ, V+FLX=VERBE+DRV=FAAIL+DRV=MAFAOUL
قَـبِّلْ, V+FLX=VERBE+DRV=FAAIL+DRV=MAFAOUL
شَأَ, V+FLX=VERBE7+DRV=FAAAIL
عَأَ, V+FLX=VERBE7+DRV=FAAAIL

Fig. 2. Example of our dictionary entries

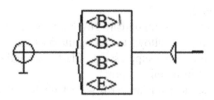

Fig. 3. Example of transducer for adverbs

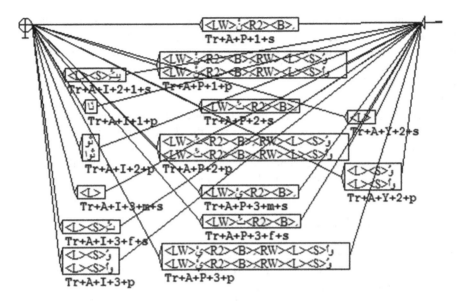

Fig. 4. Example of transducer for verbs

For example, to get the verb "شدّ" 'chadd' conjugated to the present with the second person plural: the cursor is positioned at the beginning of the word by <LW> and the two characters "ت" and "ﻮ" are added, then the word "تشدّ" 'tchadd' is obtained. Next, the cursor is advanced two characters by <R2>, the current character is deleted by <B> and the character "ﻭ" is added, then the word "تشِدّ" 'tchidd' is obtained. After, the cursor is positioned at the end of the word by <RW> and the last character is deleted, then the word "يَقُتل" is procured. Finally, the three characters "ﻮا" are added and the word "تشِدّوا" 'tchidduu' is obtained.

For adjectives, we create a transducer that presents the appropriate adjectives for the twelfth category of verbs. This transducer has a set of operators such as <L> <E>, <B> and <D>. The last operator allows the redundancy of the current character, as shown in Fig. 5.

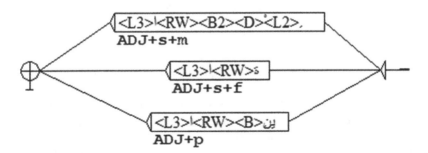

Fig. 5. Example of transducer for adjectives

To obtain an adjective in singular masculine, the character "ا" is added to the third position and the word "شَادّ" 'chaadd' is obtained. Next, the cursor is placed at the end of the word by <RW> and the last two characters are deleted by <B2> and the letter "د" is repeated by <D> and the "ة" character is added and the word "شَادِد" is obtained. Finally, the diacritic "ِ" of the second letter is added and the word "شَادِد" 'chaadid' is obtained.

In conclusion, up to now, we are developing a set of transducers containing 25 transducers: 12 transducers for verbs, 2 for adverbs (1 for interrogative adverbs and 1 for normal adverbs) and 11 for adjectives. In order to redundancy and multiplication in our transducers, we use the grouping technique of NooJ platform which places words that have common characteristics in the same node.

5   Experimentation and Evaluation

As indicated in the previous section, our lexical resources (dictionary and morphological grammars) are developed in NooJ linguistic platform [6]. Our dictionary is saved in the file "barcha.dic" that is extended by the file "barcha.nod". In fact, the file "barcha.nod" uses a set of flexional and derivational grammars based on finite transducers saved in the file "barcha.nof". In this way, we can generate from 1452 entries 150460 forms as presented in Fig. 6.

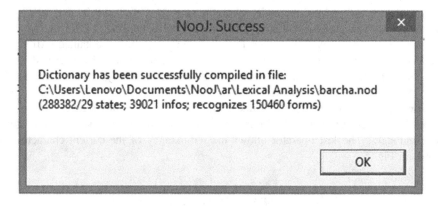

Fig. 6. Dictionary compilation

To evaluate our dictionary and our morphological grammars, we have collected a corpus from Tunisian novels and social networks. Our test corpus contains 3300 sentences and contains exactly 18134 words. The experimentation of our lexical resources is based on the recognition of Tunisian words and we focus on special grammatical categories which are prepositions, adverbs, verbs and adjectives. The obtained results are displayed in Table 6.

Table 6. Obtained results for grammatical categories

	Preposition	Interrogative adverb	Adverb other type	Verb	Adjective
Corpus18134	2494 (100%)	206 (100%)	762 (100%)	3523 (100%)	306 (100%)
Recognized word	1583 (63%)	206 (100%)	762 (100%)	3121 (88%)	306 (100%)

Table 6 shows that our resources recognize all adverbs and adjectives. However, a set of prepositions and verbs is not detected because of the agglutination phenomenon. This phenomenon will be treated later.

For example, after the linguistic analysis of the following Tunisian sentence: "نحوسوا شويه وقتاه" 'Waktaah nhawsuu chwayyah' (When we walk a little), we obtain that the word "وقتاه" (when) is recognized as an interrogative adverb "ADV+INTERR". Moreover, the recognized word "نحوسوا" (walk) is a verb "V" conjugated to the present "P" with the first person "1" plural "p". Finally, the recognized word "شويه" (a little) is an adverb "ADV" (Fig. 7).

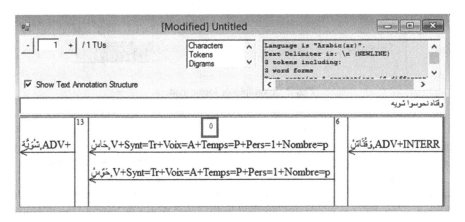

Fig. 7. Example of linguistic analysis

NooJ linguistic platform offers the patterns localization in the corpus and allows for example to locate all the different morphological and derivational forms of the verb "شدّ" "chadd" (to catch). We simply choose a NooJ regular expression and we write the expression <شد> as mentioned in Fig. 8.

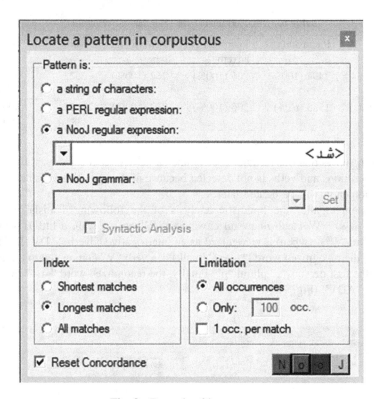

Fig. 8. Example of locate pattern

The result of this localization is presented in Fig. 9. In our case, we obtain 20 words containing verbs as يشدوا 'ychiddou' (they catch) and شديت 'chaddit' (I caught). Also, they contain adjectives like شادد 'chadid' (catcher) and شادين 'chaddin' (catchers).

In fact, our word dictionaries have different origins such as Amazigh, French, and Italian. Unrecognized words are essentially nouns that are not until now treated. In addition, unrecognized words are attached to the other words or have a typographical error. We consider that the obtained results are ambitious. They can be improved by increasing the coverage of our Tunisian dictionary and by elaborating the agglutination phenomenon and by adding other morphological rules.

Fig. 9. Result of locate pattern

6 Conclusion

In the present paper, we constructed morphological grammars for Tunisian dialect in NooJ linguistic platform, based on a linguistic study. The constructed morphological grammars recognize words having specific grammatical categories. In addition, they are based on a self-established dictionary extracted from the test corpus. Thereby, the morphological grammars are specified by a set of transducers and by adopting NooJ's new technologies as grouping. Thus, the evaluation is performed on a set of Tunisian dialect texts. The obtained results are promising since they show that our morphological grammars can efficiently treat different TD sentences despite the different origins of Tunisian words. As perspectives, we will increase the coverage of our dictionaries and will treat other grammatical categories, e.g. nouns. In addition, we would like to treat the linguistic phenomenon of agglutination for TD.

References

1. Al-Shargi, F., Kaplan, A., Eskander, R., Habash, N., Rambow, O.: Morphologically annotated corpora and morphological analyzers for Moroccan and Sanaani Yemeni Arabic. In: 10th Language Resources and Evaluation Conference (LREC 2016), Portoroz, Slovenia, May 2016, pp. 1300–1306 (2016)
2. Boujelbane, R., Khemekhem, M.E., Belguith, L.H.: Mapping rules for building a Tunisian dialect lexicon and generating corpora. In: Proceedings of the Sixth International Joint Conference on Natural Language Processing, Nagoya, Japan, 14–18 October 2013, pp. 419–428 (2013)
3. Ghezaiel Hammouda, N., Torjmen, R., Haddar, K.: Transducer Cascade to Parse Arabic Corpora. In: Silberztein, M., Atigui, F., Kornyshova, E., Métais, E., Meziane, F. (eds.) NLDB 2018. LNCS, vol. 10859, pp. 230–237. Springer, Cham (2018). https://doi.org/10.1007/978-3-319-91947-8_22
4. Harrat, S., Meftouh, K., Abbas, M., Smaili, K.: Building resources for Algerian arabic dialects. In: Fifteenth Annual Conference of the International Speech Communication Association, Singapore, 14–18 September 2014, pp. 2123–2127 (2014)
5. Mesfar, S.: Analyse morpho-syntaxique et reconnaissance des entités nommées en arabe standard. Doctoral dissertation, Thèse, Université de franche-comté, France (2008)
6. Silberztein, M.: NooJs dictionaries. In: Proceedings of LTC, Poland, 21–23 April 2005, vol. 5, pp. 291–295 (2005)
7. Tachicart, R., Bouzoubaa, K., Jaafar, H.: Building a Moroccan dialect electronic dictionary (MDED). In: 5th International Conference on Arabic Language Processing, pp. 216–221 (2014)
8. Torjmen, R., Haddar, K.: Morphological analyzer for the Tunisian dialect. In: Sojka, P., Horák, A., Kopeček, I., Pala, K. (eds.) International Workshop on Temporal, Spatial, and Spatio-Temporal Data Mining, vol. 11107, pp. 180–187. Springer, Cham (2018). https://doi.org/10.1007/978-3-030-00794-2_19
9. Zribi, I., Ellouze, M., Belguith, L.H., Blache, P.: Morphological disambiguation of Tunisian dialect. J. King Saud Univ. Comput. Inf. Sci. **29**(2), 147–155 (2017)
10. Zribi, I., Khemakhem, M.E., Belguith, L.H.: Morphological analysis of Tunisian dialect. In: Proceedings of the Sixth International Joint Conference on Natural Language Processing, Nagoya, Japan, 14–18 October 2013, pp. 992–996 (2013)

A Chinese Electronic Dictionary and Its Application in NooJ

Zhen Cai[✉]

Laboratory ELLIADD, University of Franche-Comté, 25000 Besançon, France
zhencai1122@hotmail.com

Abstract. After four years of research, our project of an electronic dictionary containing about 63,000 entries, is near completion. All the entries consist of atomic linguistic units in simplified Chinese characters, the official language of the People's Republic of China. The totality of these entries would meet the vocabulary needs of daily life. Certain scientific areas, such as mathematics and physics, have also been chosen for inclusion in the dictionary. On this basis, the grammatical categorization of the inputs has been established to clearly identify the different meanings of the entries. Furthermore, the dictionary has the potential to distinguish 15 grammatical categorizations of the Chinese language. In this way any Chinese text may be successfully analyzed using the NooJ software. The grammatical rules to ensure a more comprehensive analysis will be completed at a later stage. The grammatical structure of any sentence in Chinese can be automatically analyzed, so that the aim of assisting the learner to achieve a more complete understanding of Chinese will be realized. As a final result of the research, an effective module for segmenting the Chinese language word by word on the model of Indo-European languages should be possible, as in a Chinese sentence there is no space between two words as there is in Indo-European languages. This tool will also enable the learner to have an easier and more direct access to the Chinese language and its systems. Certain difficult words and other key words can be identified through the use of NooJ.

Keywords: Chinese atomatic linguistic unit · Electronic dictionary
Corpus · NooJ

1 Introduction

When we talk of "the dictionary", we may refer first of all to the paper dictionary, such as the Oxford English Dictionary, Oxford University Press, or the Larousse and Robert dictionaries for French. However, when we surf on the Internet and meet an unknown word, it is easier to search for the word by computer. That is why the electronic dictionary represents an important new device in daily life. In recent years, the electronic dictionary can be applied by computer or smartphone. This new technology is changing the way in which students learn a foreign language.

In this article, we will first of all discuss the advantages of the electronic dictionary in comparison with the paper dictionary. We will then explain the reasons for and the objectives of the Chinese electronic dictionary in our research, with all of the entries

© Springer Nature Switzerland AG 2019
I. Mauro Mirto et al. (Eds.): NooJ 2018, CCIS 987, pp. 75–80, 2019.
https://doi.org/10.1007/978-3-030-10868-7_7

referred to. We will subsequently explain the characteristics of the Chinese language and how the dictionary could resolve several language problems, as the electronic dictionary with NooJ could be used to split Chinese texts.

2 Precision of the Chinese Language

As our aim is to create a Chinese electronic dictionary, it is necessary to say a little about that language. Chinese is a member of the Sino-Tibetan family of languages, though it is not a single language. Chinese has many spoken varieties and also diverse forms of writing. We must therefore specify what kind of Chinese will be used for the dictionary.

First of all, we should know that there exist two kinds of Chinese in the development of its history: the first called 'Wen Yan' (文言) in Chinese and the second 'baihua' (白话), which we could translate as Classical Chinese and Contemporary Chinese respectively. Classical Chinese was used in the 19th century and also at the beginning of the 20th century, for writing the law, or in newspapers. Even today, we might find some texts written in this form. But for many people today Classical Chinese has become difficult to read fluently. From 1919, the social movement in China changed almost all texts into Contemporary Chinese. Our research is therefore to create a dictionary of Contemporary Chinese.

In ancient times, China was fragmented into small nation-states, and so the same Chinese was not spoken everywhere. For this reason, almost every city in China has its own dialect. The most famous international Chinese dialect is Chinese Guangdong. From 1955, the government began to encourage Mandarin Chinese, which is now the nation's official language, in order that all Chinese could understand one other. When we consult an internet site in Chinese nowadays, what we find is mostly two types of language according to the complexity of the writing: simplified or traditional Chinese. The simplified Chinese, simpler than traditional, is used by almost all Chinese, whereas traditional Chinese is more complex in its written form and is employed by people living in Taiwan. For our electronic dictionary, we will use simplified contemporary Mandarin Chinese, which is the mother tongue of one billion two hundred million people.

3 Grammatical Categories of Each Element in Our Electronic Dictionary

As Chinese is written in characters, the first difficulty that we encounter is the encoding system. The system used to prepare our dictionary is GB18030. All software released in China after January 1 2001 would support GB18030. It includes the GBK characters as well as additional non-Han characters, such as Tibetan, Mongolian, Uygur, etc.

Many people have thought that Chinese composes sentences by putting characters together, or that Chinese has no morphology, or even that Chinese does not have words. In reality, one character, two or several characters, even seven characters, could make up only one word. Most words in Chinese consist of one or two morphemes. In our research, we collect not only the morpheme, one of the basic units of word structure in Chinese grammar, but also the word in Chinese. Each element that we collect is the Atomic Linguistic Unit (ALU). In our electronic dictionary, we codified 15 grammatical categories such as N (Noun), ADJ (Adjective), V (Verb), ADV (Adverb), LOC (Locative case), NUM (Numeral), MOM (Classifier or Measure word), OMO (onomatopoeia), CONJ (Conjunction), PRE (Preposition), INT (Interjection), SUB (Subordination), AFF (Affix), PAR (Modal particle), PRON (Pronoun and Demonstrative). We will discuss this categorization at a later point in the article.

4   Presentation of the Electronic Dictionary

We are creating our dictionary with this purpose. 'Each entry = 1 ALU in the dictionary'. However, for the same word, we could sometimes write several entries when this word has multiple meanings. These meanings should be distinguished. We will give an example below of the word '说明'. Having consulted a dictionary and research concerning syntactic works, it is possible to give three explanations for this entry '说明':

1. explain
2. explanation
3. prove.

In the electronic dictionary, it will be described as follows:

说明, N + V
说明, V.

We consider that meaning 1 (explain) and meaning 2 (explanation) should be combined, because they represent the same meaning, the only difference between the two is that of grammatical categories. That is why these two meanings have been put together in one entry. However, when an entry has different meanings according to whether it is used as a noun or a verb, it should be separated as two ALUs. For example, with the word '干事', we describe this entry as follows:

干事, N
干事, V.

In Chinese, when "干事" is a noun, meaning the director in the department of a company, his position is more important than that of an employee, but less important than that of a boss. When this word is a verb, it means "to accomplish". So it should be separated into two entries. We know now in cases of homonymy (as in the examples cited above) that a word should be checked for different meanings. It will then have different entries (ALU). As we see from the example above, for every ALU, the first thing to be defined is the grammatical categorization for each entry. Defining the grammatical categorization is the first important step. According to Chinese linguists, all Chinese words could be placed in 12, 13 or 14 grammatical categories, each linguist having his/her own reason for the classification of these categories. We will therefore use the definition of Professor Drocourt, professor in the National Institute for Oriental Languages and Civilizations, to classify fifteen grammatical categories. As it has been already said, the sentence is a string of Chinese characters, and as we do not have a blank area in which to delimit words, the creation of a list of Chinese ALU will be helpful in segmenting Chinese. This is also a reason for the creation of an electronic dictionary.

5   The Number of Entries in Our Electronic Dictionary and Their Applications

We completed our Chinese electronic dictionary in June 2016, and over the following two years, we have applied it to the corpus many times. In this way, certain errors in the dictionary were discovered and corrected. The number of entries in the electronic dictionary may be presented in the following manner. The dictionary contains 63,000 entries (ALU). These entries cover our corpus, with a sentence producing several results. The aim of the dictionary is, for the first time, to segment successfully Chinese texts. As we know that Chinese is normally written without spaces between words and that NooJ software has no function for this, we must hope that one day NooJ will be able to split Chinese texts into a sequence of words. However, the difficulty of splitting a Chinese text into a sequence of words is a huge problem for Chinese linguists and computer scientists. As of today, the software which can split Chinese 100% correctly does not exist. We will discuss the main difficulties and give some examples from our research with NooJ. If we can resolve these difficulties, we will be able to split Chinese texts satisfactorily. First, how could a machine think and use logic like a human being? When a native Chinese reads a sequence such as '化妆和服装' huà zhuāng hé fú zhuāng (make up and disguise), he/she will split it in this way without difficulty: '化妆/和/服装' huà zhuāng/hé/fú zhuāng. But for the computer (and also for a human being), the third and the fourth characters will also form a sequence of words '和服' (a type of clothing). We should therefore establish a level of priority for these ALU. In fact, '和服' hé fú in Chinese is a rare word and is not often used. The second difficulty in splitting a text is the ambiguity of the same string of Chinese in the text, as we may see in two examples:

这个门把手坏了zhè ge mén bǎ shǒu huài le. (The hinge of this gate is broken.)
把手放开 bǎ shǒu fàng kāi. (Release the hand.)

For the human being, it is easy to know that the first sentence should be split as follows: 这个/门/把手/坏了, zhè ge/mén/bǎ shǒu/huài le, whilst the second one is: 把/手/放开 bǎ/shǒu/fàng kāi. We focus on '把手' bǎ shǒu, we see that in the first sentence it is one linguistic unit, whilst in the second it is two. How could a machine know that it is one or two units when it reads the text? In answer to this question, we may put forward a two step solution. First, as we know that when we put these two characters together, the meaning is 'hinge', we could tell the machine that if it meets a word like 'door', or 'window', it should judge immediately that the meaning of the unit is 'hinge'. Then, if there is no such word in the preceding text, and the following word after '把手' is a verb, the two characters should be split. As an example, the following solution may be proposed with the software NooJ. In 2016, on completion of the dictionary, a sentence such as 我要炒肉丝 wǒ yào chǎo ròu sī could be split with NooJ in four different ways (Fig. 1):

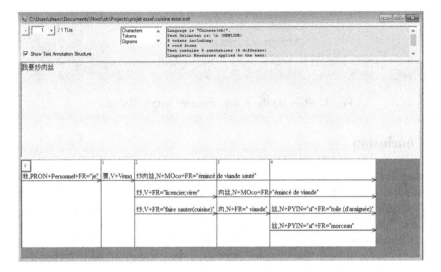

Fig. 1. Sentence with application in our electronic dictionary 2016

1. 我/要/炒肉丝 (PRON + V + N)
2. 我/要/炒/肉丝 (PRON + V + V + N)
3. 我/要/炒/肉/丝 (PRON + V + V + N + N).

Native Chinese speakers would know that the sentence could have two interpretations:

1. I want to (eat) minced meat fried.
2. I want to fry the minced meat.

In fact, the word 肉丝ròu sī is composed of two bound morphemes. It is considered a compound word and is always translated as "minced meat". In that way, we could add an operator or a program to allow this word to be a compound word. We may see the results in the figure below (Fig. 2). This sentence can therefore be split correctly:

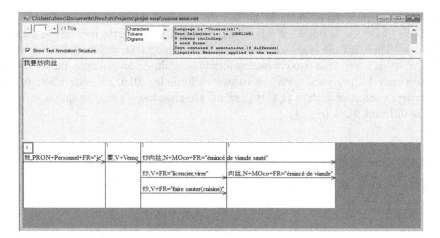

Fig. 2. Showing the results correctly with a dictionary

6   Conclusion

There are many advantages in using an electronic dictionary in comparison with paper dictionaries. We often use an electronic dictionary in our daily life. With the software NooJ, the dictionaries of several languages, such as French, English, Arabic, are available, but this is not the case for Chinese, hence our desire to fill the gap. However, as the Chinese language is completely different from European languages and does not use blank spaces to split the text, we have used the concept of ALU as particularly helpful in achieving this splitting. For each ALU we can distinguish two features: the grammatical category and the category of its construction. From this base, we can split Chinese texts effectively, and also create a model able to analyze automatically the Chinese language, and thus contribute to a variety of aspects of the field NLP, such as machine translation.

References

Introduction to Chinese Word Segmentation. http://baike.baidu.com/link?url=oFC7mKzZ1Yjjj
    Cq009qL1WHlZYNZj_VmHCvxQYwScKzaa5f-4QAH5qurOTVCabrI3z5KtWqb2DH9E8K
    mqkaXzq
Silberztein, M.: Dictionnaire électronique et analyse automatique de textes (Le système INTEX)
    Édition Masson (1993)
Silberztein, M.: La formalisation des langues, l'approche de NooJ. ISTE, London (2015)
Silberztein, M.: Formalizing Natural Languages: The NooJ Approach, Cognitive Science
    Series ISTE LTD (2016)
Silberztein, M.: NooJ Manual (2018). http://www.nooj-association.org/
Drocourt-Yang, Z.T.: Parlons chinois. Édition l'Harmattan (2007)

Syntax and Semantics

Automatic Extraction of Verbal Phrasemes in the Culinary Field with NooJ

Tong Yang[(✉)]

DILTEC (Didactiques des langues, des textes et des cultures),
Université Sorbonne Nouvelle (Paris 3), Paris, France
tong.yang@sorbonne-nouvelle.fr

Abstract. Phraseology is becoming the Achilles' heel of foreign learners. Before teaching verbal phrasemes in the culinary field, their extractions are put in the foreground. According to the needs (modeling and disambiguation) of our extraction, NooJ becomes the most appropriate software. After having implemented the lexical data in NooJ, we managed to extract the verbal phrasemes from our corpus for the teaching.

Keywords: Extraction of verbal phrasemes · Cuisitext
Disambiguation teaching · Modeling · Disambiguation

1 Introduction

Our study is part of the teaching of the FOS (French for specific purposes, 2004) to foreign cooks coming to work in French restaurants. We chose to study the lexical approach in the FOS, which, according to several authors, is unavoidable [5, 21]. The meaning of the lexicon must be studied in lexical contexts and [24] pointed out that lexical combinatory determines the meaning of a term or a lexicon. We therefore focus on the lexical combinatorics. Since the end of the 20th century, the recurrence of phrasemes (lexical combinatorics) has been taken into account by linguists: for [22], these "chunks" represent more than half of our speeches (oral and written); for [2, 25], this percentage of representation is approximately 40%. The teaching of phrasemes in specialty languages is necessary, according to several studies [7, 15, 33]. As [6] noted, foreign learners often make mistakes on these elements. Upstream of teaching, the extraction of phrasemes becomes an essential task to be solved. However, the extraction of multiple-word sequences still poses a problem in the TAL (automatic language processing) [23].

In the culinary field, the high frequency of nominal (noun + adjective) and verbal (verb + noun) phrasemes is attested through an investigation by n-gram and the first ones were extracted by NooJ [40] for the teaching. In this paper, we plan to extract verbal phrasemes from the culinary domain. We will first describe the object of our study: verbal phrasemes and then present our corpus from which we can extract the desired sequences. Then, the modeling and the disambiguation will be highlighted to achieve the automatic extraction. Subsequently, an implementation of the lexical data

© Springer Nature Switzerland AG 2019
I. Mauro Mirto et al. (Eds.): NooJ 2018, CCIS 987, pp. 83–94, 2019.
https://doi.org/10.1007/978-3-030-10868-7_8

in NooJ is shown in order to automatically extract the verbal phrasemes. To conclude, we will analyze the result of this extraction.

2 Purpose of Our Study: Verbal Phrasemes

In the 60s and 70s, phraseology arrived in Western Europe. This field of research is recent, which can explain the vagueness observed and confirmed by [2]: "Phraseology is a fuzzy part of language". This vagueness is not only about its name, but also about its definition. For example, according to [15], placed midway between lexicon and syntax, phraseology deals with polylexical signs composed of at least two words, stable, repeated and often figured. Some properties (fixedness, frequency, figurative meaning) of phrasemes are underlined in this definition, but it is still vague to define this domain. Consequently, rather than defining it by definition, we try to explain it by classification.

A number of phraseologists have addressed the issue of typology of phraseology [9, 12, 14, 16–18, 25, 26, 28]. For example, by the criterion of fixation, [28] divided phrasemes into two broad categories: "phraseological expression" and "semi-phraseological expression". The first is synonymous with idiomatic expression often used in linguistic research and the relations of the elements of a phraseological phrase are fixed. However, in a semi-phraseological expression, only one of the elements must be constrained in relation to other elements of this expression and the semi-phraseological expressions admit syntactical transformations. The typologies of [16, 17] use also this criterion of fixation. [25, 35] created, by the pragmatic criterion, the category of "pragmatemes" in his classification. According to them, pragmatemes group together the expressions associated with a situational context. Finally, the frequency criterion is taken into account in other typologies, such as those of [11, 12, 31], for example.

For the purposes of our study, we must select our own criteria according to the didactic objective, namely, the teaching of the language. Thus, in view of the intended audience, foreign learners, here is the list of criteria that we will adopt:

- The first criterion is that of fixation, because a foreign learner can not predict the continuation of a phraseme without knowing it [6]. For example, the phrase "*émietter le thon*" can hardly be predicted by a foreign learner and this phraseme is nevertheless unconsciously mastered by a native speaker.
- The second criterion that seems interesting to us is the pragmatic criterion. Because some free expressions with pragmatic value are specific to a field, for example, the expression "*préchauffer le four*" in the kitchen. It is true that, in culinary environment, the lexeme "*préchauffer*" often appears around the lexeme "*four*".
- The third important criterion is the frequency. As [34] pointed out, statistics do not define collocations but are means of assessing their significance level. So, they can help with the extraction of collocations.

We will therefore adopt these three criteria (pragmatic, syntactic and frequency) for the classification of our study. Figure 1 below illustrates this classification.

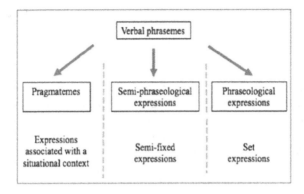

Fig. 1. Classification of verbal phrasemes

In our classification, three labels of [25, 28] are reusable: phraseological expressions, semi-phraseological expressions and pragmatemes. Phraseological expressions represent frozen or idiomatic expressions and semi-phraseological expressions include all semi-frozen phrasemes. In the identification of phraseology, high frequency expressions are taken into account, but we also check low frequency expressions as some researchers did [4, 10, 13]. Because a low frequency can hide the high relevance in a specialized field [4]. In order to extract the three types of verbal phrasemes (phraseological expressions, semi-phraseological expressions and pragmatemes) from our corpus, modeling is often presented as an effective method for easily accessing the text. In addition, the needs of the modeling then impose the choice of an appropriate software [3].

3   Modeling and Disambiguation of Lexical Data

Let's first recall that our corpus Cuisitext [36] contains both written and oral material. For the part of the written corpus, thanks to software Gromoteur, thousands of French recipes from French culinary sites (e.g., Marmiton, 750 g, Cuisine AZ) have been included. In the professional setting of cooks, speeches are also frequently oral. Thus, Cuisitext has three types of oral corpus in video format: video clips on the internet, filming in a hotel school, videos made in the kitchens of two French restaurants. The elaboration of an oral corpus imposes a transcription for the purpose of the didactic exploitation and the software CLAN was chosen to help with the transcription of the oral. The modeling is a mold with all semantic and syntactic properties and, in our study, the aim of the modeling is to carry out the extraction exhaustively. Inspired by Tutin [32], our modeling is based on observations found in Cuisitext and in dictionaries (TLFI and Petit Robert online). Concerning the collocation modeling, our study also uses the lexical function [27], a "conceptual tool for describing languages by modeling and encoding paradigmatic (semantic) and syntagmatic links" [27]. If we concretize the lexical function by the mathematical formula:

$$f(x) = y$$

x represents the argument (keyword) and y is its value. For example, the lexical function **repar** is a verb having the meaning of "prepare for" which has for keyword L as the complement of central object; the lexical function **Fact$_0$** is a realization verb. Taking the case of "thon" as a keyword, this combination of the two lexical functions can be expressed as follows:

$$\textbf{PreparFact}_0(\text{thon}) = \text{émietter}[\text{ART} \sim]$$

This lexical function helps to encode semantic and syntactic links: at the semantic level, the verb "émietter" expresses how to prepare; at the syntagmatic level, this verb is always used before the ingredient. There are also three verbal lexical functions (**Incep, Cont, Fin**) which express the three distinct phases of an event, as shown in Table 1 below:

Table 1. Correspondences between lexical functions and phases of an event

Phases of an event	Beginning	Continuation	End
Lexical functions	**Incep**	**Cont**	**Fin**

The lexical function **Incep** corresponds to the beginning of a fact, **Cont** to the continuation, and **Fin** to the end. For example,

$$\textbf{Incep}(\text{travailler}) = \text{commencer}[\text{à} \sim]$$

Since these three phasic verbs have an aspectual character and the supporting verbs (e.g., **Oper$_1$**) allow to express the time of a fact, they can perfectly match to characterize the phases of a fact. Take the keyword "cuisson" as an example, the use of the combination of phasic verbs and the verb support **Oper** is shown in Table 2 below:

Table 2. Using the combination of the phasic verbs and the verb support **Oper$_1$**

Lexical functions	Phases of an event	Case	Values
IncepOper$_1$	Beginning	cuisson	démarrer
ContOper$_1$	Continuation		prolonger
FinOper$_1$	End		arrêter

The lexical functions **IncepOper**$_1$, **ContOper**$_1$, **FinOper**$_1$ are still support verbs that can verbalize the predicative name ("cuisson") and characterize the phases of the fact ("cuisson"):

$$\textbf{IncepOper}_1(\text{cuisson}) = \text{démarrer } [\text{ART} \sim]$$

$$\textbf{ContOper}_1(\text{cuisson}) = \text{prolonger}[\text{ART} \sim]$$

$$\textbf{FinOper}_1(\text{cuisson}) = \text{arrêter}[\text{ART} \sim]$$

3.1 Lexical Modeling of Data

According to our observations on Cuisitext, the grammar of verbal phrasemes can be expressed according to four main structures as confirmed by [1] : standard construction (e.g., "reposer la pâte"), passive voice construction (e.g., "l'ail est bien haché"), relative clause construction (e.g., "carottes qu'on a déjà râpées") and construction of the pronominalization (e.g., "disposez-la", "incorporez-les"). The last construction will not be treated in this study, because this construction is easy to find (just look for the dash via a concordancer) on the one hand; on the other hand, the process of identifying pronominalized names is no longer automatic. Subsequently, the first three structures (standard construction, passive voice construction and relative clause construction) will be modeled.

Modeling of Standard Construction. As far as standard construction is concerned, there may be an insertion (e.g., an adverb) between the members. Such an insertion has been noted by [28], who described the semi-phraseological expression as a kind of "à trous" expression, but the size of this "trou" is not measurable. Regardless of the insertion (Ins), the grammar can be described as follows: (<E> represents the empty word.)

$$G = [\text{verbe} + \text{Ins ou} < E > + \text{groupe nominal}]$$

Modeling Passive Voice Construction. About passive voice construction, there are two types of times: simple time and compound time. Between the members of a "à trous" expression, there may be an Ins. The grammars of both times can be expressed as follows in Table 3:

Table 3. Grammars of passive voice construction

S	G
Simple time	[sujet + Ins ou \<E\> + \<être\> [a] + Ins ou \<E\> + participe passé]
Compound time	[sujet + Ins ou \<E\> + avoir + Ins ou \<E\> + été + Ins ou \<E\> + participe passé]
Combination of the two times	[groupe nominal + Ins ou \<E\> + avoir ou \<E\> + Ins ou \<E\> + \<être \> + Ins ou \<E\> + participe passé]

[a]The single quotation marks (\<\>) allow us to find all the occurrences of this term and its variants.

As shown in Table 3 above, two-cycle grammar can be combined into the grammar whose subject can be replaced by the nominal group.

Modeling the Relative Clause Construction. For the relative clause construction, the referent can be a nominal group and this nominal group is followed by the relative pronoun \<que\>. It could also have an insertion before the verb, as follows:

$$G = [\text{groupe nominal} + <que> + \text{Ins ou} <E> + \text{verbe}]$$

Once the three structures are modeled, we realize that the three modeled grammars can contain unwanted sequences (e.g., "travailler avec une fourchette"). Indeed, the latter can be rejected by imposing constraints in a disambiguation, so we proceed to a lexical disambiguation.

3.2 Lexical Disambiguation

In our study, lexical disambiguation is done on both nouns and verbs. At the level of nouns, we want to reject the so-called general names, for example, "fois" ("Une fois qu'ils sont dorés"), "temps" ("Le temps que les pâtes soient prêtes"), "fait" ("Du fait qu'on aime la viande"). To do this, we group the three names ("fois", "temps", "fait") under the label NL. At the level of verbs, first and foremost, we will reject intransitive verbs, for example, "rester" ("rester dans la cuisine"). In addition, we will refuse all phasic verbs, such as "commencer" ("commencer le repas"), "arrêter" ("arrêter le repas"), because all these phasic verbs are not specific to the culinary field. The lexical function makes it possible to classify all the phasic verbs in three categories: **IncepOper$_1$**, **FinOper$_1$**, **ContOper$_1$**. We adopt the label vi to collect all the rejectable verbs (phasic and intransitive) as shown in Fig. 2 below:

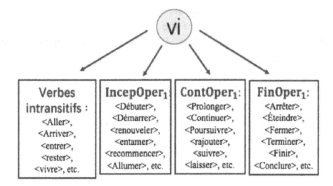

Fig. 2. Rejectable verbs under the label vi

According to the needs (disambiguation and flexibility) of our extraction, NooJ becomes the most appropriate software, because in theory, NooJ can describe all the natural languages of the world [29, 30]. Once the software is chosen, we start the implementation of lexical data in NooJ.

4   Implementation of Lexical Data

Three constructions (standard construction, passive voice construction, and relative clause construction) are expressed by three distinct paths shown in Fig. 3 below:

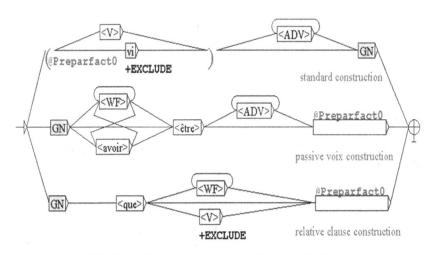

Fig. 3. Implementation of verbal phrasemes in *NooJ*

In the first path (standard construction), the colored node vi (prefixed by the character ":") makes it possible to imbricate all the rejectable verbs and the operator

(EXCLUDE) makes it possible to reject the unwanted sequences by imposing relevant constraints. We use the combination of the two tools (the colored node vi and the operator EXCLUDE) to disambiguate our verbs. In order not to repeat this procedure of verbal disambiguation in the other two paths, we use the global variables (@). In NooJ, each global variable has only one value, regardless of its place in the grammatical structure, and this value can be passed on to the NooJ generator. In our study, the global variable @**PreparFact**$_0$ represents all disambiguated verbs. Moreover, the colored node GN (nominal group) in the three paths (standard construction, passive voice construction, and relative clause construction) is also used to imbricate the grammar GN as shown in Fig. 4 below.

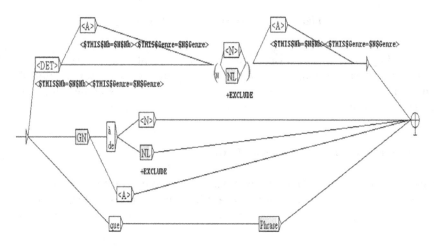

Fig. 4. Imbricated graph of the grammar GN

In Fig. 4 below, two types of variables (variable $THIS and $N) are used in the two constraints <$THIS$Nb = NNb> and <$THIS$Genre = NGenre> to check whether the adjectives match in genre and number with the names: the first constraint verifies that the adjective ($THIS) and the name ($N) have the same value for the property "Nb" (the number) and the second constraint verifies that they have the same value for the property "genre". If we apply this grammar to the expression "viande hachée", then the variable $THIS will take the value "haché" and the variable $N will take the value "viande". Of course, in this graph, the names are all disambiguated (EXCLUDE + colored node NL). In addition, recalling that, algebraic grammar allows a rule to be defined from itself. In Fig. 4 above, the imbricated graph of the GN refers to itself and this reference is recursive because the GN is part of the own graph. IT is the same case for the grammar Phrase which is part of the own graph as shown in Fig. 5 below:

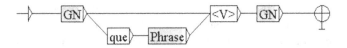

Fig. 5. Imbricated graph of the grammar Phrase

After completing the implementation of the data in *NooJ*, we launch our request.

5 Analysis of the Results

NooJ allows us to extract 1666 verbal phrasemes, one extract of which is ranked in descending order of word occurrences in Fig. 6 below.

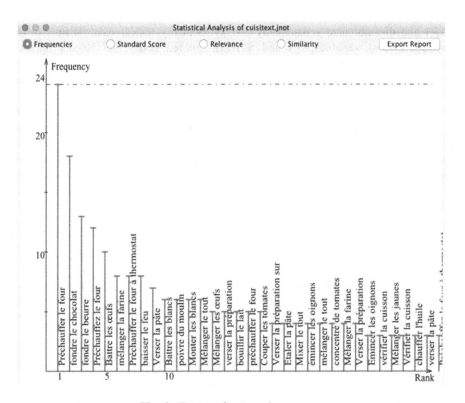

Fig. 6. Extract of extracted sequences

As we suggested at the beginning, the high frequency is taken into account in our selection of phrasemes for teaching. The number of a phraseme is the total number of all variations of a phraseme. For example, the number of the phraseme "préchauffer le four" (49 occurrences) is the total number of all variations of this phraseme: "préchauffer le four" (24 occurrences), "préchauffez le four" (12 occurrences), "préchauffer le four à thermostat" (8 occurrences) and "préchauffer le four" (5 occurrences). Our selection of verbal phrasemes for teaching stops at the threshold of two occurrences, because the phrasemes extracted of the threshold of an occurrence contain a number of irrelevant phrasemes, as "le truc m'a été donné", "rendre l'appareil", "puis les noix". But we check the phrasemes of the threshold of an occurrence for the purpose of not missing the relevant phrasemes, for example, the term "décortiquez les crevettes" appears only once in our corpus, but it is a relavant verbal phraseme. In addition, we must be wary of "false friends" in our extraction of verbal phrasemes, such as "poivre du moulin" (6 occurrences), "concentré de tomate" (4 occurrences) and the last ones are nominal phrasemes.

6   Conclusion

Verbal phrasemes are the object of our study and the lexical function allows us to model and disambiguate semantically and syntactically lexical data. Thanks to the variables (global variables, $N and $THIS), colored nodes and NooJ's operator EXCLUDE, automatic extraction of verbal phrasemes can be realized by implementing the three main constructions: standard construction, passive voice construction and relative clause construction. The selection of phrasemes for teaching is based on the frequency of their appearance and in our study, verbal phrasemes above the threshold of two occurrences are retained. The extraction of these phrasemes with NooJ can produce concordances that are useful for the teaching and learning of these structures [19, 20, 37]. We then plan to couple them to the use of mental maps [8, 38] for teaching and learning in a setting of memorization aid that we develop in three approach [39] AIP (Inductive Pure Approaches), AIG (Guided Inductive Approach), AD (Deductive Approach).

References

1. Alonso Ramos, M.: Étude sémantico-syntaxique des constructions à verbe support (thèse de doctorat). Université de Montréal, Montréal (1998)
2. Altenberg, B.: On the phraseology of spoken English: the evidence of recurrent word-combinations. In: Cowie, P.A. (ed.) Phraseology: Theory, Analysis, and Applications, pp. 101–122. Oxford University Press, Oxford (1998)
3. Aussenac-Gilles, N., Condamines, A.: Entre textes et ontologies formelles: les Bases de Connaissances Terminologiques. In: Zacklad, M., Grundstein, M. (eds.) Ingénierie et capitalisation des connaissances, pp. 153–176. Hermès, Paris (2001)
4. Binon, J., Verlinde, S., Selva, T.: Lexicographie pédagogique et enseignement/apprentissage du vocabulaire en français langue étrangère ou seconde (FLES): un mariage parfait. Cahiers de lexicologie 1(78), 1–23 (2001)
5. Binon, J., Verlinde, S.: L'enseignement/apprentissage du vocabulaire et la lexicographie pédagogique du francais sur objectifs spécifique (FOS): le domaine du francais des affaires. Études de linguistique appliquée 3(135), 271–283 (2004)
6. Cavalla, C.: La phraséologie en classe de FLE. Les Langues Modernes (1) (2009). http://www.aplv-languesmodernes.org/spip.php?article2292

7. Cavalla, C., Loiseau, M.: Scientext comme corpus pour l'enseignement. In: Tutin, A., Grossmann, F. (eds.) L'écrit scientifique: du lexique au discours. Autour de Scientext, pp. 163–182. PUR, Rennes (2013)

8. Cavalla, C., Loiseau, M., Lascombe, V., Socha, J.: Corpus, base de données, cartes mentales pour l'enseignement. In: Francfort! Peter Lang, vol. 5205, pp. 327–341 (2014)

9. Cowie, A.P.: The place of illustrative material and collocations in the design of a learner's dictionary, In: Strevens, P. (ed.) In Honour of A.S. Hornby, pp. 127–139. Oxford University Press, Oxford (1978)

10. Curado Fuentes, A.: Lexical behaviour in academic and technical corpora: implications for ESP development. Lang. Learn. Technol. **5**(3), 106–129 (2001)

11. Firth, J.R.: Modes of Meaning. Papers in Linguistics 1934-1951, pp. 190–215 (1957)

12. Gläser, R.: The grading of idiomaticity as a presupposition for a taxonomy of idioms. In: Werner, H., Schulze, R. (eds.) Understanding the Lexicon, pp. 264–279. Max Niemeyer, Tübingen (1988)

13. Gledhill, C.: Collocations in science writing. Gunter Narr Verlag Tübingen, Tübingen (2000)

14. González-Rey, I.: La phraséologie du français. Presses Universitaires du Mirail, Toulouse (2002)

15. González-Rey, I.: La didactique du français idiomatique. E.M.E, Fernelmont (2008)

16. Gross, G.: Les expressions figées en français : noms composés et autres locutions. Ophrys, coll, Paris/Gap (1996)

17. Howarth, P.A.: Phraseology in English Academic Writing: Some Implications for Language Learning and Dictionary Making. Niemeyer, Tübingen (1996)

18. Jernej, J.: O klasifikaciji frazema.397 Filogija, knjiga 20-21, Zagreb: Hrvatska akademija znanosti i umjetnosti, pp. 191–197 (1992)

19. Johns, T.: Should you be persuaded: two examples of data-driven learning. Engl. Lang. Res. J. **4**, 1–16 (1991)

20. Johns, T.: From printout to handout: grammar and vocabulary teaching in the context of data-driven learning. Engl. Lang. Res. J. **4**, 27–45 (1991)

21. Kahn, G.: Différentes approches pour l'enseignement du français sur objectifs spécifiques, numéro spécial du Français dans le Monde, Recherches et Applications, Méthodes et méthodologies, pp. 144–152. Clé International, Paris (1995)

22. Lewis, M.: Teaching Collocation: Further Developments in the Lexical Approach. Language Teaching Publications LTP, Hove (2000)

23. Luka, N., Seretan, V., Wehrli, E.: Le problème de collocation en tal. Nouveaux cahiers de linguistiques Française **27**, 95–115 (2006)

24. Mel'čuk, I., Arbatchewsky-Jumarie, N., Iordanskaja, L., Mantha, S., Polguère, A.: Dictionnaire explicatif et combinatoire du français contemporain: recherches lexico-sémantiques IV. Les Presses de l'Université de Montréal, Montréal (1999)

25. Mel'čuk, I.: La Phraséologie et son rôle dans l'enseignement-apprentissage d'une langue étrangère. Études de linguistique appliquée **92**, 82–113 (1993)

26. Moon, R.: Frequencies and forms of phrasal lexemes in English. In: Cowie, A.P. (ed.) Phraseology: Theory, Analysis, and Applications, pp. 79–100. Oxford University Press, Oxford (1998)

27. Polguère, A.: Towards a theoretically-motivated general public dictionary of semantic derivations and collocations for French. In: Proceedings of EURALEX 2000, Stuttgart, pp. 517–527 (2000)

28. Polguère, A.: Lexicologie et sémantique lexicale. Notions fondamentales. Troisième édition (première édition en 2003). Presses de l'Université de Montréal, Montréal (2016)

29. Silberztein, M.: La formalisation des langues: l'approche de NooJ. International Society for Technology in Education (2015)

30. Silberztein, M.: Formalizing Natural Languages: The NooJ Approach. Wiley, London (2016)
31. Sinclair, J.M.: Corpus, Concordance, Collocation. Oxford University Press, Oxford (1991)
32. Tutin, A.: Pour une modélisation dynamique des collocations dans les textes, pp. 207–221. Dans Euralex, Lorient (2004)
33. Verlinde, S., Binon, J., Selva, T.: Corpus, collocations et dictionnaires d'apprentissage. Langue française **150**, 84–98 (2006)
34. Williams, G.C.: Les réseaux collocationnels dans la construction et l'exploitation d'un corpus dans le cadre d'une communauté de discours scientifique, Thèse de doctorat (dir. Paul Boucher). Université de Nantes (1999)
35. Wray, A.: Formulaic Language and the Lexicon. Cambridge University Press, Cambridge (2002)
36. Yang, T.: Cuisitext : un corpus écrit et oral pour l'enseignement, colloque LOSP (Langues sur objectifs spécifiques: perspective croisées entre linguistique et didactique), Grenoble (2016). http://losp2016.u-grenoble3.fr
37. Yang, T.: La carte mentale, un outil didactique, pour l'enseignement des phrasème nominaux, communication présentée au 85ème Congrès de l'ACFAS (association francophone pour le savoir), à Montréal (2017a). https://www.acfas.ca/node/12213
38. Yang, T.: L'utilisation des concordanciers dans l'enseignement des phrasèmes nominaux, communication présentée au Colloque Jeune Chercheur (CJC) organisé par le laboratoire DyLis (Dynamique du langage in Situ) de l'Université de Rouen (2017b). https://cjcrouen2017.sciencesconf.org
39. Yang, T.: Choix et usage d'outils TAL appropriés dans l'enseignement/apprentissage des phrasèmes nominaux, communication présentée au colloque PERL – entre présence et distance. Accompagner et découvrir des pratiques pédagogiques en langues à l'université organisé par l'Université Sorbonne Paris Cité (2017c). https://perl-2017.sciencesconf.org
40. Yang, T.: Automatic extraction of the phraseology through NooJ. In: Mbarki, S., Mourchid, M., Silberztein, M. (eds.) Formalizing Natural Languages with NooJ and Its Natural Language Processing Applications. Communications in Computer and Information Science, vol. 811, pp. 168–178. Springer, Cham (2018). https://doi.org/10.1007/978-3-319-73420-0_14

Some Considerations Regarding the Adverb in Spanish and Its Automatic Treatment: A Pedagogical Application of the NooJ Platform

Andrea Rodrigo[1(✉)], Silvia Reyes[1], and Paula Alonso[2]

[1] Facultad de Humanidades y Artes, Universidad Nacional de Rosario,
Rosario, Argentina
andreafrodrigo@yahoo.com.ar, sisureyes@gmail.com
[2] Universidad del País Vasco, Donostia, Spain
alonsopaula@gmail.com

Abstract. This paper is part of the research project entitled "The pedagogical application of NooJ to the teaching of Spanish". Our particular aim is to deal with some elements of analysis concerning adverbs in Spanish, and to focus on the intersection of adverbs and adjectives, completing what we presented in previous papers -always within the range of possibilities offered by the NooJ platform-, and having the teaching of Spanish as our implementation horizon. The corpus consists of two types of texts written in Spanish, which are to be contrasted: journalistic texts and youth texts, that is, texts produced by young people. Given the low frequency of adverbs and adverbial structures in both corpora, the need to reinforce this category, the adverb, is considered.

Keywords: NLP · NooJ · Pedagogy · Spanish adverbs

1 Introduction

This paper is part of the research project entitled "The pedagogical application of NooJ to the teaching of Spanish". This project is accredited by the Universidad Nacional de Rosario, scheduled for 2017–2018, and carried out by academics and researchers of two Argentine educational institutions: the Instituto de Enseñanza Superior IES N° 28 "Olga Cossettini" and the Universidad Nacional de Rosario.

2 Our Facebook Page: *Aprendo Con NooJ* (Learning with NooJ)

The research project on which this paper relies is focused on a fundamental assumption: the democratisation of knowledge. Based on this and with the intention of promoting scientific practice, we made use of social networks by creating a Facebook page where the papers of our team and all the news about the NooJ Association and its activities are shared. Given the need to create a corpus, a Google document to be

© Springer Nature Switzerland AG 2019
I. Mauro Mirto et al. (Eds.): NooJ 2018, CCIS 987, pp. 95–100, 2019.
https://doi.org/10.1007/978-3-030-10868-7_9

completed by young people between 18 and 25 years old was created, and their consent to make use of the data was requested. The answers obtained in that document in response to the question: *"What do you think of education?"* make up the reference corpus of our proposal. It starts with a central idea: if a youth grammar exists, its characteristics must be stated. In this paper our focus will be on the presence of adverbs and adverbial constructions in the reference corpus.

3   Adverbs in the Corpus Produced by Youths

To count on a framework useful for the comparison with the corpus produced by youths (*Jov_Corp*), a corpus of opinion pieces was assembled so as to provide a standard variety of Rioplatense Spanish. When analysing the *Jov_Corp*, a low frequency of adverbs and adverbial constructions was noticed, if compared to other categories, such as nouns, verbs and adjectives. As regards the journalistic corpus, it is possible to state that there are no significant differences between categories in both corpora. This allows us to establish a first conclusion, whose implication is strictly pedagogical: it is necessary to reinforce the presence of adverbs and adverbial constructions in the texts produced by youths, principally because of the important function they perform as textual markers. Our methodological strategy involves the teaching and learning of the adverb always in relation to other categories, starting from their similarities and using the NooJ platform, created by Max Silberztein. In this respect, we mainly follow Silberztein (2015, 2016).

4   Adverbs and Adjectival Adverbs

Our approach of the teaching and learning of the adverb in Spanish consists in comparing it to other grammatical categories. Our proposal consists in inserting the use of NooJ in the description.

4.1   Adverbs in Comparison to Other Categories

For reasons of space, only the comparison between the adverb and the adjective will be discussed here, because of the many similarities they share.

From a morphological viewpoint, adjectives and adverbs share the diminutive suffix *-ito*. E.g.: adjective *bueno* (good) and diminutive *buenito* (very good); adverb *cerca* (near) and diminutive *cerquita* (very near). And they also share the superlative suffix *-ísimo*. E.g.: adjective *bueno* (good) and superlative *buenísimo* (good, great); adverb *lejos* (far) and superlative *lejísimo* (far away). It should be noted that in Rodrigo-Reyes-Bonino (2018) a morphological grammar to account for the diminutive and superlative endings of both adjectives and adverbs was presented. In addition, it is necessary to remark that adverbs in *–mente* derive from fossilised adjectives in the feminine singular. E.g.: *larga* (long) - *largamente* (longly).

From a semantic and syntactic viewpoint, adjectival adverbs constitute an intersection of both categories, i.e. of adjectives and adverbs. In the phrase *un lento movimiento* "a slow movement", *lento* (slow) is an adjective. But in the sentence *camina muy lento* "(He/she/it) walks very slowly", *lento* (slowly) is an adjective functioning as an adjectival adverb. The following subsection of our paper is devoted to this type of adverbs.

4.2 Adjectival Adverbs

Since adjectival adverbs occupy an important place in our dictionary of adverbs, it is necessary to distinguish them properly. Therefore, the feature [adjet] is added to the corresponding entries:

temprano, ADV+2a2+adjet
claro, ADV+2a2+adjet

Subtype ADV+2a2 mentioned above will be discussed next, and a grammar to remove the ambiguity between the adjective and the adjectival adverb according to their context of occurrence will be displayed in Subsect. 4.5.

4.3 Syntax of the Spanish Adverb

Following Bès (1999), the existence of nucleus adverb phrases (SADVN) and of adverb phrases (SINADV) is assumed. The classification of adverbs shown in Rodrigo (2011) and Rodrigo-Reyes-Bonino (2018) will allow us to account for adverb combinations. Moreover, an improved version of the grammar therein presented, containing a greater number of two adverb combinations, is shown below (Fig. 1).

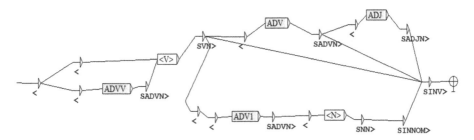

Fig. 1. Main grammar for the verb phrase (SINV), which includes a nucleus adverb phrase (SADVN) before and after the verb

Embedded graphs showing adverb combinations before the verb (Fig. 2) and after the verb (Fig. 3) are next displayed.

On the basis of the previous Main Grammar (Fig. 1) and taking into account the possible combinations of Spanish adverbs, the analysis of the following adverb phrase is proposed: *Actuaba muy abiertamente.* (V+ADV+2b2+ADV+2a1) "(He/she/it) acted very openly" (Fig. 4).

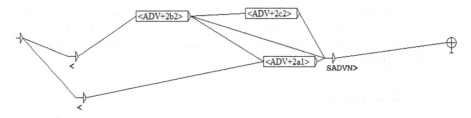

Fig. 2. Embedded graphs before the verb and inside of the nucleus verb phrase

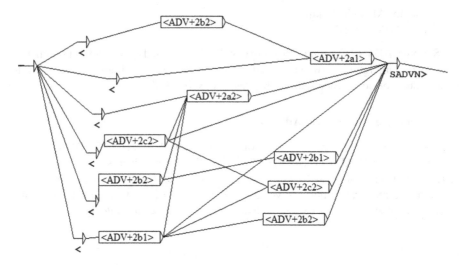

Fig. 3. Embedded graphs after the verb and outside the nucleus verb phrase

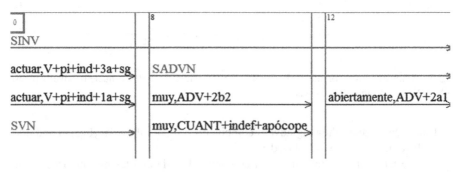

Fig. 4. Linguistic analysis of the nucleus adverb phrase *muy abiertamente*

4.4   A Grammar for Three Adverb Combinations

Although three adverb combinations are not very frequent, a possible nucleus adverb phrase will be analysed.

Fueron tratados casi exclusivamente como niños. "(They/You) were treated almost exclusively like children".

Such a structure is taken as recursive: a nucleus adverb phrase combined with two adverbs that functions as a modifier to the head of a larger nucleus adverb phrase. At the same time, this phrase -which is followed by a nucleus noun phrase- is an adverb phrase (SINADV) functioning as an adverbial complement to the passive sentence.

Next, a grammar is built with Rule Editor (Fig. 5):

```
# NooJ V5
# Syntactic grammar
#
# Input Language is: sp
# Output Language is: sp
#
# Special Start Rule: Main
#
# Special Characters: '=' '<' '>' '\' '"' ':' '|' '+' '-' '/' '$' '_' ';' '#'
#

Main = :SINADV;
SINADV = :SADVN :SNN;
SADVN = :SADVN1 :SADVN2;
SNN = <N>;
SADVN1 = <ADV+2b2> <ADV+2a1>;
SADVN2 = <ADV+2c2>;
```

Fig. 5. A grammar for three adverb combinations

4.5   Removing Ambiguity from Annotations

Given the expressions: *Sonaba claro* "(He/she/it) sounded clear", where *claro* is an adjectival adverb modifying a verb (V+ADV+2a2), and *Un pantalón claro* "A light couloured pair of trousers", where *claro* is an adjective modifying a noun (N+ADJ), a grammar to disambiguate tags (adjectival adverb after the verb in the first node, and adjective after the noun in the second node) is proposed (Fig. 6).

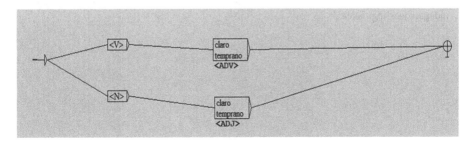

Fig. 6. A grammar to disambiguate adjectival adverbs and adjectives

5   Conclusions and Perspectives

Our intention has been to show how it is possible to focus on the teaching and learning of the adverb in Spanish by using the automatic treatment provided by the NooJ platform. Our concern has been centred on the adverb, for it is one of the grammatical categories to be reinforced in the youth grammar, according to the analysis of *Jov_Corp*. Our suggestion has been to approach the adverb always in relation with other categories, by taking into account the way it appears in real texts.

Until now we have been enriching our dictionaries and creating grammars accordingly, but from now on we will change our research focus. Instead of concentrating on grammatical categories, i.e. nouns, adjectives and adverbs, our future research project will deal with discourse strategies such as description, narration and argumentation. Our aim is to redefine the Spanish module and to group grammatical categories according to discourse skills: nouns and adjectives will play an important role in description, verbs and referential expressions in narration, and verbs and adverbs in argumentation. This new approach will be more useful for the acquisition of Spanish as a foreign language since the NooJ platform allows us to view language from a multilingual perspective, on the one hand, and will help learners to have a unified view of languages, on the other. Moreover, learners will begin to consider their own language in terms of other languages, both for the analysis or the generation of texts.

References

Bès, G.G.: La phrase verbal noyau en français. In: Recherches sur le français parlé, vol. 15, pp. 273–358. Université de Provence (1999)

Rodrigo, A.: Tratamiento automático de textos: el sintagma adverbial núcleo. Tesis doctoral. Facultad de Humanidades y Artes. UNR. Ediciones Juglaría, Rosario (2011)

Rodrigo, A., Reyes, S., Bonino, R.: Some aspects concerning the automatic treatment of adjectives and adverbs in Spanish: a pedagogical application of the NooJ platform. In: Mbarki, S., Mourchid, M., Silberztein, M. (eds.) NooJ 2017. CCIS, vol. 811, pp. 130–140. Springer, Cham (2018). https://doi.org/10.1007/978-3-319-73420-0_11

Silberztein, M.: La formalization des langues, l'approche de NooJ. Iste Ediciones, London (2015)

Silberztein, M.: Formalizing Natural Languages: The NooJ Approach. Iste Ediciones, London (2016)

Software NooJ. http://nooj-association.org/

Facebook page: Aprendo con NooJ (Learning with NooJ). http://www.facebook.com/indagacioneslinguisticas/

Expansive Simple Arabic Sentence Parsing Using NooJ Platform

Said Bourahma[(⊠)] ⓘ, Mohammed Mourchid, Samir Mbarki,
and Abdelaziz Mouloudi

MISC Laboratory, Faculty of Science, Ibn Tofail University, Kenitra, Morocco
saidbrh@yahoo.fr, mourchidm@hotmail.com,
mbarkisamir@hotmail.com, mouloudi_aziz@hotmail.com

Abstract. All Arabic sentences, both verbal and nominal, share the same main structure, which consists of two required components: the predicate and the subject, and two optional components: the head and the complement. Simple sentences are based on most basic noun phrases (simple nouns), and can be expanded in the predicate, the subject, or the complement. The expansion leads to compound parts rather than simple ones. The aim of this work is to merge our two previous parsers [2, 3], and to extend the merged parser, at the noun phrase level, to be able to parse the expansive simple sentences. Hence, we have implemented a set of syntactic grammars modeling Arabic noun phrase structures. These grammars are enriched by the agreement constraints of the noun phrase components. Using our enhanced and extended grammar, we have parsed syntactically several sentences, we have recognized both nominal and verbal expansive sentences, and we have generated their possible syntactic trees regardless of the sentence' components order. The results were satisfactory.

Keywords: Arabic sentence · Expansive sentence · Syntactic parsing
Noun phrase · Agreement constraints · NooJ platform

1 Introduction

There are two Arabic inflectional features that interface with syntax: case and mood. Both of them mark this interfacing by short vowel suffixes, "moods" when they apply to verbs and "cases" when they apply to nouns.

Government (العمل) is a syntactic principle wherein certain words cause others to inflect. Typical governors (العوامل) in Arabic are verbs, verbal nouns, verbs like nouns, active and passive participles, prepositions and other particles, etc. For instance, a mono-transitive verb takes or "governs" one direct object in the accusative case. Certain particles, such as the negative future marker "*lan*" (لن, not), requires the subjunctive mood on the next verb, and a preposition requires that its noun complement to be in the genitive case, and so on. Case (on nouns) and mood (on verbs) are the two features affected by government in Arabic [5, 6].

Agreement is where words in a phrase or a clause show feature compatibility; that is, they match or conform to each other, one reflecting the other's features [7, 8]. For instance, the verb agrees with its subject in gender, but not always in number. If the

© Springer Nature Switzerland AG 2019
I. Mauro Mirto et al. (Eds.): NooJ 2018, CCIS 987, pp. 101–113, 2019.
https://doi.org/10.1007/978-3-030-10868-7_10

verb precedes the subject and the subject is dual or plural, the verb remains singular. Thus a dual or plural noun subject when it follows the verb does not influence verb inflection for number. A feminine, singular, and human, noun takes a feminine singular adjective except some special adjectives, and so forth. In order to undertake this matching or agreement of features, one needs to be aware of the rules for agreement, and of the categories that constitute feature compatibility.

Because of these essential syntactic principles (government and agreement) that characterize the structure of words in phrases and clauses, Arabic can be seen as a language that has a network of dependency relations in every phrase or clause [6]. These relations are key components of the grammatical structure of the Arabic language.

All Arabic sentences share the same main structure, which includes four components: a head, a predicate, a subject, and a complement. In simple sentences, the predicate, the subject, and the complement, are based on simple nouns. Sentence expanding is the process of adding one or more words, phrases, or clauses to the main clause (or independent clause). In other types of Arabic sentences, the predicate, the subject and the complement can occur in compound structures.

The most important part, in the sentence, is the noun phrase; this part is defined in compound and recursive forms. The sentence expanding generally concerns the predicate, the subject, or the complement, at different levels. We have already implemented two syntactic parsers covering simple verbal and simple nominal sentences [2, 3]. The aim of this work is to extend our two previous works: In the first step, we have merged and enhanced our two parsers; in the second step, we have expanded the merged parser, at the noun phrase level, to cover expansive simple sentences.

We begin by an overview of the previous researches that concern the syntactic parsing of expansive sentences. After that, we present a study about the noun phrase structures in expansive simple sentences, and we show some implemented NooJ grammar. In section four, we present the tests and results, and we end with a conclusion and perspectives.

2 Related Works

Most of the existing researches in Arabic sentences parsing cover simple sentences. Expansive simple sentences' parsing is still in its early stages. Some works have implemented some cases of these types of sentences; however, the shortcoming in these works is in the Arabic noun phrase possible grammatical structures, sentences' types, sentences' words order, and there is no agreements constraints implemented.

In [1], Alqrainy et al. implemented a grammar checker using CFG in Natural Language Toolkit (NLTK) recursive descent (Top-Down) parser for parsing schemes constructing a parse from the initial symbol {S}. The system chooses a production rule and tries to match the input sentence's words with the chosen rule. This grammar covers verbal and nominal sentences without the head. In this work, there is no distinction between noun phrase types, definite and indefinite noun, noun phrase and prepositional phrase. The conjunction between noun phrases is not implemented.

In [4], Daimi used Prolog programming language to implement a system based on definite clause grammar for identifying the sources of several types of syntactic ambiguity in Arabic sentences with a single parse. This system analyzes the input sentence and verifies the conditions that govern the existence of certain types of syntactic ambiguities in it; the system verifies if the input sentence is ambiguous or not. The implemented grammar covers verbal sentences with one direct object, nominal ones without the head except the case of "*kana*" (to be) and its analogous verbs, and "*inna*" and its analogous particles. Noun phrases, in this grammar, are limited to the adjectival phrase and the annexation phrase with two words.

In [5] Hammo et al. used Prolog programming language too to implement a parser, based on CFG, which covers verbal and nominal sentences without the head except nominal sentences with "*inna*" (and its analogous particles) and interrogative verbal sentences. The implemented parser employs Chomsky's Government and Binding theory. The noun phrase structures integrated in this parser are limited to some cases of the adjectival phrase, the conjunctional phrase, and the annexation phrase. The rule recognizing annexation phrases as an NP recognizes also appositional phrases, but there is no distinction between these two types of noun phrase.

3   Noun Phrase Structures in Simple Expansive Arabic Sentences

In simple sentences, subjects, direct objects, and complements of prepositional/locative phrases are simple nouns. In expansive simple sentences, we can match, in these syntactic positions, a set of nouns and phrases; words of this set are compounded to form a composite structure called a Noun Phrase (NP). Noun phrases are very common cross-linguistically, and they may be the most frequently occurring phrase type.

Arabic NP structure is compound in five syntactic compounds: The annexation, الإضافة, the adjective, النعت, the corroborative, التوكيد, the apposition, البدل, the conjunction, العطف [9–11]. In the adjectival, annexation, and corroborative phrases, the noun phrase is comprised of two parts: a head noun and an expansion part. The head noun, expresses the number, gender, rationality and other features of the whole noun phrase. Into the NP, noun-pronoun or noun-adjective can show features compatibility. We have integrated the agreement constraints into the NP grammar; these constraints reject ungrammatical cases, and reduce syntactic ambiguities. The annexation phrase inherits the definiteness from the expansion part, but the adjective and the emphasis phrases can be definite or indefinite; if the head noun is definite then the phrase is definite, otherwise the phrase is indefinite. The expansion part is different from definite and indefinite noun phrases. The NP can be also defined in recursive forms, and thus, it can group many noun phrases. Table 1 presents examples of simple and expansive simple nominal and verbal sentences, the head nouns are underlined in expansive sentences.

In this section, we study the noun phrase structures occurring in expansive simple sentences. We study the agreement into each structure. And, we present their imple-mentation using NooJ's transducers with variables and syntactic constraints.

Table 1. Examples of simple and expansive simple sentences.

Simple sentences	Expansive simple sentences
كتب الطفل الحروف على اللوحتين, The child wrote the letters on the two boards	كتب الطفل الصغير الذكي الحروف العربية على اللوحتين كلتيهما, The smart young child wrote the Arabic letters on the both boards
العلوم نافعة في الحياة, Sciences are useful in life	العلوم التطبيقية كلها نافعة في الحياة اليومية, All the applied sciences are useful in daily life

3.1 The Annexation Phrase (Construct State)

An annexation phrase is a possessive/genitive construction relating an indefinite noun (or a conjunction between two or many indefinite nouns) and a noun phrase: the noun, the possessor (المضاف), grammatically heads, and possesses in semantics, the noun phrase, the possessed (المضاف إليه). The possessor is in the construct state, and the possessed has a genitive case. This construction has many comparables in English: "Noun Noun_Phrase" can be translated into "Noun of Noun_Phrase", "Noun_Phrase's Noun" or a compound "Noun_Phrase Noun" (see example (1)). The noun phrase can take another annexation phrase; therefore, the annexation phrase can be extended recursively creating what is called an *Idafa* chain. The example (2) presents an *Idafa* chain. All the words in an *Idafa* chain, except the first word, must be genitive. And all the words except for the last word must be in construct state.

(1) كتاب البنت, the girl's book.
(2) كتاب أخ البنت, the book of the brother's daughter.

3.2 The Adjectival Phrase

Another composite structure that abounds in Arabic is the adjectival phrase, which consists of tow parts: The described (المنعوت), and the adjective (النعت). The described is, generally, a noun phrase (a noun, a conjunction between nouns, or an annexation phrase). The first word of this noun phrase is the head of the adjectival phrase, which is described or qualified by adjective(s) for example in (3), numbers, verbal noun(s) for instance in example (7), relative noun(s) such as illustrated in example 6, demonstrative pronouns, prepositional/locative phrase(s) (e.g. (3)), an annexation phrase headed by an adjective for instance in (4), etc.

(3) اشتريت خاتما سميكا نفيسا من فضة خالصة, I bought an expensive thick ring of pure silver.
(4) استعمل الرجل سيارة قوية المحرك, the man used a car with a powerful engine.
(5) الجبال المغربية غنية بالمنابع المائية, the Moroccan mountains are rich in water sources.
(6) ناقش الرئيس الأمريكي أسس الديمقراطية مع مجموعة من المواطنين السود the American president discussed the democratic principles with a group of the black citizens.
(7) مررت برجال ثقة I passed by trustful men.

Adjectives and relatives, except broken plurals, and demonstratives, agree with human nouns in gender, number, case and definiteness (see example (6)). Non human plural nouns accept a feminine singular adjective, a broken plural adjective, or a feminine sound plural adjective (see Fig. 1), which means that they trigger feminine singular agreement on adjectives [9], this is demonstrated in example (5). In Arabic, some adjectives describe both feminine and masculine singular human nouns such as (شكور, thankful; صبور, patient). There is no agreement, in number and gender, between a noun and a verbal noun describing it; the verbal nouns must be singular (ثقةرجال, trustful men, see example (7)). Demonstratives in Standard Arabic occur both before and after the head noun, and agree with it in number and gender. The dual of demonstrative also agrees in case. The graph in Fig. 1 implements the agreement constraints noun-adjective.

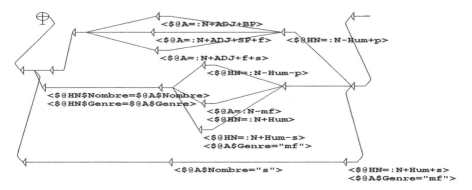

Fig. 1. Agreement constraints noun-adjective.

3.3 The Corroborative Phrase (Emphasis Phrase)

A corroborative phrase is comprised of two parts: the corroborated (المؤكد), and the corroborative (التوكيد). The corroborated take a definite or indefinite noun phrase. And the corroborated occurs with certain known words and they are the following: عين, نفس, (self), كل, جميع, أجمع, عامة, (all, whole). The corroborative and the corroborated agree in case. An attached pronoun is linked to جميع, كل, عين, نفس, and عامة; the attached pronoun must agree in number and gender with the head noun for instance in (10) [9]. The corroborative words "نفس" and "عين" can be preceded by the preposition ب, and we can insert a separate pronoun between the corroborated and the corroborative in this case (see for instance (8) and (9)). The separate pronoun also agrees in number and gender with the head noun. In addition to the six corroborative words sited above, dual nouns can be corroborated by the two words كلا, 'both', for masculine and dual nouns, and كلتا, 'both', for feminine and dual nouns. These two words agree in case with the head noun as illustrated in example (11). Another case of the corroborative consists of repeating the corroborated in the corroborative (توكيد لفظي). Figure 2 illustrates the syntactic structure of definite noun phrase corroborative, and the agreement constraints into this type of Arabic noun phrase.

(8) قام الرجل نفسه, the man himself set up.

(9) قام الرجل هو بنفسه, the man, he himself, set up.

(10) استدعى المدير العمال كلهم, the director called all workers.

(11) الدرسان كلاهما مكتوبان على السبورة, both lessons are written on the board.

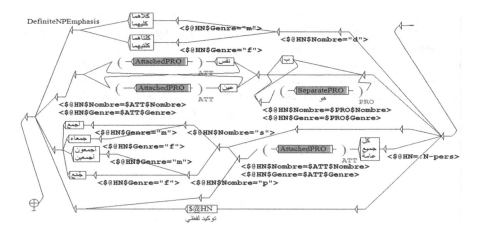

Fig. 2. Corroborative of definite noun phrase.

3.4   The Appositional Phrase

The appositive (البدل) occurs when a noun phrase is exchanged with another noun phrase or with many other noun phrases. The heads of the noun phrases in apposition agree in case. There are four types of appositive: The complete change of one thing for another (بدل الشيء من الشيء), the change of a part for a whole (بدل البعض من الكل), the change of the content for the containing (بدل الاشتمال), and the change for a mistake (الغلط بدل). See for instance (12) and (13).

(12)   كان علي أخوك البارحة في الكلية, Ali, your brother, was in the faculty yesterday.

(13)   رأيت زيدا الفرس في الحديقة, i saw Zaid, (I mean) the horse in the garden.

3.5   The Conjunctional Phrase

Conjunctional phrase is made up using conjunction particles between two or many noun phrases. Noun phrases in conjunctional phrase agree in case; the example (14) shows a conjunction between two noun phrases. The graph modeling the main structure of the noun phrase, in Fig. 3, shows the conjunctional phrase main grammar.

(14)   جاء محمد أخوك الصغير و علي الرجل المسن نفسه, Mohammed, your young brother, and Ali, the old man himself, arrived

3.6   Noun Phrase Structures in NooJ Platform

In this part, we present the noun phrase main structures, implemented in NooJ platform. Generally, noun phrases can be embedded inside each other; therefore the noun phrase is defined in recursive forms, and it can group the annexation, adjectival, appositional, conjunctional, and emphasis phrases, as illustrated in (15). Table 2 presents the noun phrase grammar represented in EBNF notation.

(15) جاء الرجل المغربي أبو بكر نفسه أخوك الكبير و زيد كاتب القصة القصيرة, the Moroccan man, Abu Baker himself, your grand brother, and Zayd, the short story's writer, arrived

Table 2. NP grammar in EBNF notation.

NP Formal Structure in Extended Backus–Naur form
NP::= AttachedPro| DefiniteNP {DefiniteNP} | IndefiniteNP {IndefiniteNP} | DefiniteNP {DefiniteNP } Conjunction CNJNP | IndefiniteNP {IndefiniteNP} Conjunction CNJNP
CNJNP::= DefiniteNP {DefiniteNP} | IndefiniteNP {IndefiniteNP} | DefiniteNP {DefiniteNP} Conjunction CNJNP | IndefiniteNP {IndefiniteNP} Conj CNJNP
DefiniteNP::= ((N+def) | AnnexationPhrase | (N+pers) | (N+Loc){DefiniteNPAdjective} {DefiniteNP} [DefiniteNPEmphasis]
AnnexationPhrase::= (N-def) DefiniteNP | (N-def) Conj CNJNoun DefiniteNP | (N-def) AnnexationPhrase
CNJNoun::= (N-def) | (N-def) Conj CNJNoun
DefiniteNPAdjective::= ADJ+def | N+RLV+def | Etc.
DefiniteNPEmphasis::= [SparatePro] ['ب'] ('نفس ' | 'عين') AttachedPro | ('كل'| 'جميع'| 'عامة') AttachedPro ['أجمع'| 'جمع'| 'أجمعين'| 'جمعاء'| Etc.] | ('أجمع'| 'جمع'| 'أجمعين'| 'جمعاء'| Etc.) | Etc.
IndefiniteNP::= (N-pers-ADJ-REL-def) {IndefiniteNPAdjective} {IndefiniteNP } [IndefiniteNPEmphasis]
IndefiniteNPAdjective::= ADJ-def | VRN-def+s | N+RLV-def | Prep IndefiniteNP | Etc.
IndefiniteNPEmphasis::= ('عامة'| 'جميع'| 'كل') AttachedPro ['أجمع'| 'جمع'| 'أجمعين'| 'جمعاء'| Etc.] | ('أجمعين'| 'جمع'| 'جمعاء'| Etc.) | Etc.

Using the grammar presented in Table 2 we have implemented the NooJ grammars recognizing noun phrases in their general case. The graph in Fig. 3 shows the main structure of the Arabic NP. A noun phrase is an attached pronoun, an indefinite or definite NP, an NP in apposition with other NPs, or an NP in conjunction with other NPs. An indefinite NP is headed by an indefinite noun, which can be expanded by the adjective (النعت) the conjunction of explanation (عطف البيان), or the corroborative of indefinite NP. A definite NP is headed by a definite noun, a noun of person and location, or an annexation phrase (see Fig. 4), the definite head can be expanded by the adjective, the conjunction of explanation, or the corroborative of definite NP. The implemented grammar in this work added new syntactic annotations in NooJ's table annotation structure; these annotations represent the grammatical role of each word in each noun phrase in the sentence.

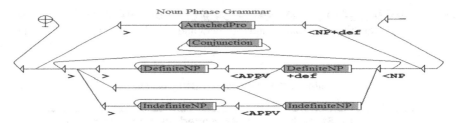

Fig. 3. Noun phrase main structure.

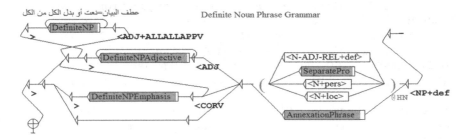

Fig. 4. Main structure of definite noun phrase.

The implemented grammar of the NP is integrated in the enhanced parser, obtained after merging our two previous parsers for parsing simple verbal and nominal sentences [2, 3]. The enhancement, in the merged parser, was where we have added the agreement constraints modeling syntactic and semantic features compatibility such as gender, number and humanness of the predicate and its subject [7, 8]. The whole implemented grammar enabled as to parse both expansive simple verbal and nominal sentences.

4   Results and Tests

The whole implemented grammar consisted of 74 graphs with 13 levels of nesting. The sub-grammar implementing the noun phrase structures consisted of 15 recursive graphs with 7 levels of nesting. The noun phrase grammar covered the 5 possible cases of the NP components and its recursive structures.

To test the syntactic parser, we have extracted a set of 500 expansive simple sentences from real texts; this set contained 200 nominal sentences and 300 verbal ones. And we have applied the parser, in the set, sentences by sentences. Figures 5, 6, 7 and 8 show an example of expansive verbal sentence. The recognized nominal sentences were 180 (90%), and the recognized verbal ones were 275 (91.66%). This is obvious since our lexical recourses are not yet completed, and thus some words figuring in the set of sentences are not yet added to the dictionary, or they are not yet recognized by our morphological resources. We also notice that some cases of noun phrases are not yet implemented.

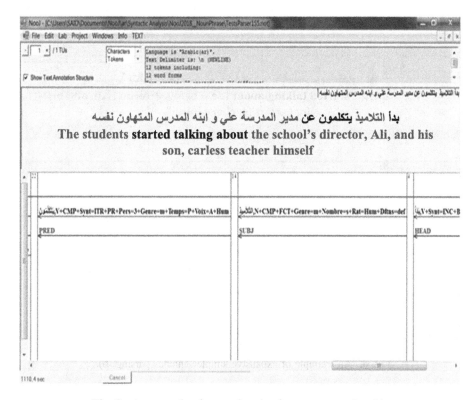

Fig. 5. An example of expansive simple sentence parsing (a).

As shown in Figs. 5, 6, 7 and 8, our syntactic grammars of the noun phrase structures add syntactic annotations in the NooJ's table annotation structure; these annotations represent the grammatical function of each word and morpheme in the noun phrase, in addition to the annotations added by the parser representing the grammatical structure of the sentence. Table 3 summarizes the abbreviations used in the syntactic annotations representing the grammatical structures of Arabic sentences treated in this work.

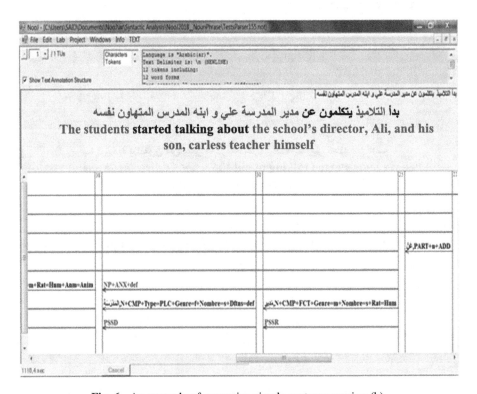

Fig. 6. An example of expansive simple sentence parsing (b).

Fig. 7. An example of expansive simple sentence parsing (c).

Table 3. Table of abbreviations.

Abbreviation	Signification
HEAD	Sentence head
PSSR	Possessor of an annexation phrase
CNJ	Conjunctional phrase
CNJP	Part of a conjunctional phrase
SUBJ	Subject of a sentence
PSSD	Possessed of an annexation phrase
DESC	Described of an adjectival phrase
ADJ	Adjective part of an adjectival phrase
PP	Prepositional phrase
PRED	Predicate of the sentence
APP	Appositional phrase
ANX	Annexation phrase
APPV	Appositive of an appositional phrase
CORD	Corroborated of a corroborative phrase
CORV	Corroborative of a corroborative phrase
VSENT	Verbal sentence
CMP	Complement of the sentence

Fig. 8. An example of expansive simple sentence parsing (d).

5 Conclusion and Perspectives

In this work, we have enhanced and merged our two parsers to parse simple verbal and nominal Arabic sentences; this enhancement was done when we have added some syntactic and semantic agreement constraints into the merged parser between the predicate and its subject. We have extended the obtained parser for parsing simple Arabic sentences to cover expansive simple ones. For that, we have expanded the noun phrase structure and implemented it in compound and recursive forms. In addition, we have enriched the NP grammar by the agreement constraints that reject ungrammatical cases. The implemented grammars add new syntactic annotations of each word in the noun phrase. This expansion enabled us to parse larger Arabic sentences applying our grammar implemented using NooJ's transducers with variables and constraints. As outputs of these transducers, we obtained the possible syntactic trees of both expansive Arabic simple verbal and nominal sentences.

As perspective, we hope to extend our parser to be able to parse more complex Arabic sentences, and after that, we can treat very important syntactic' analysis applications and semantic analyzers.

References

1. Alqrainy, S., Muaidi, H., Alkoffash, M.S.: Context-free grammar analysis for Arabic sentences. Int. J. Comput. Appl. **53**(3), 7–11 (2012)
2. Bourahma, S., Mbarki, S., Mourchid, M., Mouloudi, A.: Syntactic parsing of simple Arabic nominal sentence using the NooJ linguistic platform. In: Lachkar, A., Bouzoubaa, K., Mazroui, A., Hamdani, A., Lekhouaja, A. (eds.) ICALP 2017. CCIS, vol. 782, pp. 244–257. Springer, Cham (2018). https://doi.org/10.1007/978-3-319-73500-9_18
3. Bourahma, S., Mourchid, M., Mbarki, S., Mouloudi, A.: The parsing of simple Arabic verbal sentences using NooJ platform. In: Mbarki, S., Mourchid, M., Silberztein, M. (eds.) NooJ 2017. CCIS, vol. 811, pp. 81–95. Springer, Cham (2018). https://doi.org/10.1007/978-3-319-73420-0_7
4. Daimi, K.: Identifying syntactic ambiguities in single-parse Arabic sentence. Comput. Hum. **3**, 333–349 (2001)
5. Hammo, B., Moubaiddin, A., Obeid, N., Tuffaha, A.: Formal description of Arabic syntactic structure in the framework of the government and binding theory. Computacion y Sistemas **18**(3), 611–625 (2014)
6. Karin, C.: Ryding: A Reference Grammar of Modern Standard Arabic. Cambridge University Press, New York (2005)
7. Silberztein, M.: Formalizing Natural Languages: The NooJ Approach. ISTE Editions (2016)
8. Silberztein, M.: Nooj Manual (2008). www.nooj-association.org
9. التوابع في النحو العربي: محمود سليمان ياقوت,كلية الاداب , جامعة طنطا, مصر, (2005–2006)
10. سيبويه : الكتاب , القاهرة, بولاق (1316هـ)
11. ابن كمال الباشا : أسرار النحو ,الطبعة الثانية ,دار الفكر للطباعة و النشر و التوزيع ,فلسطين (2002)

A Construction Grammar Approach in the NooJ Framework: Semantic Analysis of Lexemes Describing Emotions in Croatian

Dario Karl[(⊠)], Božo Bekavac, and Ida Raffaelli

Department of Linguistics, Faculty of Humanities and Social Sciences,
University of Zagreb, Zagreb, Croatia
dariokarl.sl@gmail.com, {bbekavac,iraffaelli}@ffzg.hr

Abstract. The paper deals with semantic analysis of several lexemes encoding emotions in Croatian. The paper embraces the Construction grammar approach and shows how some of its basic theoretical tenets perfectly comply with the computational capabilities of NooJ. Using examples of the noun *strah* 'fear', the aim of the research is to point out the possibilities in annotating specific constructional meanings in NooJ, like different connotations of chosen lexemes, generalized uses of that constructions (their distributions in more abstract constructions like noun phrases), their relations with other constructions (other intensifiers of emotions, causative sentences etc.) and various distinctive features of their specific meanings (pragmatic features, as well as semantic and morphosyntactic), which all reflect different linguistic and cognitive phenomena in the language use.

Keywords: Construction grammar · Constructions · NooJ · Meaning Croatian language

1 Introduction

The aim of this paper is to analyze the applicability of NooJ linguistic tool in the theoretical framework of Construction Grammar (CxG). The reason for choosing the CxG as a theoretical and methodological framework was to showcase various possibilities in formalizing linguistic data in a rather simple way, while holding meaning of a construction – basic linguistic unit – as the center of the research. A corpus-based analysis enables formalization of the constructions that have a specific meaning, distinguishable from the basic meaning of a certain lexeme that is part of a construction. Taking the example of the lexeme *strah* 'fear' we show the results of implementing the NooJ tool in the C&G framework. Moreover, we point out how the constructions and various usages of the lexeme are formalized in NooJ and later on tested with randomly chosen concordances from corpora, mirroring real language usage. The main goals of the research are twofold: (a) to investigate whether NooJ has potential for recognition of specific constructions and annotate them with corresponding meaning and to what degree, (b) to see to what extent CxG can be applied as a theory in building and

© Springer Nature Switzerland AG 2019
I. Mauro Mirto et al. (Eds.): NooJ 2018, CCIS 987, pp. 114–123, 2019.
https://doi.org/10.1007/978-3-030-10868-7_11

improving existing linguistic resources providing, moreover, with information about pragmatic and semantic features. Since CxG has never been used in NooJ, the main aim of the paper is to point to the compliance of NooJ linguistic tool with a theory that revolves around meaning and has its roots in Cognitive science and cognitive linguistics.

2   Construction Grammar – A Cognitive Science-Based Theory

In the article *Regularity and idiomaticity in grammatical constructions: The case of 'let alone'*, Fillmore, Kay and O'Connor (1988) introduced the notion of a construction as a grammatical unit based on its syntactic and semantic features that cannot be described via regular 'rules' of grammar: "Constructions on our view are much like the nuclear family (mother plus daughters) subtrees admitted by phrase structure rules, except that (1) constructions need not be limited to a mother and her daughters, but may span wider ranges of the sentential tree; (2) constructions may specify, not only syntactic, but also lexical, semantic, and pragmatic information; (3) lexical items, being mentionable in syntactic constructions, may be viewed, in many cases at least, as constructions themselves; and (4) constructions may be idiomatic in the sense that a large construction may specify a semantics (and/or pragmatics) that is distinct from what might be calculated from the associated semantics of the set of smaller constructions that could be used to build the same morphosyntactic object" (1988: 501).

Accordingly, constructions, with all their syntactic, semantic, pragmatic and other features, make up the structure of language as it is. One construction can be made out of several different constructions, but its basic definition is that it can only be considered as a construction if its meaning could not be presupposed by just knowing the meaning of units within that construction: "an idiomatic expression or construction is something a language user could fail to know while knowing everything else in the language" (1988: 504).

The importance of construction as basic units in the language has been recognized also by Adelle Goldberg, who has pointed to an intertwined relationship between a verb and its arguments, (1995: 8–9; 11). It was actually Adelle Goldberg (1995; 2006) and William Croft (2001) who defined construction as any linguistic unit, regardless of its formal complexity or the level of abstractness, that has a meaning distinctive from any other in language. The increasing number of various researches shows a tendency to use constructions as keys for encapsulating and describing the entire grammatical knowledge of a speaker[1].

---

[1] For a detailed insight into differences in Construction grammar approaches and its implementation in the analysis of Croatian language structures see Katunar 2015.

2.1   Constructions and Cognitive Grammar

In a wider theoretical context of Cognitive linguistics, CxG is a theoretical and methodological framework considered as a syntactic alternative to Cognitive Grammar (Katunar 2015: 3). According to Belaj and Tanacković Faletar (2014), Cognitive Grammar considers a linguistic unit to be exclusively made of phonological and semantic pole or a connection between those two structures, whereas CxG considers linguistic form to be a syntactic structure. Within the CxG theoretical framework, the grammatical form would be a separate level in the formal structure (Belaj and Tanacković Faletar 2014: 33–34). In Cognitive Grammar the notion of grammatical form is a direct result of relation between semantic and phonological form. The other difference between these approaches is that Cognitive Grammar research is focused on schematic description of language and cognitive phenomena primarily describing the semantic pole (Katunar 2015: 36), whereas CxG is focused on formalized approaches to linguistic structures. These kinds of formalisms are considered as a theoretical and methodological backbone of our research enabling formalization of constructions in the NooJ linguistic tool. In contrast to Generative Grammar formalism, CxG formalisms include meaning, as well as pragmatic information, as core language features in describing constructions. Also, what distinguishes CxG from Generative Grammar is a negation of syntactic-centric and derivative approaches to grammar, interpreting grammatical relations as subordinate to semantic and pragmatic ones (Belaj and Tanacković Faletar 2014: 20–21). Moreover, since CxG is a usage-based model, the analysis of the language data is entirely usage based.

2.2   Usage-Based Model

Both Construction Grammar and Cognitive Grammar belong to cognitive-based usage models of language description that take language usage as a foundation for explaining mental structures of language and cognitive mechanisms connected to language (Katunar 2015: 27–28). One of the most important features of usage-based models is the importance of corpus-based research. It enables an in-depth analysis of frequencies, pointing to: (a) the linguistic structures that are more entrenched or innovative, (b) the interconnection between language and other cognitive systems and (c) the influence of language production on linguistic structures, among others (see Katunar 2015: 30–31; Barlow and Kemmer 2000).

Accordingly, we consider frequencies found in corpora as significant data that provide an insight into: (a) real language use, (b) distribution of particular lexemes in different language structures, (c) lexicalization patterns that can be defined as formalized constructions and (d) meanings conveyed by such constructions.

3   Methodology

The presented research is based on the analysis of the lexeme *strah* 'fear' that encodes the emotion of fear in Croatian language. Its distribution data were analyzed in the Croatian National Corpus (CNC)[2] and Croatian Web Corpus (HrWac)[3]. Both resources contain written texts automatically lemmatized and MSD tagged using standard heuristic methods. As a lexicographical source we used the online Croatian Language Portal (HJP) for digital overview of the already defined meanings. Defining lexeme distribution plays an important role in the context of usage-based models, especially when based on language corpus analysis. As Katunar points out (2015: 132–133), distribution is used to indicate semantic relations between two or more linguistic units (tokens in this case). Frequency data, mutual information and the logDice statistical method, for example, show if there is a semantic relation and a specific meaning that results from that distribution pattern. When a certain distribution pattern is lexicalized and its usage frequent enough, it is possible to consider it as a construction. Note that there are certain linguistic patterns that have an exact predictable meaning in all the contexts they are used in, but are still considered as a construction based on the merit of usage frequency (Goldberg 2006: 64).

3.1   Corpora Results for the Lexeme *strah*, Meaning 'fear'

The lexeme *strah* has 12 230 tokens in CNC and 177 740 in HrWaC. Its distribution patterns consist of a high frequency of prepositions:

(a) [*strah od čega*] ('fear of something') when the lexeme includes a prepositional phrase (PP)
(b) [*razlog za strah*] ('reason for fear'), when it is a part of another NP + PP
(c) [V + *bez straha*] ('without fear'), when it is a part of another V + PP
(d) [V + *u strahu*] ('in fear'), when it is a part of another V + PP construction.

It can also be found frequently next to particular verbs like:

(e) [*izazivati strah*] ('to cause fear')
(f) [*utjerati strah*] ('to instill fear')

And nouns/pronouns:

(g) [*strah koga/čega*] ('fear of somebody or something'),
(h) [*mene (N+D) je (biti) strah čega (N+G)*] ('I am/was scared of something'), being a part of a verb's argument structure

Online dictionary (HJP) has listed the following meanings:

- unpleasant emotion, state of anxiety and concern as a physiological response to a sense of danger (death, disease, punishment etc.) [*od straha da; od straha pred; u strahu od; sa strahom*] – for fear of, out of fear, with fear…

---

[2] http://filip.ffzg.hr/cgi-bin/run.cgi/first_form.
[3] http://nl.ijs.si/noske/all.cgi/first_form?corpname=hrwac;align.

- fright, reluctance or respect [*strah od starijih*] – fear of older (teenagers)
- concern for someone's safety [*u strahu zanjezin život*] – fearing for her life

Next to a couple of frozen expressions:

- *nema straha* – no need to fear
- *umrijeti od straha* – to be scared to death
- *strah i trepet* – fear and terror
- *u strahu su velike oči* – a frightened man sees danger everywhere

Taking into consideration that one of the main goals of this research was to define linguistic patterns that form constructions (Katunar 2015: 38), the distribution of the lexeme *strah* 'fear' points to several constructions which convey a specific meaning and/or are more frequent, i.e. which have a higher level of entrenchment:

- Construction [*strah za koga/što*], 'to care for something dear or someone's well-being, fearing that something bad could happen'.
- Constructions with the prepositions *od* ('of') and *prema* ('towards') and with lexemes that denote people in the meaning of 'awe': [*strah od starijih*] – 'being afraid of older people (teenagers)'; [*strah prema nastavnicima*] – 'fear of teachers'; it should be noted that the preposition *od* is mostly lexicalized in this meaning with the lexeme *strah*.
- Frequent usages of the lexeme *strah* with adjectives: [A + N] construction – the most frequent example being [*paničan strah*] ('a strong fear, panic').
- Constructions with prepositions and verbs conveying the meaning of unpleasant emotion, state of anxiety and concern as a physiological response to a sense of danger: [*strah od smrti*] – 'fear of death'; [*živjeti u strahu*] – 'to live in fear'.
- Constructions [*iz straha*] – 'out of fear' and [*zbog straha*] – 'because of fear' - a speaker can express fear as a cause that prevents a certain action.
- Frozen expressions with the aforementioned specific meanings as examples of substantive idioms, as defined by Fillmore and all.

3.2   Lexicalization Patterns

Distribution patterns of the lexeme *strah* in combination with HJP data gave us insight into the meanings that are lexicalized when the lexeme is found in different contexts. The next challenge was to analyze why and how do certain constructions acquire specific meanings. Raffaelli (2017: 175) notes that "the term lexicalization pattern comprises word-formation patterns as well as other grammatical (e.g. syntactic) patterns used in naming different concepts". Lexicalization patterns thus represent constructions as formal structures (morphosyntactic) which gain specific meanings and are shared by a larger number of speakers. Lexicalization patterns exhibit different degree of conventionalization and entrenchment (2017: 174). There is a connection between the frequency of a used construction (its distribution patterns), its level of conventionalization as a degree of speakers' shared knowledge about a certain construction and, thus, the cognitive entrenchment of that construction. In general, lexicalization is viewed as a naming process of a concept and lexicalization patterns as constructions that have been lexicalized and conceptually recognized by a large number of speakers.

Consequently, in this paper we make a clear distinction between distribution patterns (all the contexts in which a certain lexeme appears) and lexicalization patterns (distribution patterns that gain a status of constructions since they encode a specific meaning, different from lexical meaning of a certain lexeme). In NooJ, only those distribution patterns which have a high frequency of occurrences in the corpora and are considered as constructions, have been formalized and annotated.

4   Creating Grammars in NooJ

For creating NooJ syntactic grammars we have used the existing resources (dictionaries, morphological and lexical grammars) for Croatian language (Bekavac et al. 2007) that have successfully morphosyntactically annotated a large portion of tokens in Croatian texts. These annotations are described in this paper as metalinguistic generalizations that describe certain morphosyntactic, semantic and/or pragmatic categories in language. The advantage of NooJ in this theoretical and methodological framework is that it is flexible when it comes to inserting new annotations and offers different approaches to it (manually through grammars or dictionaries, but also automatically for describing wide linguistic phenomena or a specific and narrow linguistic category). Linguists actually have freedom to describe and name the category as they find appropriate, as long as it is correctly assigned in grammars later on. This functionality was used for inserting a couple of semantic annotations in the existing dictionaries and, ultimately, increased the precision of the grammars (Fig. 1).

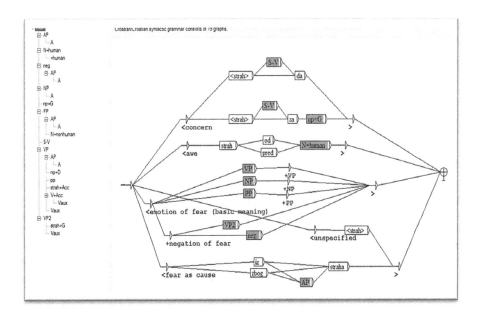

Fig. 1. NooJ syntactic grammar with annotated meanings for the lexeme *strah*

5   Results and Evaluation

Grammars were applied on 100 randomly extracted concordances from the Croatian
National Corpus (CNC) which contain the targeted lexeme. We imported extracted
concordances in NooJ and applied the existing Croatian language resources on them.
A maximum recall of 100% represented one hundred lexeme usages from the CNC
which were given an annotation, i.e. a construction was recognized by the grammar.
The precision of NooJ grammars was measured by a number of correctly assigned
annotations, both from the total recall percentage and from the total of 100 lexeme
usages that were tested (Fig. 2).

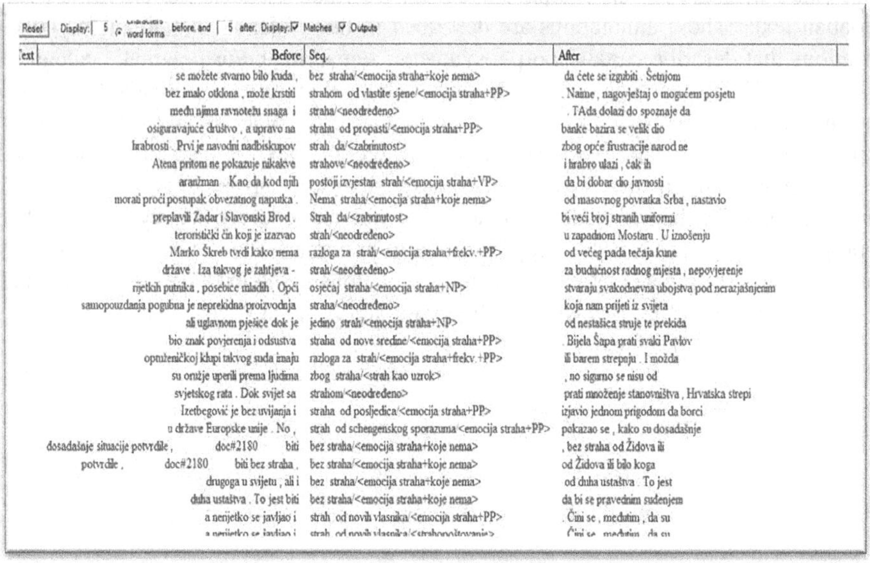

Fig. 2. Annotated concordances of the lexeme *strah*

Considering the fact that Croatian language has variable word order and that the
speakers have a possibility to insert various constituents within certain frozen
expressions and semi-frozen expressions[4], we had to be careful while creating grammars because NooJ syntactic grammars analyze only sequences of tokens. Everyday
language use does in fact enable a speaker to break even the most formal and frequent
constructions and insert various new and innovative expressions within those constructions. Those kinds of usages could have decreased the final precision of the
grammars, but since we had a statistical insight for the distribution patterns in which

---

[4] Expressions where one or more elements fully or partially vary.

the analyzed lexemes might be used, we had that kind of usages in mind and annotated their possible (re)occurrence in the grammars (Table 1).

Table 1. Recall and precision percentages of NooJ syntactic grammars comparing results of the lexeme *strah* with other lexemes describing emotions of happiness, anger and sorrow

Emotion	Lexemes	Recall	Correctly annotated usages	Total precision
Happiness	*Sreća* ('happiness')	73%	97%	71%
	Sretan ('happy')	71%	88%	63%
Anger	*ljutiti se* ('to be angry')	52%	98%	51%
	Ljut ('angry')	69%	97%	67%
Fear	*Strah* ('fear')	78%	86%	67%
	Strašan ('horrible')	76%	83%	63%
Sorrow	*Tuga* ('sadness')	100%	94%	94%
	Tužan ('sad')	61%[a]	61%	45%

[a]39 usages were not annotated, but 23 were annotated with two possible meanings.

Table 2. Recall and precision percentages for constructions containing the lexeme *strah*

Construction	Meaning	Recall	Correctly annotated usages	Precision
[*strah od čega*]	'fear of something'	23%	18%	78%
[*razlog za strah*]	'reason for fear'	3%	3%	100%
[*V (živjeti) + u strahu*]	'(to live) in fear'	6 (1)%	5%	83%
[*izazivati strah*]	'to cause fear'	/		
[*utjerati strah*]	'to instill fear'	/		
[*strah + subj. + koga/čega*]	'someone is in fear of somebody or something'	/		
[*sa strahom*]	'with fear'	2%	2%	100%
[*A + strah*]	'adjective + fear'	19%	17%	89%
[*strah od N + human (starijih)*]	'being in fear of older people (teenagers)'	2%	1%	50%
[*strah + za + koga*]	'concern for someone's safety'	4%	4%	100%
[*zbog straha*]	'because of fear' – fear as a cause	5%	5%	100%
[*nema straha*]	'no need to fear'	1%	1%	/
[bez straha]	'without fear'	13%	11%	100%
[*umrijeti od straha*]	'to be scared to death'	/	/	/
[*strah i trepet*]	'fear and terror'	1%	1%	100%
[*u strahu su velike oči*]	'a frightened man sees danger everywhere'	/	/	/
[]	Unspecified usage	22%	/	/

The total recall of all the NooJ syntactic grammars for the analyzed lexemes was 72.50%. Out of those annotated usages, NooJ grammars have correctly annotated 88% constructions and their overall precision was 65.125%. This means that over a third of lexeme usages were correctly annotated with their meaning by the grammars.

The numbers for the lexeme *strah* ('fear') roughly correspond to the overall number, but different meanings and usages of the lexemes had different results. The most frequent was the 'emotion of fear' (66 usages), 22 of them being a construction with prepositions: [*u strahu*] ('with fear') and [*od straha*] ('out of fear'). On the other hand, 'awe' had 3 usages, 'expression of concern' had 4 and 'fear as a cause for preventing actions', such as [*zbog straha*] ('because of fear') had 5, with a 100% precision (Table 2).

The results have shown that NooJ has the ability to produce high percentages of precision for automatic semantic annotation, but the question from the research itself arose about the causes that lay in the back of varying results, not just for lexemes, but for the meanings themselves, besides the possible incorrectly annotated tokens or variable word order.

6   Conclusions and Future Work

In this work we used NooJ to formalize lexicalization patterns of a chosen lexeme, describing one of the basic emotions in Croatian language. One of the biggest advantages of NooJ is the flexibility of inserting new and multiple annotations. Since we have considered annotations as being the metalinguistic generalizations of morphosyntactic, semantic and pragmatic information, NooJ makes it rather simple for a linguist to note a certain linguistic phenomenon and test it straight away. One example that was important for us was including annotation of [+human] in a large number of tokens in a simple and quick manner. It has notably increased the precision of constructions such as *strah od starijih* ('fear of older people') and helped differentiate them from *strah od smrti* ('fear of death') and other constructions with the overall meaning of 'of anxiety and concern as a physiological response to a sense of danger'.

Furthermore, NooJ grammars had a higher precision for constructions with a lower recall, while primary or basic meanings made up around 50% of lexeme usages. Also notable was the fact that the primary meanings had more lexicalized patterns, i.e. constructions formed in different prepositional, noun and verb phrases (*strah od smrti* 'fear of death', *u strahu/sa strahom* 'in fear/with fear', *osjećati strah* 'to feel fear', *iznenadan strah* 'sudden feeling of fear'...), which made them more challenging to formalize in NooJ. Other linguistic phenomena, such as causative constructions and intensifiers, were formalized in NooJ without problem (*zbog straha* 'because of fear', *silan strah* 'strong fear'...), although it would be interesting to see if it is possible to formalize argument structure constructions the way Goldberg showed in her research (1995; 2006).

In its present form our work contains only lexeme that encodes emotion of fear in Croatian language. The project described in this paper has served us as an experiment and a starting point for developing grammars for other lexemes using proposed methodology. For further research in the area of automated semantic recognition, more metalinguistic generalizations, such as pragmatic and semantic annotations, would be necessary in resources for Croatian language.

Evaluation results have shown that NooJ provides sufficient means for involving further applications of this construction-based methodology. Focusing on fine tuning of developed grammars could increase both precision and recall of results, taking into account that we experimented with highly complex language structures. Current research was based on semasiological structure, but it is also possible to analyze onomasiological structures and see how and which patterns are more likely to lexicalize a particular meaning.

References

Barlow, M., Kemmer, S.: Usage-Based Models of Language. CSLI Publications, Stanford (2000)

Bekavac, B., Vučković, K., Tadić, M.: Croatian resources for NooJ. 2007 NooJ Conference Book of abstracts

Belaj, B., Tanacković Faletar, G.: Kognitivna gramatika hrvatskoga jezika. Disput, Zagreb (2014)

Croft, W.: Radical Construction Grammar: Syntactic Theory in Typological Perspective. Oxford University Press, Oxford (2001)

Fillmore, Ch., Kay, P., O'Connor, M.C.: Regularity and idiomaticity in grammatical constructions: the case of 'let alone'. Language **64**(3), 501–538 (1988)

Goldberg, A.E.: A Construction Grammar Approach to Argument Structure. The University of Chicago Press, Chicago (1995)

Goldberg, A.E.: Constructions at Work. The Nature of Generalization in Language. Oxford University Press Inc, New York (2006)

Katunar, D.: Ustroj leksikona u konstrukcijskoj gramatici – primjer prijedloga u hrvatskom jeziku. Faculty of Humanities and Social Sciences, Doctoral thesis, Zagreb (2015)

Raffaelli, I.: Conventionalized patterns of colour naming in Croatian. In: Cergol Kovačević, K., Udier, S.L. (eds.) Applied Linguistics Research and Methodology, Proceedings from the 2015 CALS Conference, pp. 171–186. Peter Lang Verlag, Franfurt am Main (2017)

The Lexicon-Grammar of Predicate Nouns with *ser de* in Port4NooJ

Cristina Mota[1(✉)], Jorge Baptista[1,2], and Anabela Barreiro[1]

[1] L2F/INESC-ID, Lisbon, Portugal
cmota@ist.utl.pt, anabela.barreiro@inesc-id.pt
[2] Universidade do Algarve, Faro, Portugal
jbaptis@ualg.pt

Abstract. This paper provides continuity for previous efforts on the integration of complementary lexicon-grammars to expand the paraphrastic capabilities of Port4NooJ, the Portuguese module of NooJ (Silberztein 2016). We describe the integration of the lexicon-grammar of 2,085 predicate nouns, which co-occur in constructions with the support verb *ser de* 'be of' in European Portuguese, such as in *O Pedro é de uma coragem extraordinária* 'Peter is of an extraordinary courage', studied, classified and formalized by Baptista (2005b). This led to a 20% increase in the number of predicate nouns. We also extended previously created paraphrasing grammars, such as the grammars that paraphrase symmetric predicates, as well as the grammars that handle the substitution of the support verb by another support verb. Furthermore, we created new grammars to paraphrase negative constructions, appropriate noun constructions, adjectival constructions, and manner sub-clauses. The paraphrastic capabilities acquired have been integrated in the eSPERTo system.

1 Introduction

Previous research has shown that the distributional and transformational properties of adjectival and nominal predicates contained in lexicon-grammar tables can be used in paraphrasing tasks with successful results. Mota et al. (2016) describe the integration of the lexicon-grammar of human intransitive adjectives formalized by Carvalho (2007) and Mota et al. (2017) describe the integration of the lexicon-grammar of the predicate nouns co-occurring with the support verb *fazer* 'do' or 'make' formalized by Chacoto (2005).

This paper provides continuity for previous efforts on the integration of complementary lexicon-grammars to expand the paraphrastic capabilities of Port4NooJ, the Portuguese module of NooJ (Silberztein 2016). We describe the integration of the lexicon-grammar of 2,085 predicate nouns, which co-occur in constructions with the support verb *ser de* 'be of' in European Portuguese, such as in *O Pedro é de uma coragem extraordinária* 'Peter is of an extraordinary courage', studied, classified and formalized by Baptista (2005b). Many of these predicate nouns correspond to the nominalization of adjectival constructions,

© Springer Nature Switzerland AG 2019
I. Mauro Mirto et al. (Eds.): NooJ 2018, CCIS 987, pp. 124–137, 2019.
https://doi.org/10.1007/978-3-030-10868-7_12

so in those cases they are linked to the corresponding adjective in the lexicon-grammar table. This presents a major challenge in terms of integration into Port4NooJ, as in 55% of the cases where the predicate nouns have an equivalent adjectival construction, the adjective is homograph of a human intransitive adjective, already formalized in the lexicon-grammar of human intransitive adjectives. This means that one must find a way of harmonizing these entries so as not to have duplicates. However, for now, we did not tackle this challenge and will not discuss it further.

The predicate nouns that occur with the support verb *ser de* were classified into nine classes. The criteria to establish those classes are described in Sect. 3. The structural, distributional, and transformational properties represented in the lexicon-grammar table for each predicate noun led to the generation of a variety of paraphrases, which are achieved by different lexico-syntactic processes. One of these processes is the interchangeability with other elementary support verbs, such as *ter* 'have' or *haver* 'there be', and more rarely with *fazer* 'do' or 'make'. Some paraphrastic relations have also been established based on the (i) insertion of negation/negative prefixes (mainly *des-* and *in-*) on predicate nouns, (ii) complementary but analytical mechanism of negation involving the expression *falta de* 'lack of', (iii) NP restructuring, (iv) predicate nouns that can function as an adnominal adjunct of a common human noun, (v) predicate nouns most likely obtained from the reduction of complex sentence with a relative clause, and (vi) symmetric predicate noun constructions.

As in previous integration efforts, the resources gathered are to be incorporated into the eSPERTo paraphrasing system[1] and to be used in a wide variety of software applications, so as to allow rephrasing a sentence or text using different words. The evolution of eSPERTo's resources, starting from the original Port4NooJ to the current version, which integrates several lexicon-grammars, among other resources, is illustrated in Fig. 1. The combination of the different resources enables a large number of paraphrases that are increasing in volume and improving in quality. We plan to enlarge our growing database of pairs of paraphrastic units by converting more tables built (or to be built) for Portuguese or other languages at the same time as we evolve our integration of crowdsourcing and machine learning techniques to acquire raw data that require validation by linguists before integrating into the paraphrasing engine. Our methodology is based on grammar and other processes that we believe are the ones used by the human brain in processing language (Barreiro et al. 2011; Scott 2018).

2   Related Work

In our several scientific papers on the work towards increased integration of lexicon-grammar tables, we have referred to related published works on support verb constructions studied within the lexicon-grammar theory (Gross 1975,

---

[1] eSPERTo, which means 'smart' in Portuguese, stands for "**S**ystem of **P**araphrasing for **E**diting and **R**evision of **T**exts" ("*Sistema de Parafraseamento para Edição e Revisão de Texto*").

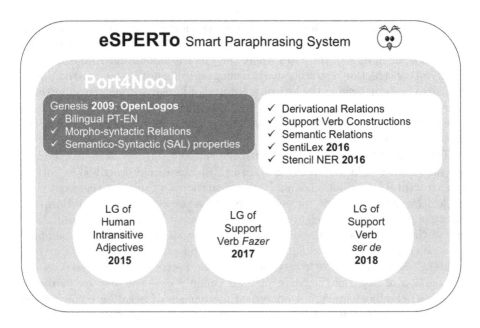

Fig. 1. Evolution of eSPERTo paraphrasing system

1996), for several Romance languages other than Portuguese (D'Agostino and Elia 1998; Laporte and Voyatzi 2008; Silberztein 1993), and contrastive studies aiming at machine translation between English and French (Salkoff 1990). Many of the studies within the lexicon-grammar framework focus on formalization of multiword units, most of them on the topic of support verb constructions. As for the Portuguese language, several detailed studies on support verb constructions have become an established theme in development cooperation, which have been presented at the last four International NooJ Conferences, addressing the integration of relations between support verbs and nominalizations (normally autonomous predicate nouns) or predicate adjective constructions. Each one of those papers also illustrates how the properties contained in the addressed lexicon-grammar tables are used in paraphrasing tasks.

The very first integration experiment by Mota et al. (2016) concerned the integration of the lexicon-grammar of human intransitive adjectives into the Port4NooJ module. After the success of this integration, we have started to integrate complementary lexicon-grammars, first the lexicon-grammar of predicate nouns, which co-occur with the support verb *fazer* (Mota et al. 2017), and now the lexicon-grammar of predicate nouns co-occurring with *ser de*. Several classes and subclasses have been defined for each one of these lexicon-grammars based on distributional and transformational properties of the predicate nouns with which each one of these verbs co-occurs. The main properties of the transformations of *ser de* that we represented in paraphrasing grammars are described in Sect. 3. As far as we know, no other similar integration efforts have been done for any other language, at least within the NooJ framework[2].

3   Lexicon-Grammar of Predicate Nouns with V_{sup} *ser de*

The lexicon-grammar of predicate nouns occurring in constructions with the support verb *ser de* 'be of' in European Portuguese, such as in *O Pedro foi de uma ajuda inestimável para a Ana* 'Pedro was of an invaluable help to Ana' was formalized by Baptista (2000, 2005b) after studying and classifying the structural, distributional, and transformational properties of 2,085 predicate nouns. The author identified seven classes of predicate nouns according to (i) the number or arguments (1 or 2) selected by the predicate noun, (ii) the syntactic (sentential/nominal) constraints, and (iii) the distributional (semantic) selection constraints on the nominal argument slots (human/non-human). Two special classes were established for: (i) nouns selecting a body-part noun as their subject, such as *Os músculos da Ana são de uma tonicidade impressionante* 'Ana's muscles are of an impressive tonicity', and (ii) constructions that have an equivalent symmetric construction, i.e., allow swapping the predicate noun's subject with its complement, such as *A Ana é de uma grande parecença com a irmã* 'A Ana is of a great resemblance to her sister'. Table 1 presents the breakdown of these nouns by classes and their basic syntactic structure. Of the many transformations formalized in this lexicon-grammar we chose a few to start creating paraphrasing grammars. In Sects. 3.1–3.7, we will briefly describe some of its properties.

3.1   Symmetry Restructuring

In symmetric predicates (see Baptista (2005a) for an overview in Portuguese), their two arguments have the same semantic role in relation to the predicate and, therefore, they can be swapped in their syntactic slots without changing the overall meaning of the sentence, e.g., *A aldeia é de uma proximidade à praia muito grande = A praia é de uma proximidade muito grande à vila* 'The village is of a great proximity to the beach' = 'The beach is of a great proximity to the beach'; or be coordinated in the same syntactic slot (the subject), e.g., *A vila é de uma grande proximidade à praia = A vila e a praia são de uma grande proximidade (uma da outra)* 'The village is of a great proximity to the beach' = 'The village and the beach are of a great proximity (to each other)'.

3.2   Support Verb Variants

Usually, the support verb occurring with a predicate noun can be replaced by lexical variants. However, that is not the case with *ser de* 'be of' which has no

---

[2] In Rassi et al. (2014, 2015), a proposal is presented for the integration of predicate noun constructions into STRING (Mamede et al. 2012), a hybrid, rule-based and statistical, natural language processing chain, specifically developed for the processing of Portuguese.

Table 1. Distribution of nominal predicates with support verb *ser de* by class attribute

Class	Count	Percentage	Structure example
SdH1	388	19%	*(Nhum)$_0$ ser de N*
			O Zé é de uma alegria contagiante
			Zé is of a contagious joy/happiness
SdH2	54	3%	*(Nhum)$_0$ ser de N Prep N$_1$*
			O Zé é da confiança da Ana
			Zé is from Ana's trust
SdNH1	363	17%	*(Nnhum)$_0$ ser de N*
			Este molho é de uma acidez exagerada
			This sauce is of an exaggerated acidity
SdNH2	30	1%	*(Nnhum)$_0$ ser de N Prep N$_1$*
			Esta substância é de uma total indissolubilidade em água
			This substance is of a total indissolubility in water
SdNPC	30	1%	*(Npc de Nhum)$_0$ ser de N*
			O rosto da Ana era de uma palidez doentia
			Ana's face was of a sick pallor
SdQ0	820	39%	*QueF$_0$ ser de N*
			Essa medida é de grande abrangência
			This measure is of broad coverage
SdQ1	308	15%	*QueF$_0$ ser de N Prep N$_1$*
			O Zé foi de uma agressividade desproporcionada para com a Ana
			Zé was disproportionately aggressive towards Ana
SdQ2	37	2%	*N$_0$ ser de N Prep QueF$_1$*
			O Zé é de uma grande habilidade para tratar das roseiras
			Ze is of great ability to treat rose bushes
SdSIM	55	3%	*N$_0$ ser de N Prep N$_1$* [symmetry]
			O Zé e a Ana são de um companheirismo exemplar
			Zé and Ana are of exemplary companionship
Total	2085		

stylistic nor aspectual variants. Nonetheless, these predicate nouns may have equivalent constructions with other elementary support verbs, mostly *ter* 'have', *haver* 'there be', and, more rarely, with *fazer* 'do, make'[3] (see examples in Table 2).

---

[3] The construction with *fazer* is not strictly a paraphrase of the construction with *ser de*, as the former only characterizes the human gesture, but not the human quality expressed by the constructions with *ser de*.

Table 2. Paraphrasing *ser de* variants

Type	Paraphrases
[Vsup=ter]	*O Pedro teve uma grande gentileza (para com a Maria)*
	Pedro had a great kindness (towards Maria)
[Vsup=fazer]	*O Pedro fez uma grande gentileza (à Maria)*
	Pedro did a great kindness (to Maria)
[Vsup=haver]	*Há no Pedro uma grande gentileza (para com a Maria)*
	There is in Pedro a great kindness (with Maria)

3.3   Nominalizations

An important source for the analysis of paraphrastic relations among sentences is *nominalizations*, that is, equivalence relations between sentences with a predicate noun and a support verb, on the one hand, and a verb or an adjective (and its auxiliary verb), on the other hand. For the most part, the predicate nouns with support verb *ser de* correspond to the *nominalization* of adjectival constructions, e.g. *O Pedro foi de uma grande crueldade para com o João* 'Pedro was of a great cruelty towards João' = *O Pedro foi muito cruel para com o João* 'Pedro was very cruel to João'. More rarely, a verbal construction can be found: *O Pedro foi de uma grande compaixão para com o João* 'Pedro was of (=had) a great compassion for João' = *O Pedro compadeceu-se do João* 'Pedro took pity on João'. It should be noted, however, that the lexical-morphological relation between a predicate noun and a verb, or between a noun and an adjective, is necessary but insufficient to establish a nominalization, with a transformational status, in the sense of Gross (1981), Harris (1981). Not only the meaning of the sentences being related must be the same, but the distributional constraints of the predicate noun on its argument domain must be similar. Establishing such paraphrastic status, thus, requires highly granular, and systematic linguistic description.

3.4   Negation

In the lexicon-grammar of *ser de*, two types of negation were formalized: (i) prefixation, i.e., possibility of adding/removing a negative prefix like *des-* or *in-* to the predicate noun; and (ii) analytic negation involving the expression *falta de* 'lack of'[4]. Table 3 illustrates these two types of negation and the paraphrastic relation between them was represented in grammars displayed in Sect. 4.2. Whenever significant differences in meaning are found between the predicates starting with different negation prefixes, the prefixed and the base forms were treated as independent lexicon-grammar entries.

---

[4] Most of the predicates having this property express human qualities/attributes.

Table 3. Paraphrasing negation

Type	Paraphrases
[in-N]	*O Pedro é de uma certa (in-)tolerância à lactose*
	Pedro is of a certain (in-)tolerance to lactose
[falta de N] (lack of N)	*O Pedro é de uma certa (falta de) tolerância à lactose*
	Pedro is of a certain (lack of) tolerance to lactose

3.5   Appropriate Nouns and NP Restructuring

The subject of the sentences with *ser de* 'be of' is many times a complex noun phrase (NP) whose head is also a predicate noun. This head may occur with its arguments, particularly its semantic/notional 'subject' argument, in the form of a prepositional phrase (PP) introduced by the preposition *de* 'of': [*A disposição destes objetos*] *é de uma certa assimetria* '[The placement of these objects] is of a certain asymmetry'. An *appropriate* relation, in the sense of Gross (1981) [pp. 113–115], Harris (1976), usually exists between the predicate noun in the subject position and the sentence's main predicate, and a *NP restructuring* operation (Guillet and Leclère 1981) is then found, which splits the noun phrase into two distinct constituents: (i) the head of the PP becomes the sentence subject, while (ii) the predicate noun (formerly the head of the subject NP) is moved to a new PP, usually at the end of the sentence. For example, in [*Estes objetos*] *são de uma certa assimetria* [*na sua disposição*] '[These objects] are of a certain asymmetry [in their placement]', the reference of the possessive determiner in the PP (*sua* 'their', in the example) is constrained, and it has to refer to the subject of the predicate noun; obviously, this possessive can not be derived from a free PP, non-co-referent to the subject. The semantic roles of the elements are then kept exactly the same in spite of the formal changes the sentence undergoes.

3.6   Manner Sub-clauses Restructuring

An interesting distributional constraint regards the subject NPs with manner operator nouns (Gross 1975) *forma, maneira* and *modo* 'manner/way' (in Brazilian Portuguese, there is also the operator noun *jeito* '*idem*'). These operators can be construed with an *infinitive* sub-clause complement introduced by preposition *de* '*of*': *A forma/a maneira/o modo* **de** *o Pedro* **fazer** *isso é de uma arrogância impressionante* 'The way **of** Pedro **doing** this is of an impressive arrogance'; or a *pseudo-relative, finite* clause, introduced by the so-called interrogative adverb *como* 'how': *A forma/a maneira/o modo* **como** *o Pedro* **faz** *isso é de uma arrogância impressionante* 'The way **how** Pedro **does** this is of an impressive arrogance'. When the predicate noun accepts these operator nouns, these sentences qualify the way a process takes place or the manner in which an action is performed, rather than expressing the attributes of a person or an object. A similar *NP restructuring* as seen above (Sect. 3.5) operates on these manner constructions, splitting the complex NP, extracting the subject of the subordinate clause to the subject of the predicate noun and leaving the operator noun as a PP manner complement: *O Pedro é de uma arrogância impressionante em_a forma/a maneira/o modo de fazer isso* 'Pedro is of an impressive arrogance in the way of doing that' *O Pedro é de uma arrogância impressionante em_a forma/a maneira/o modo como faz isso* 'Pedro is of an impressive arrogance in the way [he] does that' (Table 4).

Table 4. Paraphrasing manner sub-clauses

Type	Paraphrases
[*RestNopQueF*]	*O modo de o Pedro agir é de uma certa teimosia*
	Pedro's way of acting is of a certain stubbornness
	O Pedro é de uma certa teimosia no seu modo de agir
	Pedro is of a certain stubbornness in his way of acting
[*RestNopQueF*]	*O modo como o Pedro age é de uma certa teimosia*
	The way Pedro acts is of a certain stubbornness
	O Pedro é de uma certa teimosia no modo como age
	Pedro is of a certain stubbornness in the way he acts

3.7   Reduction of Finite Sub-clause to Infinitive and Restructuring

Other sub-clause transformations have also been represented in the lexicon-grammar, namely the possibility of an infinitive construction with operator-noun *facto* (fact), the reduction of a finite sub-clause to an infinitive and its restructuring in a way similar to the NP restructuring transformations seen above. Table 5 illustrates these phenomena.

4   Integration of Lexicon-Grammar Tables in Port4NooJ

As shown in Mota et al. (2017) and Mota et al. (2016), the integration of lexicon-grammars in Port4Nooj is a two-step process. First, one converts the lexicon-grammar tables into NooJ dictionary format, and then one builds grammars that use the linguistic knowledge encoded in the lexicon-grammar tables to identify relevant sentences or phrases and generate their corresponding paraphrases.

4.1   From Lexicon-Grammar Tables to NooJ Dictionaries

The procedure described in Mota et al. (2017) to convert the lexicon-grammar entries that occur with support *fazer* into a standalone dictionary was adopted,

Table 5. Paraphrasing of finite sub-clauses to infinitive

Type	Paraphrases
[Nop facto]	*É de uma completa evidência que a Susana está a mentir*
	It is of a complete evidence that Susana is lying
	É de uma completa evidência o facto de a Susana estar a mentir
	It is of a complete evidence the fact that Susana is lying
[Vinf]	*É de uma certa teimosia que o Pedro aja assim*
	It is of a certain stubbornness that Pedro acts in that way
	É de uma certa teimosia o Pedro agir assim
	Is of a certain stubbornness Pedro acting that way
[Rest Vinf]	*O Pedro é de uma certa teimosia em agir assim*
	Pedro is of a certain stubbornness in acting in this way

with minor adjustments, to convert the lexicon-grammar entries that occur with support verb *ser de*. The procedure is illustrated in Fig. 2.[5]

The minor adjustments were related to particularities of the lexicon-grammars properties or format that do not interfere with the overall procedure, but only with the way lexicon-grammar properties are converted into dictionary attributes. For example, the property `PfxNeg` can be filled in the lexicon-grammar entries with "-" when the predicate does not accept a negative prefix or with the value of the negative prefix, e.g., `in-`, `des-`.

The new standalone dictionary is comprised of 2,134 predicate noun entries that occur with Vsup *ser de*, corresponding to 1,376 different lemmas. Additional 797 entries await revision to be added to this version of the dictionary. They need revision of the inflectional codes, of derived adjectives or have problems with their format. The integration of this lexicon-grammar led to the creation of 450 new derivational paradigms, but there might be an overlap with paradigms created when integrating the lexicon-grammar of constructions with the support verb *fazer*.

50% of the predicate nouns in the lexicon-grammar already existed in the main dictionary of Port4Nooj. This corresponds to a 6% increase in nominal entries and 20% increase in predicate nouns. In 55% of the cases where the predicate nouns have an equivalent adjectival construction, the adjective was homograph of a human intransitive adjective, already formalized in the lexicon-grammar of human intransitive adjectives Carvalho (2007). This overlap implies harmonization of entries in order to eliminate duplicates.

It is also worth noting that 4% of the predicate noun lemmas (52) that occur with support verb *ser de* are homographs of predicate noun lemmas that occur

---

[5] As in Mota et al. (2017), the procedure allows to check whether words are compliant with the Portuguese Orthographic Agreement, but since all the words are pre-Agreement we are not using that feature and, hence, it is not described in the figure.

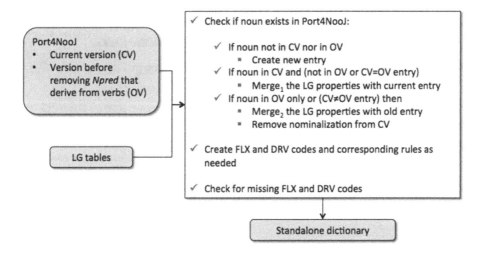

Fig. 2. Integration of LG entries in Port4NooJ

with support verb *fazer*, which had been previously integrated in Port4NooJ. Some predicates correspond to the same construction, like *O Zé é de uma patetice impressionante* 'Zé is of an impressive goofiness' seems a paraphrase of *O Zé fez uma patetice* 'Zé did a goofiness', which can be confirmed also by the fact that the entry for *patetice* accepts the Vsup *fazer* as a valid substitution for the Vsup *ser de*. Other predicate nouns, like *reserva* 'reservation' in *O Zé foi de uma grande reserva para com a Ana em relação à sua decisão* 'Ze was a of big reservation with Ana about her decision', and in *O Tó fez a reserva do bilhete* 'Tó made the ticket reservation', are not expressions of the same predicate. Further studies need to be made to see whether it is worth merging those entries together.

4.2 From Lexicon-Grammar Tables to NooJ Grammars

As we have already shown in Mota et al. (2016) and Mota et al. (2017), the process of integrating the lexicon-grammar with Port4NooJ dictionary entries is mostly automatic, but the process of creating the grammars that use the knowledge formalized in the lexicon-grammars is hand-crafted, hence, time-consuming. Some grammars can still be reused when they represent similar phenomena common to different lexicon-grammars although they usually need to be updated with the information of the newly integrated lexicon-grammar tables. The grammar that allows the substitution of the support verb by another support verb is one of such cases, as well as the grammar built to represent the equivalence between symmetric predicates, where the arguments have been swapped or coordinated. See Fig. 3 as an example of the latter. As illustrated in the figure, the equivalent adjectival constructions is also recognized and generated. In that case, the grammar guarantees the agreement in gender and in number with the subject (where the arguments have been coordinated or not) and the adjective.

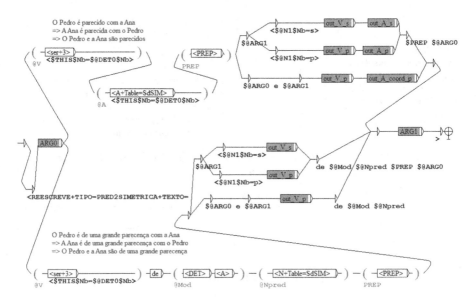

Fig. 3. Grammar for paraphrasing of symmetric constructions

Figure 4 shows the annotations that were added to the NooJ Text Annotation Structure after doing the linguistic analysis including the grammar that generates the paraphrasing of symmetric predicates illustrated in Fig. 3. Although the adjectival form *parecida* 'resembling' is feminine-singular, when swapping the argument of the adjective, it becomes masculine-singular to agree in gender-number with the noun *irmão* 'brother'; also, the adjective becomes masculine-plural to agree with the coordinated arguments, e.g. *a mulher e o irmão* 'the woman and the(=her) brother', since in Portuguese, whenever there is a masculine noun in coordinated noun phrases, the adjective is obligatorily inflected in the masculine form.

While developing new grammars, we encountered two new features that we had not encountered before: (1) we had to make use of more than one lexicon-grammar property to create the criteria to generate the paraphrase - in particular, to generate paraphrases of negative constructions, the predicate must have both attributes PfxNeg and Negfaltade, otherwise it is not enough to establish the paraphrastic relation between the two constructions; (ii) we established unidirectional paraphrases, i.e., we identify, for example, the construction A and generate the construction B; but we do not identify B and generate A - this happened when we need a larger context or a more complex analysis to be able to rephrase A given B, such as in the case of rephrasing a possessive with the appropriate noun phrase.

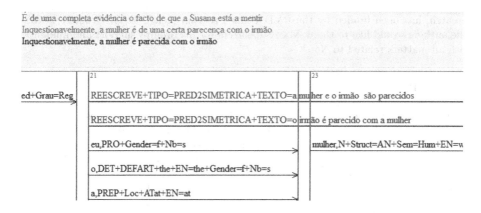

Fig. 4. Annotation and paraphrase generation of symmetric constructions

5   Conclusions and Future Work

This paper reported the progress of integration of existing lexicon-grammar tables in Port4NooJ, in continuity with previous integration efforts. This time, we have added 2,134 predicate nouns with Vsup *ser de* to our dictionary of predicate nouns, corresponding to 1,376 different noun lemmas. Half of the nouns already existed in the previous version of Port4NooJ (50%), which corresponds to a 6% increase in the number of nominal entries and a 20% increase in the number of predicate nouns for the current version of the Port4NooJ dictionary. Additional 797 entries await revision of the inflectional codes of the corresponding derived adjectives, or have format problems that require a fix prior to being added to this version. In addition, 450 new derivational paradigms were created, though some of them might overlap with paradigms already created, when integrating the predicate nouns used with the Vsup *fazer*. We have created some experimental grammars to generate production scale batches of paraphrases for different linguistic phenomena and exemplified paraphrasing with symmetric constructions in the NooJ syntactic parser. Our next steps will focus in four different axes: (i) consolidate and harmonize dictionaries, (ii) continue building lexicon-grammar-based paraphrasing grammars, (iii) review dictionaries and grammars, and (iv) integrate new lexicon-grammars, thus re-initiating the cycle. The new paraphrases can be immediately integrated in the eSPERTo system, because they are 100% precise and can serve the purposes of exploring language learning applications by using chatbots, a usage scenario in which our efforts are now engaged.

Acknowledgements. This research was supported by Fundação para a Ciência e Tecnologia (FCT), under exploratory project eSPERTo (Ref. EXPL/MHC-LIN/2260/2013). Anabela Barreiro was also funded by FCT through post-doctoral grant SFRH/BPD/91446/2012. Jorge Baptista's Ph.D. research has been funded by a scholarship under program Praxis XXI (2001–2004) and subsequent, more recent research, has been funded by the R&D Units Program (ref. UID/CEC/50021/2013). The authors would like to thank Max Silberztein for his prompt support and guidance with all matters related to NooJ.

References

Baptista, J.: Sintaxe dos Predicados Nominais construídos com o verbosuporte SER DE. Ph.D. thesis. Universidade do Algarve, Faro, Portugal (2000)

Baptista, J.: Construções simétricas: argumentos e complementos. In: Figueiredo, O., Rio-Torto, G., Silva, F. (eds.) Estudos de homenagem a Mário Vilela. Faculdade de Letras da Universidade do Porto, pp. 353–367 (2005a)

Baptista, J.: Sintaxe dos predicados nominais com 'ser de'. Fundação Calouste Gulbenkian, Fundação para a Ciência e a Tecnologia, Lisboa (2005b)

Barreiro, A., et al.: OpenLogos rule-based machine translation: philosophy, model, resources and customization. Mach. Transl. **25**(2), 107–126 (2011)

Carvalho, P.: Análise e Representação de Construções Adjectivais para Processamento Automático de Texto. Adjectivos Intransitivos Humanos. Ph.D. thesis. Universidade de Lisboa, Lisboa, Portugal (2007)

Chacoto, L.: O Verbo Fazer em Construções Nominais Predicativas. Ph.D. thesis. Universidade do Algarve, Faro, Portugal (2005)

D'Agostino, E., Elia, A.: Il significato delle frasi: un continuum dalle frasi semplici alle forme polirematiche. In: AA. VV, Ai limiti del linguaggio, Bari, Laterza, pp. 287–310 (1998)

Gross, M.: Méthodes en syntaxe: régime des constructions complétives. Actualités scientifiques et industrielles. Hermann (1975)

Gross, M.: Les bases empiriques de la notion de prédicat sémantique. Langages **15**(63), 7–52 (1981)

Gross, M.: Lexicon-Grammar. In: Brown, K., Miller, J. (eds.) Concise Encyclopedia of Syntactic Theories, pp. 244–259. Pergamon, Cambridge (1996)

Guillet, A., Leclère, C.: Restructuration deu group nominal. Langages **63**, 99–125 (1981)

Harris, Z.S.: The elementary transformations. In: Hiż, H. (ed.) Papers on Syntax. Synthese Language Library. Text and Studies in Linguistics and Philosophy, vol. 14, pp. 211–235. Springer, Dordrecht (1981). https://doi.org/10.1007/978-94-009-8467-7_9. ISBN 978-94-009-8467-7

Harris, Z.S.: Notes du Cours de Syntaxe. In: Gross, M. (ed.) Seuil, Paris (1976)

Laporte, E., Voyatzi, S.: An electronic dictionary of French multiword adverbs. In: Language Resources and Evaluation Conference. Workshop Towards a Shared Task for Multiword Expressions, pp. 31–34 (2008)

Mamede, N., et al.: STRING - a hybrid statistical and rule-based natural language processing chain for Portuguese. In: Computational Processing of the Portuguese Language (PROPOR 2012), vol. Demo Session, PROPOR, Coimbra, Portugal, PROPOR, s/p (2012)

Mota, C., Carvalho, P., Barreiro, A.: Port4NooJ v3.0: integrated linguistic resources for Portuguese NLP. In: Proceedings of the Tenth International Conference on Language Resources and Evaluation LREC 2016, Portorož, Slovenia, 23–28 May 2016

Mota, C., Chacoto, L., Barreiro, A.: Integrating the Lexicon-Grammar of predicate nouns with support verb *fazer* into Port4NooJ. In: Mbarki, S., Mourchid, M., Silberztein, M. (eds.) NooJ 2017. CCIS, vol. 811, pp. 29–39. Springer, Cham (2018). https://doi.org/10.1007/978-3-319-73420-0_3

Rassi, A., et al.: The fuzzy boundaries of operator verb and support verb constructions with dar "give" and ter "have" in Brazilian Portuguese. In: Proceedings of the Workshop on Lexical and Grammatical Resources for Language Processing (LG-LP 2014), COLING 2014, Dublin, Ireland, 24 August 2014

Rassi, A.P., et al.: Integrating support verb constructions into a parser. In: Symposium in Information and Human Language Technology (STIL 2015). SBC, Natal, Brasil (2015)

Salkoff, M.: Automatic translation of support verb constructions. In: Proceedings of the 13th Conference on Computational Linguistics, COLING 1990, Helsinki, Finland, vol. 3, pp. 243–246. ACL (1990)

Scott, B.: Translation, Brains and the Computer: A Neurolinguistic Solution to Ambiguity and Complexity in Machine Translation (2018)

Silberztein, M.: Les groupes nominaux productifs et les noms composés lexicalisés. Lingvisticœ Investig. **17**(2), 405–425 (1993)

Silberztein, M.: Formalizing Natural Languages: The NooJ Approach, p. 346. Wiley, Hoboken (2016)

Unary Transformations for French Transitive Sentences

Max Silberztein[(⊠)]

Université de Franche-Comté, Besançon, France
max.silberztein@univ-fcomte.fr

Abstract. Unary transformations are transformations that link one sentence to another, keeping the same semantic material. This paper presents a system that formalises a subset of Harris' transformations for French, in particular the transformations described in the lexicon-grammar table #1, which describes a hundred auxiliary, modal and aspectual verbs. Other, more general transformations will be described as well.

Keywords: NooJ · Transformations · Automatic paraphrasing

1 Introduction

Transformational Grammars were introduced by Harris (1968) in order to describe relations between sentences that share the same semantic material. For instance, the two sentences "Joe loves Mary" and "Mary is loved by Joe" share the same predicate (*to love*) and the same arguments (*Joe* and *Mary*), even though their structure is different. There might be some semantic difference between the two sentences linked by a transformation; for instance, the two sentences in:

Joe loves Lea. Joe does not love Lea.

are transformed sentences, even though they are not synonymous: a difference in meaning is allowed, as long as it is the same for any pair of sentences for a given transformation. Transformations are symmetric by nature; for instance, a system capable of putting an active sentence in the passive form must also be capable of parsing a passive form and then re-construct its original active form. For the purpose of automatic processing, it is convenient to describe transformations as asymmetric operators, e.g.:

(a) *Joe loves Lea* [Neg]→ *Joe does not love Lea*
(b) *Joe does not love Lea* [Neg^{-1}]→ *Joe loves Lea*

Typically, Natural Language Processing (NLP) applications will use transformations such as (a) to produce texts from a given semantic representation,[1] whereas transformations such as (b) are used to parse a complex sentence and produce its semantic representation.

---

[1] Silberztein (2017) shows how to automatically produce a large number of sentences from relatively elementary statements represented as predicates in *Friend Of A Friend* (FOAF) data bases.

© Springer Nature Switzerland AG 2019
I. Mauro Mirto et al. (Eds.): NooJ 2018, CCIS 987, pp. 138–151, 2019.
https://doi.org/10.1007/978-3-030-10868-7_13

Transformations are not only applied to elementary sentences; they can also be applied to more complex sentences that are themselves produced by other transformations. Hence, a sentence can be the result of a chain of transformations. For instance:

Joe loves Lea [Neg]→ *Joe does not love Lea* [Pro1]→ *Joe does not love her*
[Cleft0]→ *It is Joe who does not love her* [Preterit]→ *It is Joe who did not love her.*

Reciprocally, in order to analyse a complex sentence to produce an elementary predicate, one needs to perform a series of transformations, e.g.:

It is her who might have been loved by Joe
$[Pro^{-1}]$→ *It is Lea who might have been loved by Joe*
$[Cleft^{-1}]$→ *Lea might have been loved by Joe*
$[Modal^{-1}]$→ *Lea has been loved by Joe*
$[Tense^{-1}]$→ *Lea is loved by Joe*
$[Passive^{-1}]$→ *Joe loves Lea*

Note finally that transformations might involve more than one sentence. For instance, binary transformations link one complex sentence to two sentences, e.g.:

Joe sees Lea + Mary sees Lea [Coord0]→ *Joe and Mary see Lea*
Joe was sleeping + Lea came [When]→ *Joe was sleeping when Lea came*
Lea is sleeping + Joe tells Mary [Sub]→ *Joe tells Mary that Lea is sleeping*

In this article, I present a set of French unary transformations.

2 Unary Transformations

In the following examples, I have used the NooJ linguistic development environment[2] to develop a set of linguistic resources in order to perform transformations for tenses, pronominalisation, extraction, negation, passivation, transformations associated with a set of verbs that generalise the notion of auxiliary verbs (e.g. modal and aspectual verbs), as well as mandatory orthographical transformations.

2.1 Tenses

I have described 7 simple tenses:

Léa dort [PrésentIndicatif]→ *Léa dort*	*Lea sleeps*
Léa dort [PrésentSubjonctif]→ *(que) Léa dorme*	
Léa dort [PrésentConditionnel]→ *Léa dormirait*	*Lea would sleep*
Tu manges [PrésentImpératif]→ *Mange (!)*	*Eat!*
Léa dort [Imparfait]→ *Léa dormait*	*Lea was sleeping*
Léa mange [PasséSimple]→ *Léa mangea*	*Lea slept*
Léa dort [Futur]→ *Léa dormira*	*Lea will sleep*

---

[2] See Silberztein (2016b).

I have not added the *Imparfait du subjonctif* tense (e.g. *Léa dormît*) used in literary or classical XVIIIth century French, because it is no longer used in modern French.[3] There are 4 basic compound tenses:

Léa dort [PasséComposé]→ *Léa a dormi.*	*Lea has slept*
Léa dort [PlusQueParfait]→ *Léa avait dormi.*	*Lea had slept*
Léa dort [FuturAntérieur]→ *Léa aura dormi.*	*Lea will have slept*
Léa dort [PasséConditionnel]→ *Léa aurait dormi.*	*Lea would have slept*

Most verbs use the auxiliary verb *avoir* (*to have*), but some require the auxiliary verb *être* (*to be*), e.g.:

Léa vient [PasséComposé]→ *Léa est venue.*   *Lea has come*

In pronominal constructions, all verbs require the auxiliary verb *être*, e.g.:

Léa a lavé sa main [VPron]→ *Léa s'est lavé la main.*   *Lea has washed her hand*

The compound tenses *Passé du subjonctif* (e.g. *Que Léa ait dormi*), *Plus-que-parfait du subjonctif* (e.g. *Que Léa eût dormi*) and *Passé de l'impératif* (e.g. *Aie dormi!*) are not used in modern French.

I have generalised tenses to the following constructions, with *être en train de*, *aller* and *venir de* treated as auxiliary verbs[4]:

Léa dort [PrésentIndicatifProgressif]→ *Léa est en train de dormir*   *Lea is sleeping*
Léa dort [PrésentSubjonctifProgressif]→ *(que) Léa soit en train de dormir*
Léa dort [PrésentConditionnelProgressif]→ *Léa serait en train de dormir*
Léa dort [ImparfaitProgressif]→ *Léa était en train de dormir*
Léa dort [FuturProgressif]→ *Léa sera en train de dormir*
Léa dort [FuturProchePrésentIndicatif]→ *Léa va dormir*   *Lea is going to sleep*
Léa dort [FuturProchePrésentSubjonctif]→ *(que) Léa aille dormir*
Léa dort [FuturProchePrésentConditionnel]→ *Léa irait dormir*
Léa dort [FuturProcheImparfait]→ *Léa allait dormir*
Léa dort [FuturProcheFutur]→ *Léa ira dormir*
Léa dort [PasséProchePrésentIndicatif]→ *Léa vient de dormir*
                                         Lea has just finished sleeping
Léa dort [PasséProchePrésentSubjonctif]→ *(que) Léa vienne de dormir*
Léa dort [PasséProchePrésentConditionnel]→ *Léa viendrait de dormir*
Léa dort [PasséProcheImparfait]→ *Léa venait de dormir*
Léa dort [PasséProcheFutur]→ *Léa viendra de dormir*

---

[3] A 1976 Ministerial decree promotes the use of the *présent du subjonctif*, instead of the imparfait du subjonctif, e.g. *Joe aimerait qu'elle vienne* instead of *Joe aimerait qu'elle vînt*.

[4] *Lea is going to sleep:* Some of these sentences are ambiguous. For instance, *Léa ira dormir* (*Léa is going to sleep*) can mean that she will be getting ready to sleep (*aller* as an auxiliary verb), or that she will go somewhere to sleep (*aller* as a movement verb).

One might want to formalise the application of composed tenses on these auxiliary verbs, as in:

[Progressif][PasséComposé]→ ? *Léa a été en train de dormir.*   *Lea has been sleeping*
[FuturProche][PasséConditionnel]→ *Léa serait allé dormir.*

Lea would be going to sleep

However, these sentences are better described as results of a combination of two transformations. Note that not all combinations of transformations are allowed, e.g.[5]:

[PasséProche][FuturAntérieur]→ **Léa sera venu de dormir.*

Lea will have just finished sleeping
[FuturProche][PlusQueParfait]→ **Léa était allé dormir.*   *Lea was going to sleep*

In the same way, the application of two or more auxiliary verbs to a sentence would be described by a composition of several elementary transformations, e.g.[6]:

[FuturProche][Progressif]→ *Léa va être en train de dormir.*

Lea is going to be sleeping
[Progressif][FuturProche]→ * *Léa est en train d'aller dormir.*
[PasséProche][Progressif][FuturProche]→ ?*Léa vient d'être en train d'aller dormir.*

Lea has just been going to sleep

In total, I have implemented 26 elementary transformations to describe French tenses.

2.2   Pronominalisations, Extractions, Negations and Passivation

The most frequent French pronouns in written texts are: *elle, elles, en, eux, il, ils, la, le, les, leur, lui, on, se.*[7] A subject noun phrase can be pronominalised via one of these transformations:

Joe mange [Pron0_il]→ *Il mange*	*He eats*
Les enfants mangent [Pron0_ils]→ *Ils mangent*	*They eat*
Léa mange [Pron0_elle]→ *Elle mange*	*She eats*
Les amies mangent [Pron0_elles]→ *Elles mangent*	*They eat*
Joe mange [Pron0_lui]→ *lui mange*	*He eats*
Quelqu'un mange [Pron0_on]→ *On mange*	*Someone eats*
Trois personnes sont venues [Pron0_NB]→ *Trois sont venues*	*Three came*

---

[5] **Léa était allé dormir:* This sentence is correct only if *aller* is interpreted as the movement verb, as in *Lea was getting to her bedroom in order to sleep.* However, the auxiliary verb *aller* used to express the near future as in *Lea was on the verge of sleeping* cannot be expressed by this sentence.

[6] **Léa est en train d'aller dormir:* Ibid.

[7] I have not described the pronouns *je, tu, me, nous, te, vous* in this study. The pronoun *on* is often used as a variant of *nous: nous mangeons = on mange (we are eating).* There are over 200 other pronouns (e.g. *aucun, celui-ci, certains, n'importe qui, personne, plusieurs,* etc.) that are described in Gross (1986) and have been integrated in a syntactic grammar by Silberztein (2003).

An object noun phrase can be pronominalised via one of these transformations:

Joe donne le pain à Léa [Pron1_le] : → *Joe le donne à Léa*   Joe gives it to Lea
Léa donne la cuillère à Joe [Pron1_la]→ *Lea la donne à Joe*
Joe donne les pains à Léa [Pron1_les]→ *Joe les donne à Léa*   Joe gives them to Lea
Lea donne trois pains à Joe [Pron1_NB]→ *Léa en donne trois à Joe*
Lea gives three of them to Joe
Joe donne du pain à Léa [Pron1_en]→ *Joe en donne à Léa*   Joe gives some to Lea

An indirect object noun phrase can be pronominalised via one of these transformations:

Joe donne un pain à Léa [Pron2_lui]→ *Joe lui donne un pain*
Léa donne des pains aux amis [Pron2_leur]→ *Léa leur donne des pains*
Lea gives them some bread
Léa parle de Joe [Pron2_delui]→ *Léa parle de lui*   Lea speaks about him
Joe parle de Léa [Pron2_d'elle]→ *Joe parle d'elle*
Léa parle des amis [Pron2_d'eux]→ *Léa parle d'eux*
Joe parle des amies [Pron2_d'elles]→ *Joe parle d'elles*

Finally, a locative noun phrase can be pronominalised via one of these transformations:

Léa va à Paris [PronLoc_y]→ *Léa y va*   Lea goes there
Léa vient de Paris [PronLoc_en]→ *Léa en vient*   Lea comes from there

Extractions can be used to add focus to the subject noun phrases:

Joe voit Léa [Extraction0s]→ *C'est Joe qui voit Léa*   It is Joe who sees Lea
Les enfants voient Léa [Extraction0p]→ *Ce sont les enfants qui voient Lea*

It is not possible to combine [Pron0_il] with [Extraction0s], nor or [Pron0_ils] with [Extraction0p] when the subject is masculine:

Joe mange la pomme [Pron0_il][Extraction0s]→ **C'est il qui mange une pomme*
Les enfants mangent les pommes [Pron0_ils][Extraction0p]→ **Ce sont ils qui mangent les pommes*

One must add a specialised transformation to produce the correct sentence:

Joe mange la pomme [Pron0_il][Extraction_lui]→ *C'est lui qui mange la pomme*
It is he who is eating the apple
Les enfants mangent les pommes [Pron0_eux][Extraction0_eux]→ *Ce sont eux qui mangent les pommes*   It is they who are eating the apples

Transformations [Extraction0s] and [Extractions0p] can always be applied when the subject is feminine, even when pronominalised in *elle*, e.g.:

Léa mange la pomme [Pron0_elle][Extraction0s]→ *C'est elle qui mange la pomme*
It is she who is eating the apple

Extractions can be used to add focus to the object noun phrases:

Léa voit Joe [Extraction1s]→ *C'est Joe que Léa voit*   It is Joe that Lea sees
Joe voit les enfants [Extraction1p]→ *Ce sont les enfants que Joe voit*

Finally, extractions can also be used to add focus to any indirect prepositional phrases:

Joe donne une pomme à Léa [ExtractionPrép]→ *C'est à Léa que Joe donne une*
pomme   It is to Lea that Joe gives an apple
Joe a reçu un cadeau de Léa [ExtractionPrép]→ *C'est de Léa que Joe a reçu un*
cadeau   It is from Lea that Joe received an apple
Léa vit à Paris [ExtractionPrép]→ *C'est à Paris que Léa vit*
                                              It is in Paris that Lea lives
Léa vient de Paris [ExtractionPrép]→ *C'est de Paris que Léa vient*
                                              It is from Paris that Lea comes

The main negation adverbs are *guère, jamais, pas, plus*. The adverb *point* is used in literature or classical XVIIIth French, but is no longer used in modern French.

Joe vient [Négation_guère]→ *Joe ne vient guère*   Joe seldom comes
Léa vient [Négation_jamais]→ *Léa ne vient jamais*   Lea never comes
Joe vient [Négation_pas]→ *Joe ne vient pas*   Joe is not coming
Léa vient [Négation_plus]→ *Léa ne vient plus*   Lea no longer comes

The main negation determiners are *aucun, guère de, jamais de, pas de, plus de*. Negation determiners can be used inside object noun phrases, e.g.:

Joe mange des fruits [Négation_aucun]→ *Joe ne mange aucun fruit*   Joe eats no fruit
Léa mange des fruits [Négation_guère]→ *Léa ne mange guère de fruit*
                                              Lea seldom eats fruits
Joe mange des fruits [Négation_jamais]→ *Joe ne mange jamais de fruit*
                                              Joe never eats fruits
Léa mange des fruits [Négation_pas]→ *Léa ne mange pas de fruit*
                                              Lea does not eat fruits
Joe mange des fruits [Négation_plus]→ *Joe ne mange plus de fruit*
                                              Joe no longer eats fruits

However, only the determiner *aucun* can be used in a subject noun phrase:

Des chats sont venus [Négation0_aucun]→ *Aucun chat n'est venu*   No cat came
Des chats sont venus [Négation0_pas]→ **Pas de chat n'est venu*

There are four passive forms in French:

Joe mange une pomme [Passif_par]→ *Une pomme est mangée par Joe*
An apple is being eaten by Joe

Ces histoires fatiguent Léa [Passif_de]→ *Léa est fatiguée de ces histoires*
Lea is tired of these stories

Trois personnes sont venues [Passif_il]→ *Il est venu trois personnes*
There came three people

On mange une pomme [Passifz]→ *Une pomme est mangée*
An apple is being eaten

In total, I have implemented 10 pronominalisations, 7 extractions, 10 negations and 4 passive transformations.

2.3   Lexicon-Grammar Table #1

Harris (1970) studied verbs that can be inserted without modifying the distributional constraints between a verb and its arguments, named them *operators* and noted them *U*. For instance:

This demonstration surprises Joe→ *This demonstration continues to surprise Joe.*

For the verb *to surprise*, the set of nouns that can occur in its subject (i.e. *events*) and the set of nouns in its object complement (i.e. *people*) are not modified if one adds the verb *to continue*.

This situation is similar to adding the auxiliary verb *to have* to a verb in order to construct a sentence in the present perfect tense:

This demonstration surprises Joe→ *This demonstration has surprised Joe.*

For French, these verbs have been studied by Gross (1999), and listed and described in the lexicon-grammar table #1:[8] they include the four traditional auxiliary verbs *avoir, être, aller, venir*, modal verbs such as *devoir* (*must*), aspectual verbs such as *continuer* (*to continue*), as well as 100 other verbs that share with auxiliary verbs some semantic and syntactic characteristics, such as *oser* (*to dare*), *hésiter* (*to hesitate*), etc. See extract in Fig. 1 below. Each entry of the table can be seen as corresponding to one transformation, e.g.:

Joe mange [choisir]→ *Joe choisit de manger*   *Joe chooses to eat*
La pluie tombe [risquer]→ *La pluie risque de tomber*   *It might rain*

Each entry of the table is also associated with 18 structures and distributional constraints, described in binary columns in the table. In effect, each verbal entry of table #1 might potentially trigger 11 transformations, that I have implemented as such:

---

[8] Cf. Gross (1975). The actual table contains 119 entries; I have not implemented locutions nor semi-frozen expressions. I have used an updated version of the table, published by Sagot and Tolone (2009). In the following, I will use the symbol <AUX> for these verbs.

	N0=Nhum	N0=Nnr	Ppv0		aux=avoir	aux=être	N0estVppW	N0u	Prép	N1="que P"	N1="que Psubj"	Tp=tc	Tc=passé	Tc=présent	Tc=futur	Vc=devoir	Vc=pouvoir	Vc=savoir	Ppv	
1																				
2	+	+	<E>	devoir	+	-	-	-	<E>	-	-	-	+	+	-	+	+	-		Il doit neiger en ce moment à Gap
3	+	-	<E>	pouvoir	+	-	-	-	<E>	-	-	-	-	+	-	-	-	-		Il peut toujours pleuvoir (<E>+j'ai mon parapluie)
4	+	+	<E>	devoir	+	-	-	-	<E>	-	-	+	+	+	+	+	-			Max doit partir
5	+	+	<E>	être	+	-	-	-	pour	-	-	-	-	+	-	-	-	-		Max était pour partir quand il s'est mis à pleuvoir
6	+	+	<E>	pouvoir	+	-	-	-	<E>	-	-	+	+	+	+	+	+			(Max+le livre) peut passer entre les barreaux
7	+	-	<E>	pouvoir	+	-	-	-	<E>	-	+	-	-	-	-	-	+			Max peut réussir
8	+	-	se	prendre	-	+	-	-	à	-	+	-	-	-	-	+				Max se prend à (rêver+espérer)
9	+	-	<E>	aller	-	+	-	-	jusqu'à	-	+	-	-	-	-	-				Luc est allé jusqu'à insulter Léa
10	+	+	<E>	aller	-	-	-	-	<E>	-	-	-	-	+	+	+	-			La chaise va tomber
11	+	+	ne	aller Nég	-	+	-	-	sans	+	+	-	-	+	+	-				Cette mesure n'ira pas sans créer des troubles
12	+	-	<E>	passer	+	-	-	-	pour	-	+	+	-	+	+	+	-			Ida en passera par faire la vaisselle
13	+	+	<E>	daigner	+	-	-	-	<E>	-	+	-	-	-	-	-				Il a daigné pleuvoir
14	+	+	<E>	manquer	+	-	-	-	de	-	+	-	-	-	+	+	-			Il a manqué (<E>+de) pleuvoir
15	+	+	<E>	partir	-	+	-	+	pour	+	-	-	+	+	-	+				La pluie est partie pour durer
16	+	-	se	presser	-	+	+	+	de	-	+	-	-	-	-	-				La pluie ne se presse pas de tomber
17	+	+	<E>	menacer	+	-	-	-	de	-	+	-	-	+	+	-				La pluie menace (<E>+de tomber)
18	+	-	ne se	gêner Nég	-	+	+	-	pour	+	-	+	+	-	-					La pluie ne se gêne pas pour tomber
19	+	+	n'en	finir Nég	+	-	-	-	de	-	+	-	-	-	-	-				La pluie n'en finit pas (<E>+de tomber)
20	-	+	<E>	refuser	+	-	-	-	de	-	+	-	-	-	-	-				La pluie refuse de tomber
21	+	+	<E>	risquer	+	-	-	-	de	-	-	+	+	+	+	+	+			La pluie risque de tomber
22	+	+	<E>	arrêter	+	-	-	-	de	-	+	-	-	-	-					Luc arrête de travailler
23	+	+	<E>	cesser	+	-	-	-	de	-	+	-	-	+	+	+	-			Max a cessé de dormir
24	+	+	<E>	finir	+	-	-	+	de	-	+	-	-	-	-					Max a fini de ranger
25	+	+	<E>	finir	+	-	-	-	par	-	+	-	-	+	+	+				Max a fini par ranger
26	+	-	<E>	négliger	+	-	-	-	de	-	+	-	-	-	-					Max a négligé de se laver
27	+	-	<E>	omettre	+	-	-	-	de	-	+	-	-	-	-					Max a omis de fermer la porte
28	+	-	<E>	oser	+	-	-	+	<E>	-	+	-	-	-	-	+	+			Max a osé venir
29	+	-	<E>	oublier	+	-	-	-	de	-	+	-	-	-	-					Max a oublié de venir
30	+	+	<E>	stopper	+	-	-	+	de	-	+	-	-	-	-					Max a stoppé de faire des bêtises
31	+	-	<E>	trouver	+	-	-	-	à	-	+	-	-	-	-					Max a trouvé à faire quelque chose
32	+	-	<E>	partir	-	+	-	-	à	-	+	-	-	-	-					Max est parti à rire
33	+	-	<E>	achever	+	-	-	-	de	-	+	-	+	-	-					Max achève de peindre le mur
34	+	-	<E>	avoir	+	-	-	-	à	-	+	-	+	-	+					Max aura à se déplacer
35	+	-	<E>	choisir	+	-	-	+	entre	-	-	-	+	+	-	-				Max choisi entre faire ça et faire autre chose
36	+	-	<E>	commencer	+	-	-	+	à	-	+	-	-	+	+	+				Max commence à dormir
37	+	+	<E>	commencer	+	-	-	-	par	-	+	-	-	+	+	+				Max commence par dormir
38	+	+	<E>	continuer	+	-	-	+	à	-	+	-	-	+	+	+				Max continue à dormir
39	+	+	<E>	continuer	-	-	-	-	de	-	+	-	-	+	+	+				Max continue de faire des bêtises
40	+	-	<E>	hésiter	+	-	-	-	à	-	+	-	-	-	-					Max hésite à venir

Fig. 1. Lexicon-grammar table #1

Joe mange [N0 AUX Prép Vinf]→ *Joe commence à manger*   Joe is starting to eat
Léa mange [N0 se AUX Prép Vinf]→ *Léa se prend à manger*
Joe mange [N0 ne AUX que Prép Vinf]→ *Joe ne demande qu'à manger*
Léa mange [N0 n'en AUX pas Prép Vinf]→ *Léa n'en finit pas de manger*
Joe mange [N0 ne se AUX pas Prép Vinf]→ *Joe ne se gêne pas pour manger*
Léa mange [N0 AUX à W]→ *Léa est décidée à manger*
Joe mange [AUX de devoir]→ *Joe cesse de devoir manger*
Lea mange [AUX à pouvoir]→ *Léa continue à pouvoir manger*
                                                            Lea continues to be able to eat
Joe mange [AUX savoir]→ *Joe doit savoir manger*   Joe must know how to eat
Léa mange [N0 AUX]→ *Léa arrête (= Léa arrête de manger)*
                                                    Lea stops (= Lea stops eating)
Joe mange [Ppv]→ *Joe le peut (= Joe peut manger)*
                                            Joe can do it (= Joe can eat)

2.4   Orthographical Transformations

14 transformations, performed at the orthographical level, take care of various mandatory elisions and contractions:

> *le arbre* [Elision_l]→ *l'arbre*
> *la architecture* [Elision_l]→ *l'architecture*
> *jusque à* [Elision_jusqu]→ *jusqu'à*
> *me aide* [Elision_m]→ *m'aide*
> *ne approche* [Elision_n]→ *n'approche*
> *se aide* [Elision_s]→ *s'aide*
> *te aide* [Elision_t]→ *t'aide*
> *à le directeur* [Contraction_au]→ *au directeur*
> *à lequel* [Contraction_auquel]→ *auquel*
> *à les directeurs* [Contraction_aux]→ *aux directeurs*
> *à lesquels* [Contraction_auxquels]→ *auxquels*
> *à lesquelles* [Contraction_auxquelles]→ *auxquelles*
> *de le pain* [Contraction_du]→ *du pain*
> *de des tables* [Contraction_de]→ *de tables*
> *de les tables* [Contraction_des]→ *des tables*

Some of these transformations can be combined, e.g.:

jusque à lesquelles [Contraction_auxquelles][Elision_jusqu]→ *jusqu'auxquelles*

3   Implementation

In total, we have 26 tenses, 20 pronouns, 7 extractions, 10 negations, 4 passive forms, 14 orthographical transformations, and 11 operators, i.e. 91 transformations. In order to implement them, a straightforward solution would be to construct 91 NooJ grammars that recognize a given elementary sentence, and then produce the corresponding transformed sentence, such as the **[Passif_par]** grammar in Fig. 2 below.

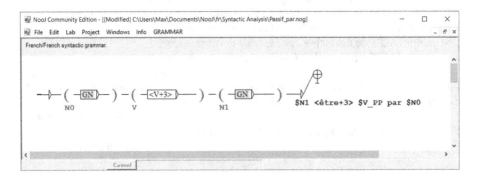

Fig. 2. [Passive_par] transformational grammar

This grammar recognizes a sentence constituted by a noun phrase (e.g. *Joe*), followed by a verb conjugated in the third person (e.g. *aime*), followed by a noun phrase (e.g. *Léa*) and then produces the sequence constituted by the second noun phrase (stored in variable **$N1**), the auxiliary verb *être* conjugated at the third person (**<être +3>**), the verb in its past participle form (**$V_PP**), the preposition ***par*** followed, finally, by the first noun phrase (**$N0**).

Transformations are not applied only to elementary sentences: they can also be applied to complex sentences that have themselves been produced by other transformations. Note that the [Passive_par] graph in Fig. 2 cannot handle a negative sentence (e.g. *Joe n'aime pas Léa*) nor a sentence conjugated in the Passé composé tense (e.g. *Joe a aimé Léa*). In order to fully describe the Passive transformation, we would need to add, for each sentence already transformed, another specific [Passive_par] graph. Hence, if *n* is the number of transformations, one would need to construct $n \times n$ graphs to process all sentences that have already been transformed once, $n \times n \times n$ graphs to process all sentences that have already been transformed twice, etc. As there is no limit on the number of transformations that can be applied to a given sentence, nor even any limit on the number of times a given transformation can be applied, the potential number of graphs to construct is therefore infinite. If T is the finite set of transformations, the set of graphs one would need to construct to account for every transformations is T*.

However, not all combinations of transformations are possible; for instance, it is not possible to apply a [Passive] transformation to a sentence that is already in a passive form. In consequence, the set of graphs, while infinite in size, is strictly included in T*: it constitutes itself a complex formal language.[9]

It is for these reasons that Silberztein (2016a) proposed a new mechanism to formalise all the combinations of transformations that can be applied to the elementary sentence *Joe loves Lea*, in order to produce over 3 million sentences.

3.1   A Generic Grammar

We will now generalize the grammar that recognizes the sentence *Joe loves Lea* described by Silberztein (2016a) to a generic transitive structure: NP V NP (any noun phrase, followed by any verb, followed by any noun phrase).[10]

To construct the general transformational grammar, one needs to replace in the initial grammar all occurrences of the verb *to love* with the more generic lexical symbol <V> (any verb). All the corresponding inflected (e.g. *loved*) and derived forms

---

[9] Transformations like Passive [P] or Negation [N] can be applied more than once, if they are interlaced with the reverse transformations $[P]^{-1}$, e.g. $[P][N][P]^{-1}[N]^{-1}[P]$. It is not possible to describe these types of constraints in a Context-Free grammar.

[10] Of course, not all verbs can enter in transitive sentences. Thanks to Prof. Mauro-Mirto for the following remark: the grammar recognizes certain sentences that contain an intransitive verb, e.g. *Luc est un policier*. These sentences still accept several transformations, e.g. [Negation_pas]: *Luc n'est pas un policier*, [Extract_N0]: *C'est Luc qui est un policier*, whereas other transformations will have to be deactivated, e.g. [Extract_N1] **C'est un policier que Luc est*, [Passif_par] **Un policier est été par Luc*.

(e.g. *lover*) must be replaced as well with the corresponding symbol (e.g. <V+PP> for past participle form), provided that the verb has these forms.

The Lexicon-Grammar table #1 shown in Fig. 1 represents not 11, but 11 × 110 transformations. For instance, the following three sentences are actually produced by different [N0 AUX Prép Vinf] transformations:

Joe mange→ Joe continue de manger (AUX =: continuer)
Joe mange→ Joe finit de manger (AUX =: finir)
Joe mange→ Joe hésite à manger (AUX =: hésiter)

In order to avoid implementing the 1,210 transformations explicitly, I have implemented the 11 generic transformations, using NooJ grammars that are indexed to the Lexicon-Grammar table #1's lexical entries, using NooJ's symbol <U+LG1>. Each of the 11 transformations can then be accessed using NooJ's compound variables that access each transformation as a distinct property.

For instance, the transformation [Ppv] is described as the feature **+Ppv** in the dictionary. Therefore, if $AUX is the operator, AUXPpv is true if $AUX is associated with the feature **+Ppv**, false if not. The constraint <AUXPpv> can then be used to activate or deactivate a path in the transformational grammar.

Other types of constraints account for the agreement of the subject and the AUX verb, e.g. <$N0$Nb=AUXNb> and the subject and the past participle form of the AUX verb when the auxiliary verb is *être*, e.g.: *Lea s'est efforcée de manger*.

The grammar contains 17 graphs, including the one that describes the tense of the auxiliary verb, see Fig. 3.

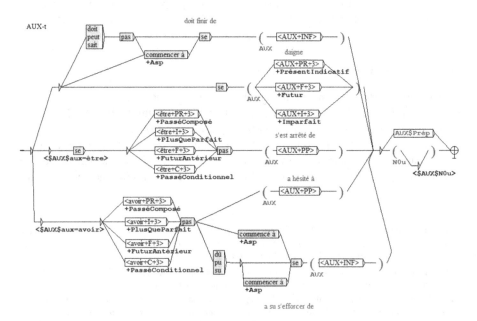

Fig. 3. Graph for the AUX conjugation

If one submits a given sentence to NooJ (e.g. *Joe regarde Léa*) and a given auxiliary verb (e.g. *oser*), the complete transformational grammar produces over 4,000 sentences. Running the system over the whole lexicon-grammar table #1 would therefore produce over 400,000 sentences. Here are a few examples of sentences produced by the grammar:

Joe a osé regarder Léa,**P+oser+Pron1+PasséComposé**
C'est elle qui est regardée par Joe,**P+Extr1+Pron1+PrésentIndicatif+Passifpar**
Joe avait commencé à oser la regarder,**P+Asp+oser+PlusQueParfait+Pron1**
Joe had started to dare looking at her

There are a few problems:

- double or triple negation makes some sentences stylistically difficult, or even incorrect, e.g.:

?Ce n'est pas Joe qui n'a pas fini de regarder Lea
?It is not Joe who has not finished looking at Lea
*Ce n'est pas Joe qui n'a pas fini de ne pas regarder Lea
*It is not Joe who has not finished to not looking at Lea

Because a negation can be applied to any of the verbs that occur in the transformed sentence, the grammar describes all potential negations. One could add a "stylistic" component to the system, so that NooJ does not produce more than one negation in a given sentence.

- When an auxiliary verb is accompanied itself by another auxiliary verb, as well as by one of the three verbs *devoir, pouvoir* or *savoir*, it is not clear where exactly the tense must be applied. For instance, the three following sentences could be produced by a [PasséComposé] transformation:

Joe a dû finir de s'occuper de Léa	*Joe had to stop looking after Lea*
Joe doit avoir fini de s'occuper de Léa	*Joe must have stopped looking after Lea*
*Joe doit finir de s'être occupé de Léa	**Joe must stop to be looking after Lea*

At this point, only the first sentence has been produced by the grammar.

- There are many more tenses, aspects and modal constructions than the ones described in lexicon-grammar table #1. For instance, the auxiliary verb can itself be preceded by an aspectual verb, itself preceded by an auxiliary verb, such as in sentence:

(Joe a) commencé à s'efforcer de (manger des légumes).
(Joe) has started to try to eat (vegetables)

– A large number of 3-verb combinations are not described by the lexicon-grammar table, which is 2-dimensional in nature, for instance:

> *Joe devrait arrêter d'***oser** *regarder Léa* vs.
> *Joe n'***ose** *pas arrêter de devoir regarder Léa* vs.
> *Joe n'arrêtera pas de devoir* **oser** *regarder Léa*

It is a similar problem to the one described in Silberztein (2003), when converting the lexicon-grammar tables used to describe constraints between determiners and pre-determiners: the lexicon-grammar tables are perfectly suited to describe constraints between two components, but they are not powerful enough to describe constraints between three or more elements. NooJ's grammars are better suited than lexicon-grammar tables to describe complex constraints.

4   Conclusion and Perspectives

In this paper, I have shown that it is possible to build a large transformational grammar that can perform 91 transformations, as well as any combination of them. The grammar formalises the behaviour of the 110 generalized auxiliary verbs that are described in the lexicon-grammar table #1.

This first grammar is crude, as it does not take the main verb's properties into account (see Footnote 9). The properties needed to make sure the grammar parses only sentences that contain a verb compatible with each structure can be found in the LVF dictionary.[11] The easiest way to develop the transformational grammar would be to add the intransitive verbs described in tables #31, #33, #34 and #35, cf. Boons et al. (1976).

A second step will be to construct an equivalent grammar for the movement verbs described in table #2, e.g.:

> *Joe mange une pomme* [partir]→ *Joe part manger une pomme*
> *Joe is leaving to eat an apple*

More generally, one will need to design a system capable of performing binary transformations, i.e. a system that can parse a complex sentence and analyse it as two elementary sentences, and reciprocally, produce a complex sentence from two elementary ones.

References

Boons, J.-P., Guillet, A., Leclère, Ch.: La structure des phrase simples en français: classes de constructions intransitives. Droz, Genève (1976)

Dubois, J., Dubois-Charlier, F.: Les Verbes Français. Disponibles à partir du site (2017). www.modyco.fr

---

[11] See Dubois and Dubois-Charlier (2017).

Gross, M.: Méthodes en syntaxe: régime des constructions complétives. Herman, Paris (1975)

Gross, M.: Grammaire transformationnelle du français: 2 Syntaxe du nom. Cantilène, Malakoff (1986)

Gross, M.: Sur la définition d'auxiliaire du verbe. In: Langages, n° 135, pp. 8–21 (1999). http://www.persee.fr/doc/lgge_0458-726x_1999_num_33_135_2199

Harris, Z.S.: Mathematical Structures of Language. Wiley, New York (1968)

Harris, Z.S.: The elementary transformations. In: Harris, Z.S. (ed.) Papers in Structural and Transformational Linguistics. Formal Linguistics Series, pp. 482–532. Springer, Dordrecht (1970). https://doi.org/10.1007/978-94-017-6059-1_26

Sagot, B., Tolone, E.: Intégrer les tables du lexique-grammaire à un analyseur syntaxique robuste à grande échelle. In: Actes de la conférence TALN 2009 (2009)

Silberztein, M.: Finite-state recognition of the French determiner system. J. French Lang. Stud. **13**(02), 221–246 (2003)

Silberztein, M.: *Joe Loves Lea*: transformational analysis of direct transitive sentences. In: Okrut, T., Hetsevich, Y., Silberztein, M., Stanislavenka, H. (eds.) NooJ 2015. CCIS, vol. 607, pp. 55–65. Springer, Cham (2016a). https://doi.org/10.1007/978-3-319-42471-2_5

Silberztein, M.: Formalizing Natural Languages: The NooJ Approach. Wiley-ISTE, London (2016b)

Silberztein, M.: From FOAF to English: linguistic contribution to web semantics. In: Proceedings of the Linguistic Resources for Automatic Natural Language Generation, LiRA@NLG Workshop at INLG2017 (2017). http://aclweb.org/anthology/W/W17/#3800

Natural Language Processing
Applications

A Set of NooJ Grammars to Verify Laboratory Data Correctness

Francesca Parisi[✉] and Maria Teresa Chiaravalloti

Institute of Informatics and Telematics,
National Council of Research, Cosenza, Italy
{francesca.parisi,maria.chiaravalloti}@iit.cnr.it

Abstract. Semantic interoperability in clinical processes is necessary to exchange meaningful information among healthcare facilities. Standardized classification and coding systems allow for meaningful information exchange. This paper aims to support the accuracy validation of mappings between local and standardized clinical content, through the construction of NooJ syntactical grammars for recognition of local linguistic forms and detection of data correctness level. In particular, this work deals with laboratory observations, which are identified by idiosyncratic codes and names by different facilities, thus creating issues in data exchange. The Logical Observation Identifiers Names and Codes (LOINC) is an international standard for uniquely identifying laboratory and clinical observations. Mapping local concepts to LOINC allows to create links among health data systems, even though it is a cost and time-consuming process. Beyond this, in Italy LOINC experts use to manually double check all the performed mappings to validate them. This has over time become a non-trivial task because of the dimension of laboratory catalogues and the growing adoption of LOINC. The aim of this work is realizing a NooJ grammar system to support LOINC experts in validating mappings between local tests and LOINC codes. We constructed syntactical grammars to recognize local linguistic forms and determine data accuracy, and the NooJ contextual constraints to identify the threshold of correctness of each mapping. The grammars created help LOINC experts in reducing the time required for mappings validation.

Keywords: NooJ · Semantic annotation · LOINC

1 Introduction

Nowadays electronic healthcare systems provide advanced technological infrastructures to support data exchange and pooling. Nonetheless, an effective communication between systems is not yet fully realized as still many healthcare settings use idiosyncratic local codes and names to identify the same clinical concepts. Clinical classification and coding systems describe concepts through standardized labels identifying them through unique codes. Among them, LOINC [1] is the main standard for coding laboratory and clinical observations. Its use requires that local codes are mapped to standardized codes so that equivalent concepts are aligned and can be easily understood and reused by other systems. This mapping process is cost and time-consuming as involves for many hours domain experts to find the right association

© Springer Nature Switzerland AG 2019
I. Mauro Mirto et al. (Eds.): NooJ 2018, CCIS 987, pp. 155–166, 2019.
https://doi.org/10.1007/978-3-030-10868-7_14

between local and standard codes. Trying to make easy and speed up this task, many mapping support tools and methodologies had been developed overtime. A lot of attention is focused on the mapping phase, as it is fundamental to foster the standard adoption, likewise mappings double checking is important to verify their accuracy.

The work described in this paper arises from the need to help LOINC Italia experts to manage the great amount of mappings they have to double check to validate them. After the Prime Minister Decree n. 178/2015 entered into force, a lot of public and private laboratories started the process of aligning their local tests to LOINC, often requiring assistance to LOINC Italia for training and validation. This have burdened LOINC Italia experts with a great amount of work, as their validation work follows a bottom-up approach, starting from each local test and the information associated with it, and using them to gradually narrow the research, without looking at the code already identified by the laboratorian, to check then if the LOINC code autonomously identified corresponds to the one chosen by the mapper. This method proved to be advantageous because it allowed to retrace the path carried out by the mapper to identify the most appropriate LOINC code and, therefore, to check for any issues that might have come across. Nonetheless this work is manually performed and hardly quantifiable in terms of time (and consequently costs) as it depends on the completeness of the information available in the local catalogue. If tests are described in detail, it is easy to refine the results until arriving to the LOINC code candidate for the mapping. Nevertheless, the reality is that laboratory catalogues are often incomplete and full of acronyms and abbreviations. It requires that experts dedicate more time to fully understand the exact clinical object of the test to determine if it was correctly mapped. Having a tool for automatic recognition of local linguistic forms would be an important step in helping LOINC experts involved in the mappings validation. In this paper we describe the creation of a NooJ grammar system to allow the automatic recognition of Italian local linguistic forms and, starting from them, the detection of specific correctness levels of the mappings between local tests and LOINC codes. By using NooJ contextual constraints we identified thresholds of correctness to determine the level of accuracy of each mapping and decide, on the basis of the assigned score, if the mapping has to be reviewed by LOINC experts or can be considered surely correct.

This paper is structured as follows. Section 2 offers an overview of the LOINC standard and presents a review of the related works; Sect. 3 describes the NooJ application realized; Sects. 4 and 5 are dedicated to present results and conclusions.

2 Background

LOINC codes are uniquely assigned numbers and LOINC names are defined *fully specified* because they contain all the information needed to certainly identify a test, distinguishing it from others who might apparently seem identical. These names are given by the concatenation of six fundamental axis:

1. Component: the substance that is measured (e.g., sodium, glucose, etc.);
2. Property: the measurement type;

3. Timing: it distinguishes measurements made at a given time by those covering a time interval;
4. System: the type of sample on which the observation is performed;
5. Scale: the scale of measurement;
6. Method: the method used in test performing.

The LOINC database has more than 80,000 codes (v. 2.64 - June 2018) and it is translated in 13 languages and 21 linguistic variants. The first LOINC Italian translation was released in 2010 following the part based translational approach [2]. Since then, refinements, based on the analysis of the outcomes of the automatic translation process, produced other releases (the last one in December 2017).

To use LOINC, domain experts are required to map their laboratory tests to the codes of the standard, which convey the same semantic meaning. It is not only an informatics matter, but it requires a deep knowledge of both the destination terminology structure and the way in which the tests are actually realized. This is a non-trivial task because local catalogues contains idiosyncratic names and codes and they are not always complete of all the details required by the standard. Even if some studies [3] propose an incremental approach to mapping, it remains a time consuming and, consequently, cost effective process. Because of this, a lot of supporting tools and techniques had been developed overtime. Regenstrief Institute (the LOINC Standard Development Organization) releases the free program RELMA (REgenstrief LOINC Mapping Assistant), which offers different functionalities to help users in finding the right LOINC code, such as a test frequency rank [4], the Intelligent Mapper [5] and the Community Mappings [6] repository. The goodness of the Intelligent Mapper was tested in a comparative study [7] with a vector space model-based program for mapping local diagnostic radiology terms to LOINC, and in a German study [8] aimed at proving its validity also on non-English languages. Zollo and Huff [9] proposed a mapping approach that aims to map local catalogues to LOINC by cross-referencing the matching codes. They demonstrated that if two local tests match in all the information they carried, and one of them is correctly mapped to LOINC, then this mapping could be inherited by the other. Fidahussein and Vreeman [10] approach is based on supervised machine learning and information retrieval using Apache's Maxent and Lucene to show that the collective knowledge contained in a complete dataset of local terms mapped to LOINC can be used to support mapping new local terms. Lau et al. [11] presented a methodology study for automatically mapping local terms to LOINC by using parsing, logic rules, synonyms, attribute relationships and the frequency of mapping to a specific LOINC code. One of the rare study [12] that evaluates mapping correctness, focuses on the analysis of the mappings performed by three large healthcare facilities in order to individuate common errors that occur during mapping operations and define possible mapping improving approaches. Nonetheless it does not address the issue of the time required to double check performed mappings and verify their accuracy before input them into an healthcare system for data exchange.

3   The NooJ Application

Following paragraphs describe the development of the NooJ grammar system to support LOINC Italia experts in evaluating the mapping accuracy. It is presented the methodology used for corpus construction and grammars definition and the strategy for automatize the data accuracy control, through contextual constraints.

3.1   The Corpus Construction

The corpus used as reference for training the system is composed of 8 laboratory test datasets mapped to LOINC. It includes 375 local tests, which were structured on the model of the six main LOINC axes. It was not performed a normalization phase as the intent of the NooJ application we want to develop is properly to recognize local linguistic forms, thus avoiding the request to pre-process laboratory catalogues before the mappings and so relieving LOINC experts from the effort of interpreting local acronyms, abbreviations and conventions. We decided to focus on 33 different types of laboratory tests, so to better control the dictionaries and grammars definition and then eventually extend the developed methodology to the others. We choose some of the tests that usually have in our experience an high level of variability in the name description. We selected all the tests rows belonging to the following categories: *Acido Urico, Acido Vanilmandelico, Alanina, Albumina, Azoto, Bilirubina, Calcio, Cloro, Colesterolo, Creatinina, Emoglobina, Epinefrina, Estradiolo, Estrone, Follitropina, Fosfatasi alcalina, Fosfato, Glucosio, Aspartato transaminasi, Alanina transaminasi, Fattore di crescita insulino simile, Insulina, Lattato deidrogenasi, Potassio, Pregnenolone, Progesterone, Prolattina, Proteina, Sodio, Trigliceridi, Urobilinogeno, Vitamina D*. Starting from them, we constructed dictionaries in which the morphological proprieties of local linguistic forms were described and flexional grammars associated to them. Therefore, the corpus is composed by a set of textual data records in which the local test parameters (test name, sample, method, time, scale and type of result) are linked with the mapped LOINC code. Each test is considered such a sentence. The order of the elements is predetermined: each sentence has in first position the test name and in the last one the mapped LOINC code. The absence of textual context gave the possibility to apply the formal grammars recognition rules exactly to the correct category, being sure to find it in a specific position. The textual context could, indeed, create a lot of ambiguity especially in specialist domain applications, on the contrary a structured text avoids this problem and makes the results more accurate.

3.2   The NooJ Dictionaries and Flexional Grammars

For recognizing all local linguistic forms in terms of simple lexical units or compound terms, we constructed a set of dictionaries to identify specific terminology used for each clinical test parameter [13]. In particular, in the dictionaries we considered all the local linguistic forms associated to the same LOINC axis. Each lexical unit was described considering its morphologic, syntactic and semantic characteristics as well as its flexions. The added value given by NooJ is the possibility to associate local linguistic forms and standardized tags from LOINC, by using the semantic properties associated to the lexical units. In particular, for each lexical unit in the dictionaries, we defined a semantic property containing the value of the corresponding LOINC parameter. This allows also the domain experts' knowledge formalization.

The "Analyte.dic" dictionary contains Atomic Lexical Units (ALUs), which are all local linguistic forms placed at the beginning of the sentences and reporting the local idiosyncratic names corresponding to the LOINC Component. Each linguistic form was described using morphologic and semantic proprieties. In particular, the properties "+Analita" and "+CORE" were associated for identifying the specific category and the semantic property "+Component" for assigning the corresponding value for the LOINC Component (See Fig. 1).

Fig. 1. Example of simple ALUs structure in the Analyte.dic

The definition «Conalbumina,N+Analita+CORE+Component=Conalbumina Ab. IgE» means that the local form *Albumina* is associated to the LOINC Component *Conalbumina Ab.IgE*. Going beyond this simple case, this domain is full of ambiguities, i.e. the definitions «Calcio,N+Analita+CORE+Component=Calcio» and «Calcio, N+Analita+CORE+Component=Calcio.ionizzato» report the same ALU that could be associated to different Component. In this case, there is not a rule that determines if the local form *Calcio* refers to *Calcio* or *Calcio.ionizzato*. Other simple categories such as acids, acronyms and synonyms were represented in the corpus respectively by the properties "+AC", "+Acronimi", and "+SIN". The corpus contains also compound ALUs as multi-words and morphemes. For example, the ALU *Emoglobina A1* refers to the LOINC Component *Emoglobina A1/Emoglobina.totale* reporting a ratio («Emoglobina A1,N+Analita+CORE+Component=Emoglobina A1/Emoglobina.totale»). The same is for the ALUs followed by specific symbols as %, i.e. the ALU *albumina%* refers to the ratio *Albumina/Proteina.totale* («Albumina%,Albumina/Proteina.totale, N+Analita+CORE+Component=Albumina/Proteina.totale»). For the morphemes category, we considered the suffixes *-emia* and *-uria*. These lexical units provide information about other LOINC axis. The suffix *-emia* suggests the value *Blood* (*Sangue* in Italian) of LOINC System and related sub specifications, while the suffix *-uria* suggests the value *Urine* (*Urina* in Italian). Example of morphemes are: «Glicemia,Glucosio, N+Analita+Component=Glucosio+System=Sangue» and «Azoturia,Azoto,N+Analita+ Component=Azoto+System=Urine». The annotation of local morphemes allows also managing ambiguities. In fact the LOINC database contains different sub specifications for *Blood*, often not detailed in the local test definition. For example *-emia* can refer to different kinds of *Blood* (i.e. *Venous blood*, *Arterial blood*, etc.) thus creating ambiguity. In this case, the semantic annotation rules created are able to consider only the element matching with the corresponding element in the associated LOINC code.

The dictionary describes also specific categories such as acids and acronyms. The first are always reported in LOINC definitions with the suffix *-ato*: «Acido metilippurico, Metilippurato, N+Analita+AC+Component=Metilippurato». Acronyms are associated to the official LOINC extended test definitions: «Fsh,Follitropina,N+Analita+Acronimo +Component=Follitropina».

The NooJ dictionaries allow managing the synonyms too. For example, the local form *Emoglobina glicata* is synonym of *Emoglobina A1c* used in LOINC definition, as «Emoglobina glicata,Emoglobina A1c,N+Analita+SIN+Component=Emoglobina A1c».

The "LOINC elements" dictionary contains values of the other LOINC axis. Following the same rules and structure of the Analyte dictionary, it defines the possible values for the parameters System, Scale, Property, Timing and Method. The description of these elements allows formalizing a lot of deductions starting from the values present in the local linguistic form. For example, the local unit of measure could suggest values for Scale, Property and Timing. This kind of formalizations allows deducing values of the LOINC axis even when they are not explicitly reported in local databases. Other important parts of speech considered for this purpose are the adjective in combination with the analyte definition. They are included in this dictionary and associated with the official LOINC axis value it refers to. For example, the adjective *urinario* suggests the value *urine* for the System.

In addition, LOINC codes are formalized by associating all the official elements they represent. This association allows to measure data accuracy and annotate only the correct parts without ambiguities. The realized formal grammars work on local data, transforming them in LOINC language and matching it with standard values associated to a specific LOINC code. The following example reports the formalization of a specific code: «21305-8,NUM+Code+Component=Glucosio+Property=MCnc+Timing=24h+System= Urine+Scale=Qn+Method=Absent». For each ALU we constructed a flexional grammar, according to the specific Syntax used in NooJ. In particular, flexional grammars allow recognizing all the morphologic variations of the lexical units. For example, the multi-words could have different variations (See Table 1).

Table 1. An example of flexional grammars: the multi-words flexion.

Multi-word flexion	
<E>/m+s|<B>i<P><B>i/m+p	<E>/m+s|<B>hi<P><B>i/m+p
<E>/m+s|<B>o/m+s|<B>i/m+p	<E>/f+s|<B>e<P><B>e/f+p

3.3   The Context-Free Formal Grammars

The context-free grammar is a regular grammar composed of a set of recursive rules used to generate patterns of strings. In this work the structure of hierarchical context-free grammars is described in NooJ to produce the semantic annotation rules sequence

[14, 15]. The basic idea concerns the transformation of local terms set used by laboratories to describe their tests into the official LOINC language to control the mapping accuracy. Each local term is stored in a specific variable together with the value of the corresponding semantic property. For example, local test name is stored in the variable "V1" that contains its value and annotates the value of the corresponding semantic property "+Component". The "starting point" is represented by the terms in the local databases and formalized in the NooJ dictionaries. The prediction rules are defined with a specific NooJ syntax establishing which semantic properties values will appear in the final annotation, so the "ending point" is represented by the terms chain recognized by the fixed rules. Table 2 reports the values stored by each variable (with reference to the linguistic category associated in the dictionary), the production rules and the terms chain obtained. For example, in the first row "N+Analita" is a linguistic category described in the dictionary, "+Component=A" is the semantic property associated during the dictionary formalization, "V1$Component" is the production rule for semantic annotation, "A" is the term obtained starting from V1. Row number 3 presents a particular case of production rule as it produces the value *Present* or *Absent* depending on the presence or absence of the value of the Method axis.

Table 2. Semantic annotation variables and annotation rules.

Number	Semantic annotation Variables	Production rules	Language obtained
1	V1 = (N+Analita+Component=A)	V1$Component	**A**
2	V2 = (N+UnMis+Property=B +Timing=C)	V2$Property V2$Timing	**B+C**
3	V3 = (N+Metodo+Method=D)	+Method=Present +Method=Absent	**D**
4	V4 = (N+Campione+System=E)	V4$System	**E**
5	V5 = (N+Risultato+Scale=F)	V5$Scale	**F**

The final annotated chain will have the form «LOINC+Component=A+Property=B +Timing=C+Method=D+System=E». The following figures (See Figs. 2, 3, 4, 5, 6, 7 and 8) show the complete structure of the realized system in NooJ. The "LOINC_E-LEMENTS" grammar is composed of 6 hierarchical sub grammars producing the final terms chain. Each yellow highlighted element represents the higher level of the related specific hierarchical grammar.

Fig. 2. The LOINC grammar

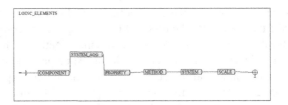

Fig. 3. The "LOINC_elements" grammar

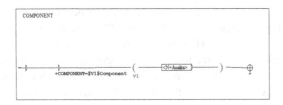

Fig. 4. The "Component" sub grammar

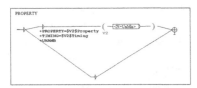

Fig. 5. The "Property" sub grammar

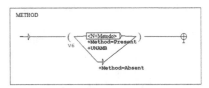

Fig. 6. The "Method" sub grammar

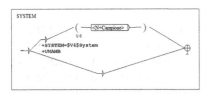

Fig. 7. The "System" sub grammar

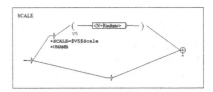

Fig. 8. The "Scale" sub grammar

The figure below (See Fig. 9) shows an example of semantic annotation of a record in the corpus.

Fig. 9. Example of semantic annotation

3.4   The Control of Data Accuracy: The Contextual Constraints

The language obtained after the semantic annotation rules application is compared with the values associated to the corresponding semantic properties described by the mapped LOINC code. This process allows identifying and storing the accuracy level of each local test. For example, considering the code description: «555,NUM+Code+**Component=A**+Property=Bb+Timing=Cc+**Method=D+System=E**» and the language obtained after semantic annotation application: «LOINC+**Component=A**+Property=B +Timing=C+**Method=D+System=E**», the contextual constraints produce a specific correctness level, in this case equal to "+EL=3" (matched elements are in bold). The final annotation will be: «LOINC+Component=A+Property=B+Timing=C+Method=D +System=E+EL=3». For each record, the final part of the formal grammar stores in the variable C the value of the mapped LOINC code recognized in the text and allows comparing the obtained language with the values of the semantic property associated to the specific LOINC code. Table 3 shows the matching rules applied to control data accuracy. They allow to annotate for each test the number of elements that match between the local linguistic forms and the values of the axis of the mapped LOINC code. The semantic annotation is obtained if and only if the matching rules (constraints) are satisfied.

Considering for example the local test description «Proteinuria delle 24h mg/24h Urine Numerico 2889-4» and the associated variables:

– V1 = Proteinuria,Proteina,N+Analita+Component=Proteina+System=Urine
– V2 = mg/24h,N+UnMis+Property=MRat+Timing=24h+Scale=Qn
– V4 = Urina,N+Campione+System=Urine
– C = 2889-4,NUM+Code+Component=Proteina+Property=MRat+Timing=24h +System=Urine+Scale=Qn+Method=Absent the obtained semantic annotation will be: *«LOINC+Component=Proteina+Property=MRat+Timing=24h+Method=Absent +System=Urine+Scale=Qn+EL=3».*

Constraints make direct comparison between local and LOINC official elements to determine their matching. There are also Help constraints which operate on the deduced values, as they allow passing to the higher accuracy level by controlling the values

Table 3. The matching rules applied to control data accuracy levels.

Number	Constraints	Semantic annotation
1	CComponent=V1$Component	**+EL=1**
2	CComponent=V1$Component CProperty=V2$Property	**+EL=2**
3	CComponent=V1$Component CProperty=V2$Property CSystem=V4$System	**+EL=3**
4	CComponent=V1$Component CProperty=V2$Property CSystem=V4$System CTiming=V2$Timing	**+EL=4**
5	CComponent=V1$Component CProperty=V2$Property CSystem=V4$System CTiming=V2$Timing CScale=V5$Scale	**+EL=5**
6	CComponent=V1$Component CProperty=V2$Property CSystem=V2$System CTiming=V2$Timing CScale=V5$Scale CMethod=V6$Method	**+EL=6**

deduced from different parameters. This kind of constraints frequently deals with the adjectives in the test definition, which could suggest values for the System. It allows to double check the correctness of the value associated to the System axis.

4   Results

The system for supporting mapping validation, based on semantic rules set, allows controlling the data accuracy referring to a specific domain. The work presented gives an important contribution in formalizing the experts knowledge in evaluating the associations between the standard linguistic forms used in LOINC and the local linguistic forms used by laboratories. This formalization deals also with the reasoning behind the deduction of specific values, which is proper of the human expertise. The formalization of the considered linguistic elements in NooJ allows having a lot of information about the analyzed datasets. It works as a question-answering system and allows querying the data. It is possible to get different kinds of information such as: "how many times laboratories define their tests only through the test name", or "how many times they report the information about the used method". These query operations are possible only through a precise recognition of all the different elements in the local databases. As the local linguistic forms cannot always be used as research strings because they are idiosyncratic, the semantic recognition of local linguistic forms used by laboratories allows to easily find the subset of codes candidate for mapping. Furthermore, the semantic rules application reduces the set of possible correct codes as research parameters increment. The results obtained after constraints definition allow verifying the entire data trend in terms of accuracy and reducing the analysis time. It is possible to determine the level of correctness for each mapping and so refer back to the laboratories those that need to be improved. Table 4 shows the accuracy level scored by each test of the corpus.

Table 4. The accuracy level scored by each test of the corpus.

Level	Total number	Stopped at level	Passed to higher level
1	346	146	
2	200	101	17 (level 3 HELP)
3	82	5	1 (level 4 HELP)
4	76		23 (level 5 HELP)
5	53	27	
6	26		

The chance to have an automatic selection of those mappings with an high correctness level (about the 60% out of the total) speeded up the entire validation process.

The realized NooJ application allows also constructing an automatic collection of local linguistic forms stored in a specific XML database and usable for other analysis. The XML file contains both the starting local language and the language obtained after the rules application. The content of each XML LOINC element is represented by the local test description associated to the LOINC code. Each element is associated to the accuracy level reported as the last attribute "EL".

5   Discussion and Conclusions

The work presented in this paper represents an important result in helping the validation process of local tests mapped to LOINC. The realized NooJ grammars allow reducing the time required for codes validation, while preventing potential human errors. As discussed in Sect. 2, prior studies presented automatic or semi-automatic mapping support tools and techniques. Despite the slightly different application domain, all of them require expert review to double check computer-generated results, while our approach reduces time required for mapping validation by automatically validating all the mappings that gained a top level accuracy score. The developed NooJ application allows to automatically identify one of the main common mapping errors, also described in [12]: a more specific test mapped to a more general concept. In fact, thanks to the use of the created dictionaries and grammars, it annotates all the elements of the local name that have to find correspondence into the LOINC name to be considered as correct. Differently from the cited mapping accuracy study, our system does not perform a validation based only on the names, but it automatically considers all the LOINC axis. Even if semantic annotation is not new in automated or semi-automated tools for language analysis and comparison in the LOINC mapping efforts, this is the first time it is applied to the mapping accuracy validation. Actually, for what is in our knowledge, the same LOINC producers do not have a system to control the clinical quality of the performed mapping around the world. Everything is left to the mappers competence or, as in Italy, to local organizations responsible for the standard implementation. The system presented is a first attempt to create a support tool for speeding up the mapping validation process, which is fundamental to avoid that erroneous mappings vehicle erroneous clinical concepts thus invalidating the semantic interoperability effort. In the future, the work could be extended to support laboratorians in mapping operations, but it would need some more adjustments of the defined rules as this activity is performed without a precise one to one comparison, as in mapping accuracy control, but having all the LOINC codes as potential reference. This system would be then helpful for both laboratorians involved in the mapping operations and LOINC experts for mappings validation.

References

1. McDonald, C.J., Huff, S.M., Suico, J.G., et al.: LOINC, a universal standard for identifying laboratory observations: a 5-year update. Clin. Chem. **49**, 624–633 (2003)
2. Vreeman, D.J., Chiaravalloti, M.T., Hook, J., McDonald, C.J.: Enabling international adoption of LOINC through translation. J. Biomed. Inform. **45**(4), 667–673 (2012)
3. Vreeman, D.J., Finnell, J.T., Overhage, J.M.: A rationale for parsimonious laboratory term mapping by frequency. In: AMIA Annual Symposium Proceedings, pp. 771–775 (2007)
4. Regenstrief Institute, Inc., Common LOINC Laboratory Observation Codes. http://loinc.org/usage/obs. Accessed 15 Sep 2018
5. Vreeman, D.J., McDonald, C.J.: Automated mapping of local radiology terms to LOINC. In: AMIA Annual Symposium Proceedings, pp. 769–773 (2005)
6. Dixon, B.E., Hook, J., Vreeman, D.J.: Learning from the crowd in terminology mapping: the LOINC experience. Lab Med. **46**(2), 168–174 (2015)
7. Vreeman, D.J., McDonald, C.J.: A comparison of Intelligent Mapper and document similarity scores for mapping local radiology terms to LOINC. In: AMIA Annual Symposium Proceedings, pp. 809–813 (2006)
8. Zunner, C., Bürkle, T., Prokosch, H.-U., Ganslandt, T.: Mapping local laboratory interface terms to LOINC at a German university hospital using RELMA vol 5: a semi-automated approach. J. Am. Med. Inf. Assoc. **20**(2), 293–297 (2013)
9. Zollo, K.A., Huff, S.M.: Automated mapping of observation codes using extensional definitions. J. Am. Med. Inform. Assoc. **7**(6), 586–592 (2000)
10. Fidahussein, M., Vreeman, D.J.: A corpus-based approach for automated LOINC mapping. J. Am. Med. Inform. Assoc. **21**(1), 64–72 (2014)
11. Lau, L.M., Johnson, K., Monson, K., Lam, S.H., Huff, S.M: A method for the automated mapping of laboratory results to LOINC. In: AMIA Annual Symposium Proceedings, pp. 472–476 (2000)
12. Lin, M.-C., Vreeman, D.J., McDonald, C.J., Huff, S.M.: Correctness of voluntary LOINC mapping for laboratory tests in three large institutions. In: AMIA Annual Symposium Proceedings, pp. 447–451 (2010)
13. Silberztein, M.: La formalisation des langues, l'approche de NooJ. ISTE, London (2015)
14. Chomsky, N.: Structures syntaxiques. Le seuil, Paris (1957)
15. Husser, R.: Foundations of Computational Linguistics. Springer, London (2014)

A Semantico-Syntactic Disambiguation System of Arabic Movement and Speech Verbs and Their Automatic Translation to French Using NooJ

Mariem Essid[1]([⊠]) (iD) and Hela Fehri[2]([⊠])

[1] University of Gabes, Gabès, Tunisia
Mariemessid2@gmail.com
[2] MIRACL Laboratory, University of Gabes, Gabès, Tunisia
hela.fehri@yahoo.fr

Abstract. In this paper, we propose a rule-based method whose purpose is to remove the semantico-syntactic ambiguity of Arabic movement and speech verbs and to translate different disambiguated verbs into the French language. This method consists of two main phases: a phase of semantico-syntactic disambiguation and a phase of automatic translation from Arabic to French.

The semantico-syntactic disambiguation phase can be subdivided into three main steps. The first step is to analyze and adapt the syntactic patterns used for nominal sentences. The second step is to identify a dictionary of Arabic movement and speech verbs and a dictionary of Arabic names based on syntactic patterns. As for the third step, it consists in identifying the disambiguation transducers based on the identified dictionaries, a morphological grammar and syntactic patterns. These transducers make it possible to remove the ambiguity of the verb by assigning it an Arabic meaning.

The purpose of the automatic translation phase is to improve the phase of semantico-syntactic disambiguation since the assignment of an Arabic meaning to a verb is not always sufficient to disambiguate it. This phase is based on the identifying of translation transducers based on the treatment of some problems related to the translation from the Arabic language to the French language, the identified dictionary of Arabic movement and speech verbs and a dictionary of French verbs.

The ideas of the proposed approach were validated by a prototype implemented in JAVA and using the NooJ platform.

The experimentation of the two phases enabled us, on the one hand, to test the feasibility of the realized system and secondly, to discern the limits encountered. Metrics of evaluation: F-measure, Precision and Recall allowed us to evaluate the phase of disambiguation. The comparative study with other famous translators supporting the Arabic language such as Google, Reverso and Babylon showed us that the prototype gave satisfactory results.

Keywords: Semantico-syntactic disambiguation · Automatic translation
Arabic language · NooJ

© Springer Nature Switzerland AG 2019
I. Mauro Mirto et al. (Eds.): NooJ 2018, CCIS 987, pp. 167–179, 2019.
https://doi.org/10.1007/978-3-030-10868-7_15

1   Introduction

The on-line textual contents of the Arabic language know an evolution with more than 20 000 web sites and hundreds of millions of users. With this evolution, the need has quickly been felt to rely on linguistic techniques to better meet the different needs of users, which opens the way for new domains of search, among these domains are semantico-syntactic disambiguation and automatic translation, which are the most difficult tasks to be performed by a computer and which present challenges for researchers so far.

The semantico-syntactic disambiguation in its broadest definition is the determination of the correct meaning of a polysemous word according to the rules by which linguistic units combine in sentences. It is considered a catalyst for the automatic translation task which consists in transforming a word or set of words from a source language to a target language.

The lack of electronic resources and rigorous studies for the standard Arabic language, the richness of this language and the disagreement in some cases between the French language and the Arabic language make the task of semantico-syntactic disambiguation and the task of automatic translation more difficult.

In this paper, we propose a rule-based method whose purpose is to remove the semantic ambiguity of Arabic movement and speech verbs and to translate different disambiguated verbs into the French language to support the task of disambiguation.

The remainder of this paper is organized as follows: we begin by giving a brief overview of the state of the art. After that we describe the strategy used to disambiguate the different Arabic movement and speech verbs and the strategy used to translate verbs to the French language. Then we present the experimentation and the evaluation results obtained with a test corpus. Finally, we will conclude with some perspectives.

2   Related Works

Three major groups of approaches are usually adopted for the semantic disambiguation:

The first is the symbolic approach that is based on human intuition with manual construction of analysis models. From the research on using this approach, we mention the work of (Bouhriz et al. 2016) who developed a semantic disambiguation system for Arabic language based on the use of Arabic WordNet lexical database (AWN). Also, we can cite the work elaborated by (Brun et al. 2005) who developed a system that relies on the use of Oxford-Hachette French Dictionary (OHFD) as a semantically labeled corpus for the semantic lexical disambiguation of words in French.

The second approach is the numerical approach which is based on the automatic development of analysis models based on large volumes of data. From the research on using this approach, we mention the work of (Merhbene et al. 2014) who proposed a semi-supervised semantic disambiguation system for the Arabic language. Also, we can cite the work elaborated by (Gaume et al. 2004) who developed a disambiguation system which is based on an algorithm that calculates a semantic distance between the words of a dictionary.

The third approach is the hybrid approach that combines the numerical approach and the symbolic approach to exploit the strengths of two approaches. From the research on using this approach, we mention the work of (Abacha et al. 2011) that allows disambiguating of the semantic relationships between two medical entities.

3   The Proposed Method for Disambiguation

As shown in Fig. 1, the proposed method for disambiguation is composed of two main steps: The identification of dictionaries based on syntactic patterns and the identification of disambiguation transducers based on the identified dictionaries, a morphological grammar and syntactic patterns.

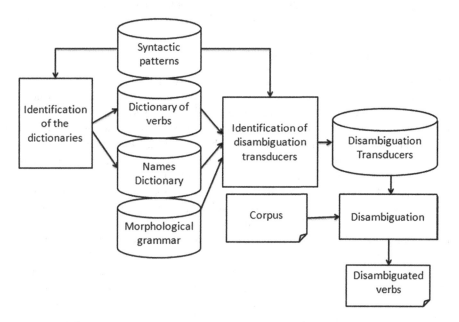

Fig. 1. Proposed approach for semantico-syntactic disambiguation

3.1   Syntactic Patterns

The syntactic patterns exploit the arrangement of different constituents of sentences where verbs of movement and speech exist to determine the proper meanings of these verbs and their translations into the French language.

We relied on the use of the syntactic patterns of (Lahyani 2013) for verbal sentences who identified in total 72 main patterns that can generate 390 sub-syntactic patterns.

To better describe these syntactic patterns, we will present the following example:
Pattern 1:= < كلام يحقق أعمالا لغوية – نادى > (<Words that do language work – to call>;)

The pattern 1 describes spoken verbs whose purpose is to express words that accomplish linguistic work and that have the meaning of "to call". This pattern can generate 8 sub-patterns. Among these sub-patterns we can mention:

Pattern 1.1:= if < [بشر] | ب | [بشر] |صاح> then صاح= نادى; صاح = appeler;

In the sub-pattern 1.1, we have: if the speech verb "صاح" [saha] is followed by a human name which is followed by a preposition "ب" [bi] followed by a human name then this verb has the meaning of "نادى" [nada] (to call). This verb can be translated to the French language to "appeler". Among the forms generated by this sub-pattern, we can cite: صاح أحمد بأخيه (Ahmad called his brother).

We refined the syntactic patterns of (Lahyani 2013) by adapting them to nominal sentences to have more satisfied results. This adaptation consists of changing the location of the noun that follows the verb to the first position (just before the verb).

3.2 Identification of Dictionaries

This step consists in identifying two dictionaries based on syntactic patterns: the first is a dictionary of movement and speech verbs and the second is a dictionary of nouns.

To identify the dictionary of movement and speech verbs, we used the Arabic dictionary of (Fehri 2016) which contains in total 9257 verbs including more than 400 movement and speech verbs. We have enriched the entries that characterize the different ambiguous verbs, cited in the syntactic patterns, by adding some features (syntactic codes) useful for disambiguation and translation.

The used dictionary contains different features that represent linguistic information that describes a verb. Among this information, we can cite: the grammatical category of entry, the model of derivation to recognize the forms derived from the contained lemma, the model of flexion to recognize the inflected forms of the contained lemma and the type of the verb (transitive, intransitive …). We have added other features such as the semantic feature that defines the class of the verb (movement or speech verb), syntactical construction, the correct translation, and the Arabic meaning of the verb.

We have built a dictionary of names that allows describing of the different names that can follow or precede a verb based on the different syntactic patterns.

Each entry in the dictionary contains the different features that represent the grammatical category of a noun, its semantic feature, and its grammatical number.

3.3 Identification of Disambiguation Transducers

This step consists in transforming syntactic patterns into transducers allowing disambiguation by assigning to a verb the correct Arabic meaning.

Note that we used the morphological grammar of (Fehri 2012) to solve the problem of agglutination related to the Arabic language.

The main transducer identified is intended to classify sentences. As shown in Fig. 2, we distinguish in total 2 sub-graphs in this transducer: The first sub-graph: "PhraseNominale" which groups disambiguation transducers adapted for nominal sentences where the subject precedes the verb. As for the second sub-graph:

"PhraseVerbale", it groups the disambiguation transducers for verbal sentences where the verb precedes the subject.

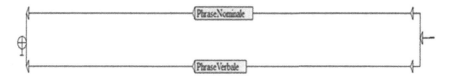

Fig. 2. Main transducer for sentence classification

Note that each path of a sub-graph describes a set of disambiguation rules. The Fig. 3 shows some sub-graphs imbricates in the graph "PhraseVerbale".

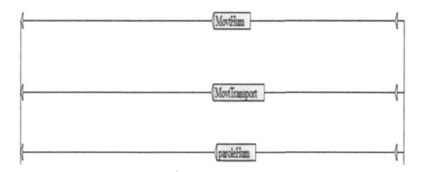

Fig. 3. Extract of sub-graphs imbricates in the graph "PhraseVerbale"

These sub-graphs make it possible to group the disambiguation rules based on the semantic feature that defines the verb used as well as the semantic feature that defines the noun that follows the verb. The grouping of the rules makes it possible to clarify our work and subsequently to facilitate the enrichment, modification and re-use of the transducers according to the objective to be achieved.

Note that each sub-graph contains other sub-graphs where each path of sub-graph describes a syntactic sub-pattern.

To illustrate the transformation of syntactic sub-patterns into transducers, we present Fig. 4 where we detail the sub-graph "paroleHum".

As shown in Fig. 4, we have automated the different sub-syntactic patterns by transforming them into transducers. These transducers provide disambiguating of the verbs by identifying the words preceding them and/or following them.

For example, the framed graph represents the sub-pattern:

If < صاح] | بشر [ب] | بشر[> then صاح; نادى= صاح = appeler;). In this graph we have: The annotation <V + Word + const79> represents the verb "صاح" [saha] which is saved in the variable $c8 (the saving in a variable allows us to display and process the

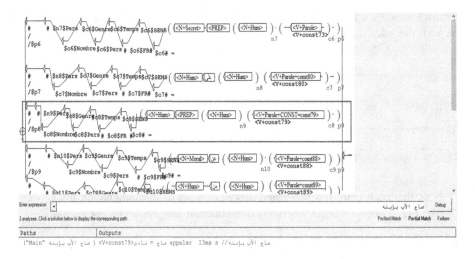

Fig. 4. Sub-graphs imbricates in the sub-graph "paroleHum"

entry), the annotation <N + Hum> represents the name "بشر" [bacharon] which represents the subject of the sentence which is saved in the variable \$n9, the annotation <PREP> represents the used preposition ("ب") that directly follows the subject, the annotation <N + Hum>, that follows the preposition, represents the used complement, the annotation /\$c8\$SENS displays the meaning assigned to the verb, the annotation /\$c8\$FR displays the French translation of the verb, the annotations /\$c8\$Temps, /\$c8\$Pers, /\$c8\$Genre, and /\$c8\$Nombre are used to display information about conjugation of the verb and the annotation /\$n9\$Pers displays the number of the subject.

The French translation, information about conjugation of the verb and the number of the subject are useful only for the transition from the disambiguation phase to the translation phase and will not be displayed later in the experimental part.

If there is a sentence that respects the presented graph then, the verb used in this sentence has the meaning of "نادى". For example, the sentence: "بابنه الأب صاح" (The father called his son) respects the graph presented, which allows us to have the result at the end of Fig. 4: the verb "صاح" means "نادى".

In Fig. 5 we present the assignment of the same verb "صاح" to another construction and another meaning. This figure allows for better understanding our disambiguation approach.

As illustrated in Fig. 5, the same verb "صاح" [saha] in the sentence: "صاح الأب إبنه على" (the father shouted at his son) is assigned to the meaning "صاح" (to shout) and not "نادى" (to call). This change in meaning is due to the change of the preposition used which prevented to follow the path framed in Fig. 4 and to verify another path which corresponds in this case to the path framed in Fig. 6. This path represents the pattern: صاح = صاح then <صاح> [بشر] | [على + في] (بشر) | [صاح]> if < hurler;).

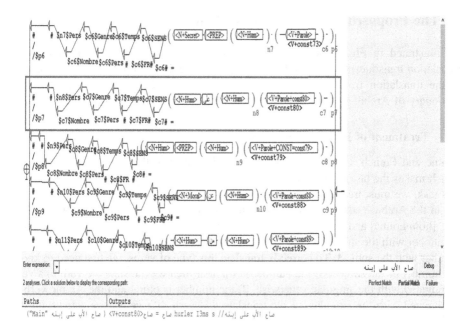

Fig. 5. Sub-graphs imbricates in the sub-graph "paroleHum"

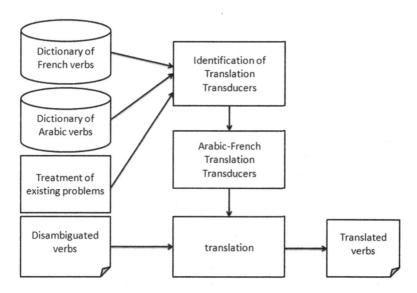

Fig. 6. Proposed approach for translation

The assignment of an Arabic meaning to a verb is not always sufficient to disambiguate it because there are verbs that keep the same meaning even by changing the constituents of the sentences where they are. That's why we used the translation task to improve the disambiguation task.

4   The Proposed Method for Translation

As illustrated in Fig. 6, our translation approach is based on the identification of translation transducers based on the treatment of the existing problems that are related to the translation from the Arabic language to the French language, the identified dictionary of Arabic movement and speech verbs and a dictionary of French verbs.

4.1   Treatment of Existing Problems

Arabic and French, two different languages, do not have the same vision of reality which makes the task of translation non-trivial. Indeed, for the purpose of carrying out this task, we must treat some existing problems.

In the Arabic verbal sentence, using the third personal pronoun of the plural "هم" / "هن" [hom/honna] and the dual personal pronoun "هما" [houma], the verb does not agree in number with the subject unlike the French language where the verb always agrees in number with the subject. To correctly translate this type of verbs, we first need to know the number of the subject: if the number is singular then we translate the verb to a verb conjugated with the singular, otherwise, if, the number is plural and the Arabic verb is conjugated with the singular, so we translate this verb to a verb conjugated with the plural.

In the French language, there are no dual personal pronouns unlike the Arabic language. For this we replace the Arabic dual personal pronoun "هما" with "ils/ells" [they] and the Arabic dual personal pronoun "أنتما" [antouma] with "vous" (you).

4.2   Identification of Translation Transducers

The transducers allow us to translate the verbs of the Arabic language into the French language by respecting their inflections. To do this, we need the bilingual dictionary of identified verbs and another dictionary of French verbs that contains the different verbs used and its inflections in the proper times and with the different personal pronouns. That's why we used the monolingual automatic dictionary "_dm" (Trouilleux 2011) which contains 61666 entries.

Figure 7 shows our main translation transducer which contains at total 7 graphs.

This transducer contains sub-graphs that translate the verbs of the Arabic language into the French language by conjugating them with different personal pronouns and at the correct time.

The Fig. 8 shows different paths in the graph «Présent».

As shown in Fig. 8, disambiguation phase outputs that indicate verb translation, information about the Arabic verb inflection and the number of the Arabic subject are used as annotations to link the disambiguation phase to the translation phase.

For example: In the first graph, if there is a verb (<V>) followed by the word "P3fs" or "P3ms" or "P5" which represent information about the flexion of the Arabic verb followed by "p" which represents the number of the subject or, the verb is followed by "P5" only (in the nominal sentence, we do not identify the grammatical number of the subject since it is useless) then, we conjugate the verb in the present with the 3rd

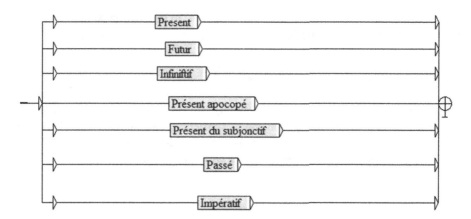

Fig. 7. Main transducer of translation

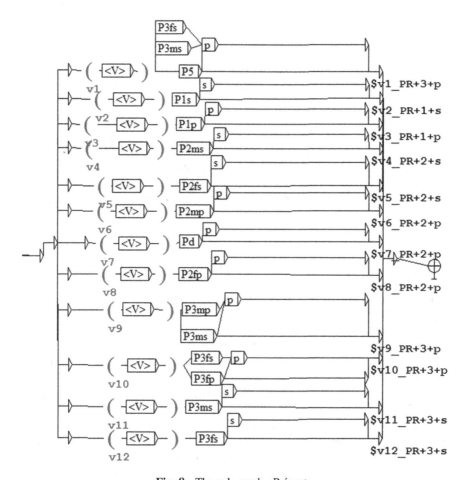

Fig. 8. The sub-graph «Présent»

personal pronoun of the plural. This makes it possible to translate an Arabic verb to the French language by respecting its flexion.

5   Experimentation and Evaluation

The experimentation of the tool of disambiguation and translation of verbs is carried out in a java application, using noojapply, syntactic grammars and specialized dictionary that have already been designed and edited with the NooJ platform.

The Fig. 9 shows Home interface of the java application.

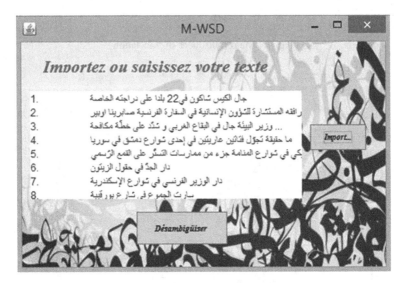

Fig. 9. Home interface

As shown in the Fig. 9, disambiguation is done by importing or entering a sentence or a set of sentences.

We test the validity of our presented disambiguation and translation method by using an application corpus. The texts of the used corpus are articles of the press, books, magazines and blogs downloaded from the net. These texts contain 4710 words that include more than 400 occurrences of movement and speech verbs.

The application of our disambiguation system allows us to obtain the result illustrated in Fig. 10.

As shown in Fig. 10, the disambiguation is done by affecting to the verb its proper Arabic meaning.

For example, the movement verb "جرى" [jara] that exists in position 299 of the text file is assigned to the meaning "جرى" (run). As long as the same verb "جرى" that exists in position 337 is assigned to the meaning "سال " (flow).

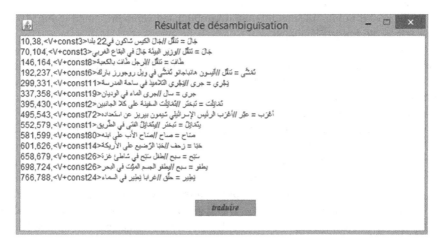

Fig. 10. Extract of the obtained result of disambiguation

The results in Fig. 10 are interpreted by calculating the following metrics: precision, recall, and F-measure (F1). Table 1 illustrates the obtained reults.

Table 1. Interpretation of the result of obtained disambiguation

Precision	Recall	F1
0,9730	0,6295	0,7644

The result obtained is satisfactory, but it shows the existence of some unsolved problems. Some of these problems are related to the lack of some names in the dictionary, the no treatment of the case of intransitive verbs, the case of coreference, the case of presence of punctuation in the sentence or the case of sentences which do not respect the following order: verb-subject-preposition-object complement or subject-verb-preposition-object complement.

The application of the translation transducers allows us to obtain the result illustrated in Fig. 11.

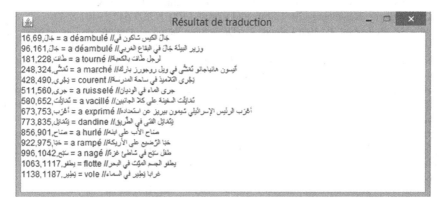

Fig. 11. Extract of obtained result for the translation

As illustrated in Fig. 11, the different disambiguated verbs presented in Fig. 10 are translated to the French language.

Our translation tool for movement and speech verbs provides 52% of well trans-lated verbs. This result shows the existence of some unsolved problems. Some of these problems are related to the absence of vowels (for example if the verb "تمايل" [tamayala] (wobble) does not contain vowels, it can be understand as a verb that is conjugated in the imperative, in the past or in the infinitive).

We compared our translation tool with famous translators who support the trans-lation from Arabic to French. Thanks to the treatment we have done on the different verbs, our developed tool for the translation of movement and speech verbs gives more correct results than that of Google, Babylon and Reverso. For exemple for the input "يَجْري التّلاميذ في ساحة المدرسة", the developed tool translate the verb "جَرى" to [courent], Google translate the input to [Les élèves *sont* dans la cour de l'école], Babylon translate the input to [Les élèves *à la place* de l'école] and Reverso translate the input to [*Étant* élèves dans la cour le yard scolaire].

6   Conclusion

We have developed a tool for semantico-syntactic disambiguation and translation of movement and speech verbs which is based mainly on syntactic patterns.

The phases of disambiguation and translation have been separated: the translation starts once the disambiguation is completed. The goal is to improve the rate of re-use of designed grammars.

The integration of the disambiguation module in online translation systems allows us to obtain more consistent results.

We propose in future works to use other resources useful for the Arabic language to increase the performance of our method.

References

Ben Abacha, A., Zweigenbaum, P.: A hybrid approach for the extraction of semantic relations from MEDLINE abstracts. In: Gelbukh, A. (ed.) CICLing 2011. LNCS, vol. 6609, pp. 139–150. Springer, Heidelberg (2011). https://doi.org/10.1007/978-3-642-19437-5_11

Bouhriz, N., Benabbou, F., Ben Lahmar, E.: Désambiguïsation sémantique de l'arabe basée sur WordNet. In: 4th Day on Information and Modeling Technologies, TIM 2016 (2016)

Brun, C., Jacquemin, B., Segond, F.: Exploitation de dictionnaires électroniques pour la désambiguïsation sémantique lexicale. TAL **42**(3/2001), 667–691 (2005)

Fehri, H., Zaidi, M., Boudhina, K.: Création d'un dictionnaire des verbes NooJ open source pour la langue Arabe. Report of the end of studies project. Higher Institute of Management of Gabes (2016)

Fehri, H.: Reconnaissance automatique des entités nommées arabes et leur traduction vers le français. Ph.D. thesis, University of Franche-Comté and University of Sfax (Tunisia) (2012)

Gaume, B., Hathout, N., Muller, P.: Désambiguïsation par proximité structurelle. TALN, Fes (2004)

Lahyani, I.: الأفعال المتعدّية بحرف إلى فضلة واحدة قيود التوارد و الانتقاء. Ph.D. thesis, University of Sfax (Tunisia) (2013)

Merhbene, L., Zouaghi, A., Zrigui, M.: Approche basée sur les arbres sémantiques pour la désambiguïsation lexicale de la langue arabe en utilisant une procédure de vote. In: 21st Automatic Processing of Natural Languages, Marseille (2014)

Trouilleux, F.: Le DM, a French dictionary for NooJ. In: Proceedings of the 2011 International NooJ Conference (2011)

NooJ Grammars and Ethical Algorithms: Tackling On-Line Hate Speech

Mario Monteleone[(⊠)]

Dipartimento di Scienze Politiche, Sociali e della Comunicazione,
Università degli Studi di Salerno, Fisciano, Italy
mmonteleone@unisa.it

Abstract. The definition of "on-line hate speech" covers all forms of expression that propagate, incite, promote or justify hatred based on intolerance, including that expressed in the form of discrimination and hostility against minorities. Moreover, the concept of hatred includes other sub-concepts such as Homophobia, Racism, Chauvinism, Terrorism, Nationalism, Tolerance/Intolerance, and so on. Specifically, on-line hate speech is used in cases of cyber-harassment, to harm others deliberately, repeatedly and aggressively, in a way so to weaken victims psychologically. To contrast this phenomenon, EC has allocated a relevant amount of H2020 funds for the completion of specific research projects, the goal of which is the construction of computer tools to locate, evaluate and eventually block on-line hate speech. Today, the automatic tackling of online hatred is a daily-performed operation on Social Forums like Facebook, Twitter and Instagram. However, the algorithms these Social Forums use are stochastic/statistical, therefore not suitable to contextualize syntactically and semantically the words used inside posts. Therefore, with on-line hate speech tackling, statistical algorithms may produce inaccurate or even false results, with rather serious consequences.

Keywords: NooJ · NooJ finite-state automata/transducers
On-line hate speech · Ethical algorithms · Rule-based algorithms
Statistical algorithms

1 Definition of Algorithm

An algorithm is an executable process or a set of detailed and unambiguous instructions that must be carried out in a particular order to attain a specific result. Its main function is to effect change in accordance with the procedural and behavioral definition embodied within its formal rendering. The word "algorithm" comes from the name of the 9th century Persian and Muslim mathematician Abu Abdullah Muhammad ibn Musa Al-Khwarizmi.

1.1 Formal Algorithms vs. Informal Algorithms

Algorithms may be classified as formal or informal. Formal algorithms are intended to be readable by machines, therefore are written in formal languages. On the contrary, informal algorithms [1] are intended to be understandable by humans, and are written

© Springer Nature Switzerland AG 2019
I. Mauro Mirto et al. (Eds.): NooJ 2018, CCIS 987, pp. 180–191, 2019.
https://doi.org/10.1007/978-3-030-10868-7_16

in natural and/or iconic language. In this sense, an informal algorithm is any natural language oral/written procedure describing how to attain a goal, going from all gastronomic recipes to the assembly instructions for an Ikea piece of furniture. Largely, formal and informal algorithms share many definition traits, because they establish how the achievement of a given result is the direct consequence of the sequential application of specific instructions. Finally, the main difference between formal and informal algorithms stands in the expression tool, that is, formal language versus natural and/or iconic language.

Indeed, contrary to formal ones and due to the use of natural language, informal algorithms are almost always open to interpretation. Therefore, in order to carry out correctly their functions and procedures, it is necessary to use the cognitive elements of the human system, balancing cognition and practice. As for the human system, it is based on two main aspects: selective resonance and free will. By means of free will, human system shows itself more oriented toward informal algorithms than formal ones. Free will also makes selective resonance possible, implying that the process embodied within the informal algorithm may be treated in a subjective manner. Only certain components may become integral within the system built. Others components may be interpreted and revised, some may be discarded in their entirety. Hence, the process conveyed by informal algorithm is subjected to change based upon the condition of the will of a given recipient. Its subsequent conveyance to another human is therefore pre-filtered: free will allows a freedom of expression which cannot be achieved through the formality of formal algorithms.

While Algorithmics is the science that studies formal algorithms, there are several disciplines that study informal ones, as for instance: Logics, Philosophy, Cognitivism, Psychology, Psychoanalysis, Psychiatry and, last but not least, Computational Linguistics.

1.2 Today's Use of Algorithms

Today, for their research and activities, many disciplines make use mostly of stochastic/statistical algorithms, which are a direct creation of Computational Statistics. This kind of Statistics have developed with the increase in the complexity of the random data generated by the main fields of application related to Biology, Medicine, Finance, Information Processing, and others. It relies on the use of estimation algorithms rather than formal resolution techniques, like for instance Ontologies and Knowledge Management Systems exploiting rule-based Natural Language Processing (NLP) tools. Many and diverse are the applications and functions of stochastic/statistical algorithms. As for Computational Linguistics, for instance and among others, we have, chunking, named entity extraction, part-of-speech tagging, word alignment in machine translation, spell checking, parsing, document classification, anaphora resolution, topic modeling and keyword extraction, word sense disambiguation, and stemming.

1.3   Ethical Algorithm: Definition, Functions, Applications and Controversies

According to [2], many, but not all, algorithms implicitly or explicitly comprise essential value judgments, which means that they are ethical. For instance, if two algorithms are designed to perform the same task, such as classifying a cell as diseased or non-diseased, they are essentially value-laden if one cannot rationally choose between them without explicitly or implicitly taking ethical concerns into account. This means that an algorithm cannot be designed without implicitly or explicitly taking a stand on ethical issues, some of which may be highly controversial.

Besides, [3] states that an algorithm comprises an essential value-judgment if and only if, everything else being equal, software designers who accept different value-judgments would have a rational reason to design the algorithm differently (or choose different algorithms for solving the same problem). When an algorithm is designed to accomplish a specific purpose, its ethical character depends on the evaluation of this purpose. For example, is it right to enable facial recognition of gays, autonomous weapons systems, subprime credit models, sex robots, or targeted advertising aimed at exploiting psychological weakness of vulnerable populations? The answers to these questions are all parts of an algorithm's character. An algorithm cannot possibly avoid having an ethical character when the overwhelming likelihood is that the algorithm will be used for a specific purpose. Ethical issues can also be an unavoidable part of an algorithmic model's construction. Some researchers note that choosing which of several competing algorithms to use requires taking ethical concerns into account. For instance, setting a certain threshold for whether a cell should count as diseased or not depends on the ethical value of avoiding false positives versus false negatives. Other researchers restrict the functional form of an algorithm so that it can be easily explained to those affected by it. The algorithm itself embodies the value judgment that some sacrifice of accuracy is worth the gain in intelligibility. Gaps between the design and operation of algorithms and our understanding of their ethical implications can have severe consequences affecting individuals as well as groups and whole societies.

In a formal sense, algorithms should consider all variations of a given problem, but some problems are difficult and you may not be able to get a reasonable solution in an acceptable time. In these cases, you can often get a solution that is not too bad much faster, by applying arbitrary choices (reasonable assumptions). Therefore, ethical algorithms are also supposed to be heuristic [4], which means that they use an approach to problem solving, learning, or discovery that employs a practical method not guaranteed to be optimal or perfect, but sufficient for reaching an immediate goal. Heuristic methods can be used to speed up the process of finding a satisfactory solution, or mental shortcuts that ease the cognitive load of making a decision. Examples that employ heuristics: a rule of thumb, an educated guess, an intuitive judgment, a guesstimate, stereotyping, profiling, or common sense. A heuristic is always a kind of algorithm, but one that will not explore all the possible states of the problem, or that will begin by exploring the most probable ones.

As for algorithms, heuristics calls into question another important doubt: to what extent can the ethical algorithms be "neutral"? That is, are they able to quickly offer a balanced response to the problems they analyze? This question becomes crucial if we think that with regard to ethical algorithms [5], a very important aspect is that today, in information societies, operations, decisions and choices previously left to humans are increasingly delegated to algorithms, which may advise, if not decide, about how data should be interpreted and what actions should be taken as a result. More and more often, algorithms mediate social processes, business transactions, governmental decisions, and how we perceive, understand, and interact among ourselves and with the environment. Human beings decide less and less; more and more, decisions are let to algorithms that return scores, indices, predictions, which become judgments. The application fields may vary, and include personnel selection, granting of bank loans and mortgages (in terms of applier's reliability), predictive police (in the USA, establishing the degree of danger of a criminal), access to US universities, targeted advertising and evaluation of teachers.

Today, especially philosophers and sociologists support the non-neutrality and unreliability of algorithms in general, and of ethical ones in particular. For instance, [6] states that algorithms are not neutral, and that this is a problem that we cannot underestimate. The mathematical models that decide our lives are not objective, as we believe. On the contrary, they are arbitrary, ideological, irresponsible and devoid of any transparency. Algorithms are usually more objective than humans are, but that does not mean we should trust them wholeheartedly. They may be wrong, for example, when they learn from faulty data, and even the best ones are not omniscient: for many problems, it is simply not possible to have always the right answer. For example, learning algorithms are generally better than human doctors are for diagnosis, so I would prefer an algorithm to do so; but there is no absolute guarantee that it is correct, so I would prefer to know how he arrived at these conclusions. With algorithms, we end up being judged not based on who we are, but on whom we resemble to, where we come from, or what we believe in. In the algorithmic meat grinder, the individual becomes expendable at group regularities; and if it is an exception, worse for him. As Sociology and History teach, this is the matrix of all racism, of every social injustice. Even if algorithmic decisions are presented as neutral, effective, objective and reliable, and so on, we certainly need to have a broader view of the internal structure of the algorithmic systems in which we live. Similarly, we need to develop an analysis of the cultural relevance of the algorithm concept, what that represents, what it does and what it can reveal.

Cathy O'Neil [7] stresses how algorithms slam the door to millions of people, often for the most insipid reasons, and do not offer the possibility of appeal. Moreover, according to Michael Luca, Jon Kleinberg, Sendhil Mullainathan [8], algorithms do not understand compromises. They pursue resolutely individual goals, are capable of making predictions, but do not eliminate the need for caution when making connections between cause and effect; they do not replace controlled experiments. What they can do is extremely powerful: they identify structures that are too thin to be detected by human observation, and use these models to generate accurate insights and better guide decision making. The challenge for us is to understand their risks and limitations and, through effective management, unleash their considerable potential.

2   On Line Hate Speech

On-line hate speech covers all forms of expression that propagate, incite, promote or justify hatred based on intolerance, including that expressed in the form of discrimination and hostility against minorities. The concept of hate includes other sub-concepts, as for instance homophobia, racism, sciovinism, terrorism, nationalism, or tolerance/intolerance. More specifically, hate speech occurs in cases of cyber-harassment, to harming others deliberately, repeatedly and aggressively, in order to weaken psychologically the individuals who are the victims.

On line hate speech is a much more widespread behavior than one might imagine. As shown on [9], according to the Anti-Defamation League and based on a broad set of keywords (and keyword combinations) to capture anti-Semitic language, between August 2015–July 2016 in the USA there were 2.6 million tweets containing language frequently found in anti-Semitic speech. These tweets had an estimated 10 billion impressions (reach), which may contribute to reinforcing and normalizing anti-Semitic language on a massive scale. Also, at least 800 journalists received anti-Semitic tweets with an estimated reach of 45 million impressions. The top 10 most targeted journalists (all of whom are Jewish) received 83% of these anti-Semitic tweets. 1,600 Twitter accounts generated 68% of the anti-Semitic tweets targeting journalists; 21% of these 1,600 accounts have been suspended in the study period, amounting to 16% of the anti-Semitic tweets. Sixty percent of the anti-Semitic tweets were replies to journalists' posts (11% were regular Tweets and 29% retweets). In other words, anti-Semitism more often than not occurred in response to journalists' initial posts.

There was a significant uptick in anti-Semitic tweets in the second half (January–July 2016) of this study period. This correlates to intensifying coverage of the presidential campaign, the candidates and their positions on a range of issues. There is evidence that a considerable number of the anti-Semitic tweets targeting journalists originate with people identifying themselves as Trump supporters, "conservatives" or extreme right-wing elements. The words that show up most in the bios of Twitter users sending anti-Semitic tweets to journalists are "Trump," "nationalist," "conservative," "American" and "white." This finding does not imply that Mr. Trump supported these tweets, or that conservatives are more prone to anti-Semitism. It does show that the individuals directing anti-Semitism toward journalists self-identified as Trump supporters and conservatives. While anti-Semitic tweets tended to spike in the wake of election-related news coverage, the language used in the anti-Semitic tweets was not solely election-related. Many tweets referenced classic anti-Semitic tropes (Jews control the media, Jews control global finance, Jews perpetrated 9/11, etc.). This suggests that while the initial provocation for anti-Semitic tweets may have been at least nominally election-related, the Twitter users generating targeted anti-Semitism may have used news events as an excuse to unleash anti-Semitic memes, harassment, etc. The words most frequently used in anti-Semitic tweets directed at journalists included "kike," "Israel," "Zionist," and "white" etc., an indication that the harassment may have been prompted by the perceived religious identity of the journalist.

As for Europe, and considering only young people [10], it s possible to state that 1 out of 3 have already been cyber-harassed at least once. 78% of Lesbian Gay Bi Trans (LGBT) have already encountered hate speech online. 70% of the targets of hate speech were an LGBT audience (highest percentage). 80% of these speeches were mostly made on social networks. 69% of young people do not know how to cope, react or who to ask for help when they are victims of cyber hate. As for Italy, a recent research highlighted that in Italy the presence of racist texts and speeches is remarkable, even in newspapers as well as in their Web sites/logs. Among the results highlighted, in addition to the close link between hatred and racism, religious intolerance, ultra-conservative politics and nationalist pressures, there is also the low level of education of those who participate in the debates on Italian immigration/reception policies.

2.1 Stochastic/Statistical Algorithms vs. On-Line Hate Speech: The European Community and the «Facebook Affair»

In order to tackle on-line hate speech, through the H2020 program [12] and for the year 2018, the EC has allocated 32.9 million euros [13] for carrying out specific research projects. One of the main goal of this initiative is the construction of computer software, tools and routines that can locate, evaluate and eventually block hate speech online. Furthermore, in May 2017 [14], the same European community had congratulated Facebook, Twitter and YouTube for the progress made in controlling on line hate content. As is known, social media generally perform content analysis using stochastic/statistical algorithms. However, and in a surprising way, on June 28, 2017, an article entitled "Facebook's Secret Censorship Rules Protect White Men from the Hate Speech but not Black Children" [15] revealed how the algorithm used by Facebook was not able to distinguish between hate speech and legitimate political expression. Actually, this algorithm had not banned the following text: "Hunt them, identify them, and kill them. Kill them all. For the sake of all that is good and righteous. Kill them all." On the contrary, it had banned the text: "All white people are racist. Start from this reference point, or you've already failed." Without wanting to carry out content analysis, in this specific case the disparity of choice is clearly unbalanced. This confirms what previously stated on the unreliability of the ethical algorithms, as well as the stochastic/statistical ones. Moreover, if related to the amount of funds allocated by the European Community to tackle on line hate speech, the inaccuracy of the result just mentioned appears even more serious. Therefore, on such basis, two main questions arise: How do we have to structure a good algorithm to tackle hate speech online? Also, is it possible to reckon automatically and precisely the "slur/hatred coefficient" of a given sentence/text?

3 Algorithms, Ethics and NLP

As it is known, Ethics is a philosophical discipline of value judgments concerning the fundamental reflections on which morality will establish its norms, limits and duties. It is characterized by normative, prescriptive or evaluative statements, among which there are categorical imperatives. Unlike the sciences, ethics is based on factual judgments formulated in descriptive statements, among which are hypothetical imperatives. In the absence of a categorical imperative, an ethical formulation is a fault of logic called naturalistic paralogism, which actually confuses a judgment of fact with a normative judgment. The naturalistic paralogism thus passes from the judgment "x does y" to the judgment "x must do y". It is an error of logic occurring especially in ethics when we base a normative judgment on a state of fact.

For philosophers such as Aristotle and Kant, Ethics is about defining what needs to be. As a consequence, an ethical algorithm should be an automatic procedure that, in relation to a problem, especially concerning relations between human beings, finds the solution more "just and balanced". However, we have seen how such a result does not seem to be achievable by means of stochastic/statistical algorithms, and this calls into question a different NLP approach to tackle correctly on-line hate speech, that is to say the use of algorithms based on the formalization of the morphosyntactic rules of a given language, (for instance, NooJ Grammars in the form of FSA/FST). As we will see, such approach may lead us to build a correct Sentiment Analysis useful to reckon automatically, with a very minimal margin of error, the "slur/hatred coefficient" of a given sentence/text.

As for NLP, in Fig. 1 [16], we summarize the methodological and functional differences between the Machine Learning (statistically based) and Grammar Engineering (rule based) approaches.

Two approaches to NLP

Approach	Pros	Cons
Machine Learning (based on keywords)	• Good for document-level • High recall • Robust • Easy to scale • Fast development (if data available)	• Requires large annotation • Course-grained • Difficult to debug • Fail in short messages • Only shallow NLP • No understanding
Grammar Engineering (based on sentence structure)	• Good for sentence level • Handles short messages well • High precision • Fine-grained insights • Easy to debug • Parsing and understanding	• Requires deep skills • Requires scale up skills • Requires robustness skills • Moderate recall (coverage) • Parser development slow

Fig. 1. Differences between Machine Learning and Grammar Engineering NLP approaches.

In the following pages, we will show NooJ efficacy to tackle on-line hate speech. As it is well known, NooJ is an NLP environment based on grammar engineering (i.e. on Lexicon-Grammar syntacto-semantic rules formalization [17, 18]). It embeds all the necessary tools to avoid misleading and fake results (see "The Facebook Affair"), and to build an efficient and reliable Sentiment Analysis to tackle on-line hate speech. Also, it is an excellent hybridization between informal and pure algorithms, as concerns their both construction and application.

4 Hate Speech and Sentiment Analysis

Sentiment Analysis, also known as opinion mining, is the automatic analysis of a large amount of textual data in order to deduce the different feelings, or even the psychological attitudes, expressed in such texts by their authors. This kind of analysis has appeared at the beginning of the 2000s. It is having a growing success, mainly because the feelings extracted can be the subject of statistics on the general feeling of a community, including hate. In this sense, is crucial the abundance of data coming from the most known social networks as Twitter and Facebook.

In the following pages, we will give a concrete example on how to build an efficient Sentiment Analysis routine in NooJ [18]. As for the lexical and semantic aspects, the main step to take is the creation of a specifically tagged electronic dictionary of insults, including simple words, compound words, and phraseology. As for the syntactic aspects, it is fundamental to formalize Italian negation grammar[1] system into NooJ finite-state automata/transducers.

As for lexical entries and phraseology, we will use the following semantic tags: Ig = generic slur; Ir = racial slur; Is = sexist/homophobe slur; Id = defamatory slur; Gren = ethnic/national group; GrenInd = indicative adjective for an ethnic/national group; Prd = undefined predeterminer/quantifier; Qual = quality; Modo = manner adverb. As for the syntactic analysis, we will use the following value tags: EXN (extremely negative, value = −4); ON (very negative, value = −3); MN (average negative, value = −2); NG (negative, value = −1); NE (neutral, value = 0); PO (positive, value = +1); MP (average positive, value = +2); OP (very positive, value = +3); EP (extremely positive, value = +4). The expected results of our NooJ Sentiment analysis will be, in a given text or set of texts, the calculation of the statistical weight of the slurs tags, to drive an automated text storage, together with the creation of a dedicated database. Another expected result will be the combinatorial calculation of the labels of the single elements inserted in syntactic patterns, to obtain their evaluation in terms of sentiment analysis.

---

[1] Because of the complexity of the subject, it is not advisable to propose here an exhaustive analysis of the Italian negation grammar, which basically is also a subject well exposed in the literature and on the Web. However, it is important to stress here that Italian is a multiple-negation language: in sentences, propositions and expressions, the presence of two negative elements is not interpreted as a double denial equivalent to an affirmation of truth, as it is in Logic. This means that to evaluate hate speech in Italian, the analysis of declarative sentences may be not sufficient, and that the formalization of the negation grammar will be mandatory.

5   Tackling On-Line Hate Speech with NooJ

Figure 2 shows some sample entries of the NooJ Italian slur dictionary. We can see how each entry is tagged with both semantic and value tags, which can be used in NooJ concordance and standard score analyses to weight and graphically represent the hate content in a given text or set of texts:

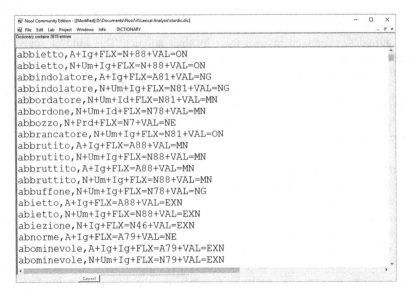

Fig. 2. A sample of the NooJ Italian slur dictionary.

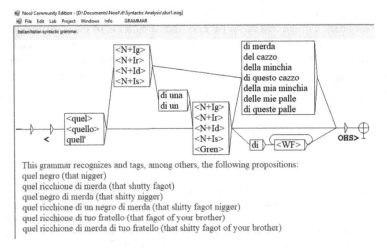

Fig. 3. A sample of hate speech tackling grammar.

Semantic tags can also be used to read and identify specific syntactic patterns containing hate expressions. Figure 3 shows a finite-state transducer which tags as OHS (on-line hate speech) a set of racial and homophobic slurs as for instance "that shitty nigger" or "that shitty fagot of your brother":

In NooJ grammars, variables can be used to sum up slurs value tags and provide numerical results useful for evaluating the hate contents of a given text, as shown in Fig. 4:

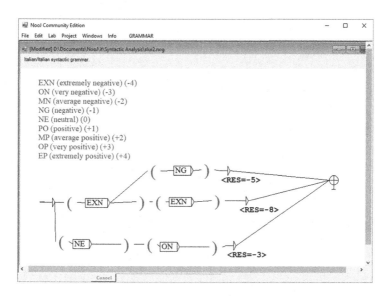

Fig. 4. Variables for the evaluation of hate contents.

A tag of control, as the OHS=CHECK of Fig. 5, may be useful in the case of negative sentences containing hate expressions, as for instance *non è assolutamente un negro del cazzo* (definitely he is not a fucking nigger), the sentiment analysis of which is positive. However, the OHS=CHECK can be used by human controllers to validate the results achieved automatically:

Finally, as for ambiguous sentences which have apparently a positive sentiment analysis, it is possible to build some "interpretative grammars" that give more importance to the insults used rather than to the semanto-syntactic structure of the sentences, as shown in Fig. 6.

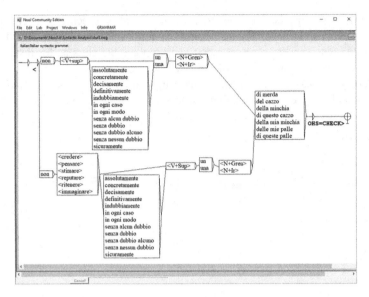

Fig. 5. OHS=CHECK finite-state transducer.

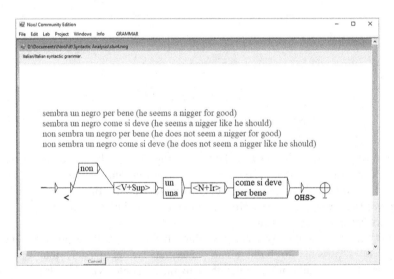

Fig. 6. A sample of interpretative grammar.

6 Conclusion: Possible Applications

We have seen that the statistical algorithms created to tackle on-line hate speech may produce inaccurate or even false results. On the contrary, the adoption of algorithms with the formalization of morphosyntactic rules, that is the use of NooJ finite-state automata/transducers, can be useful to locate, weight and tag precisely online texts that incite hatred. Such grammars could support different kinds of Information Technology tools, both online (servers with free access for the detection of sites inciting hatred), and offline (standalone software module; browser plug-in to; CMS modules for online newspapers pages, discussion forums, or blogs; open API module for website builders; analysis modules to be used also on personal pages or social forum groups; evaluation and validation modules for the e-mails of public bodies, and local administrations).

Finally, as for our current research, the next steps to take will be an enrichment of the linguistic resources to be used, that is the slur dictionary and the grammars. In addition, we will achieve a more deep study of the syntactic patterns susceptible to contain hate speech, especially those concerned by the Italian negation grammar.

References

1. http://psiometrics.com/greatdiesis/archive/algdefinition.html
2. Kraemer, U.A.F., van Overveld, C.W.A.M., Peterson, M.B.: Is there an ethics of algorithms? Ethics Inf. Technol. **13**(3), 251–260 (2011). https://doi.org/10.1007/s10676-010-9233-7
3. https://www.cio.com/article/3232395/analytics/ethical-principles-for-algorithms.html
4. https://en.wikipedia.org/wiki/Heuristic
5. Mittelstadt, B.D., Allo, P., Taddeo, M., Wachter, S., Floridi, L.: The ethics of algorithms: mapping the debate. In: Big Data & Society, pp. 1–21, July–December 2016. http://journals.sagepub.com/doi/pdf/10.1177/2053951716679679
6. http://www.pensierocritico.eu/algoritmi.html. (translation by the author)
7. www.theguardian.com/technology/2017/jul/16/how-can-we-stop-algorithms-telling-lies
8. www.hbs.edu/faculty/Pages/item.aspx?num=50204
9. www.humanrightsfirst.org/blog/hate-speech-online-2016-review
10. www.rtbf.be/info/societe/detail_un-campagne-pour-lutter-contre-le-cyber-harcelement-chez-les-jeunes?id=8146623
11. Scoppetta, C., Alfieri, A., Merenda, F., Lay, S., Colasanto, A., Manna, R.: From language to social perception of immigration. In: Mbarki, S., Mourchid, M., Silberztein, M. (eds.) NooJ 2017. CCIS, vol. 811, pp. 213–224. Springer, Cham (2018). https://doi.org/10.1007/978-3-319-73420-0_18
12. http://ec.europa.eu/research/participants/portal/desktop/en/opportunities/rec/topics/rec-rrac-online-ag-2018.html
13. http://ec.europa.eu/research/participants/portal/desktop/en/opportunities/rec/topics/rec-rrac-online-ag-2018.html#budgetTable
14. http://www.lefigaro.fr/secteur/high-tech/2017/06/01/32001-20170601ARTFIG00142-haine-en-ligne-la-commission-europeenne-salue-les-progres-de-facebook-twitter-et-youtube.php
15. https://www.propublica.org/article/facebook-hatespeech-censorship-internal-documents-algorithms
16. www.linkedin.com/pulse/pros-cons-two-approaches-machine-learning-grammar-engineering-wei-li/
17. Gross, M.: Les bases empiriques de la notion de prédicat semantique. In: Formes syntaxiques et prédicats sémantiques, Langage, 15e année, n. 63, Paris, Larousse, pp. 7–52 (1981)
18. Silberztein, M.: La formalisation des langues. L'approche de NooJ. ISTE, London (2015)

Pastries or Soaps?

A Stylometric Analysis of Leonarda Cianciulli's Manuscript and Other Procedural Documents, with NooJ

Sonia Lay[(✉)]

Dipartimento di Scienze Sociali Politiche e della Comunicazione,
Università di Salerno, Fisciano, Italy
sonia.lay84@gmail.com

Abstract. This paper focuses on the analysis of Leonarda Cianciulli's manuscript, an Italian serial killer better known as "The Soap-maker of Correggio", who murdered three women (Faustina Setti, Francesca Soavi, Virginia Cacioppo) between 1939 and 1940 and, according to her confessions, turned their bodies into soap and teacakes. The authenticity of her biographical memoirs have been disputed for a long time: many scholars claim they were written by people that aimed at persuading the Court of Assize to limit the effects of the charge of murder, because she studied up to the elementary school and probably wasn't able to write such a document of more than 700 pages. Data extracted from the manuscript were compared to other procedural documents, the interrogatories and the letters she wrote to her son while she was in the criminal asylum. This analysis is based on the methodology and the tools of Computational Linguistics, and has three main objectives:

- to evaluate the assumptions of non-reliability of the manuscript, supported by different scholars and experts who examined the document;
- to define a stylometric profile of the woman;
- to detect the most significant traits of her "magical thinking".

Specifically, the analysis was carried out with the NooJ software, and has led to the construction of local grammars able to mine different information about her rituals and obsessions, her murder weapons and methods, her writing style and most used expressions. The identification of stylistic markers plays an important role in forensic linguistics: preferences for certain grammatical constructions, contractions, spelling and punctuation, together with the presence of linguistic mistakes, can provide relevant indicators to make inferences about the author's motivations and characterization. The analysis gives a detailed portrait of a tormented woman, whose real motives generate arguments and debates among scholars even today.

Keywords: Forensic linguistics · Cianciulli · Deviant behavior
Information extraction

© Springer Nature Switzerland AG 2019
I. Mauro Mirto et al. (Eds.): NooJ 2018, CCIS 987, pp. 192–203, 2019.
https://doi.org/10.1007/978-3-030-10868-7_17

1 Preliminary Operations

All the documents have undergone preliminary operations aimed at favoring data processing and computational analysis [7]. Firstly, text cleaning was performed to remove unnecessary information, such as page numbers, comments of the Court during the interrogatories, indexes of judicial cases. The so obtained texts were subsequently saved in .txt files with Notepad ++ editor.

A linguistic analysis was carried out in order to get the most frequent tokens: the three corpora showed the predominance of terms related to the semantic field of "family", with a particular focus on the word "mother" (Tables 1, 2 and 3).

Table 1. Tokens in the manuscript

Frequency	Tokens
1633	mio
1200	mia
545	madre
530	casa
448	miei
410	marito
319	figli
264	figlio
227	Peppino
203	Ina
192	padre
165	cuore
160	Dio

Table 2. Tokens in the interrogatories

Frequency	Tokens
35	mio
27	mia
27	Soavi
19	figlio
17	Setti
16	miei
15	disse
13	casa
13	figli
12	madre

Table 3. Tokens in the correspondence

Frequency	Tokens
24	Peppino
19	mia
16	padre
15	mio
12	madre
12	Iddio

2   The Text Analysis

2.1   A Mother's Love

Through the "locate a pattern function", sequences containing the expressions "my mother" were searched in all the texts, in order to figure out information on the relationship between Leonarda and her parent. The following specific regular expression includes a disjunction operator, which separately returns all the occurrences of the sequences, and the angular brackets for each form, that make it possible to identify the related inflections:

<mia> <madre>|<madre> <mia>

All the concordances tell of an unhealthy bond, full of hate, fear and superstition. As several sequences show, Leonarda believed that her mother had cursed her because she married a man, Raffaele Pansardi, against her will:

"In Salerno, I met my husband and fell madly in love with him - My mother opposed our marriage because she wanted to give me her nephew - I got married anyway and my mother threw a curse on me" [3].

Moreover, in her declarations it is possible to find a strong duality with reference to the representation of motherhood, where an unfriendly and hostile figure depicted by the term "mother" is opposed to the benevolent and careful image of a "mum".

2.2   Norina and Nardina

Leonarda Cianciulli referred to herself alternately as "Nardina" or "Norina", names that her father and mother respectively had attributed to her [1]. We submitted a regular expression query to the three corpora:

Norina|Nardina

The results of this interrogation revealed a higher frequency for the name "Norina". Actually, Leonarda may have developed two different personalities but clearly identified herself more with the female figure conceived by her mother: Norina was active, impulsive and ready to protect her children at all costs; Nardina represented the suffering mother who relied on Norina to solve her problems and defend her family.

A representative synthesis of the inner conflict that tormented the woman is clearly exemplified by the following concordance:

"In my family my mother called me Norina because she hated my father's father, whose name was Leonardo; my father instead called me Nardina - My sisters, to please them both, called me Ina" [4].

3 Magical Thinking

3.1 Introduction

A semantic extension operation was performed on the concept of "magical thinking", through an accurate consultation of different sources. The so obtained semantic field provided us with essential elements for the next phase, which aimed at identifying the most peculiar aspects of her disturbed personality (Fig. 1).

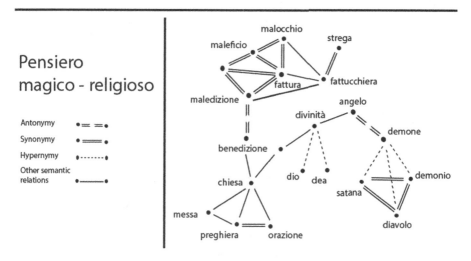

Fig. 1. A small portion of the semantic extension

3.2 Rituals, Spells and Hells

A syntactic grammar on ritualism was built in order to focus on the origins of her superstitious beliefs and suggestibility. Rituals.nog automaton has been provided with two metanodes that include synonyms of the term "witch" and has allowed the detection of different syntactic combinations:

- (<DET>|<A>)<N>(dell'|<del>)<N>: la predizione della gitana;
- (<DET>|<A>)<N>(<A>|<ADV>)<V>: la gitana mia aveva;
- (<DET>|<A>)<N><WF>*<N>: un chiromante prestigiatore che faceva miracoli;
- (<DET>|<A>)<N>(<A>|<ADV>)<V>: gran Dio cosa potevo; il diavolo zoppo replicò;
- (<DET>|<A>)<N>(<E>|<A>|<N>|<ADV>|<CONG>)<V>: le diavolesse dicono.

In the most relevant concordances, Cianciulli declares that she was helped by a Romany fortune teller to save her children from her mother's curse and recalls the myth of the "goddess Thetis": she identified herself with the Greek goddess Thetis who bathed her children in the river Stige to make them immortal.

Therefore she was not a goddess, so she planned a personal strategy that consisted in making human sacrifices.

4   Suspicious Sweets: The Crime Scene Investigation

4.1   Introduction

This section proposes syntactic grammars aimed at retrieving information that gave us the possibility to reconstruct the crime scene, through the comparison of the admissions made by Leonarda in different contexts. Specifically, an automaton including several embedded graphs was built (Fig. 2).

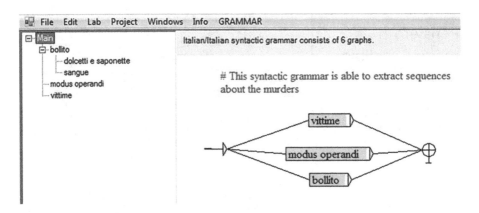

Fig. 2.   Structure of omicidi.nog syntactic grammar

4.2   A Focus on the Victims

The first two graphs, :vittime and :modus operandi, were able to return information about the victims and concordances that specifically deal with murder planning and strategies (Fig. 3).

The possible syntactic combinations contemplated by the two graphs are shown below:

- <V>*(<DET>|<A>)<N>: *commettere quei delitti, commettere i delitti;*
- <DET>(<E>|<A>)<N>(<E>|<A>|<ADV>)<V>*: *la martire sorseggiava, il cadavere mezzo tagliato;*
- <V>(<E>|<DET>)<N>: *diceva assassina.*
- <V>(<DET>|CONG)<N>(<E>|<PREP><DET><N>): spezzare un dito, spaccassero il cranio, spezzare il cuore dal dolore;

modus operandi

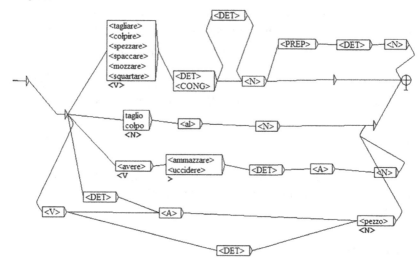

Fig. 3. Modusoperandi graph

- <N><PAA><N>: taglio al ginocchio;
- <avere>(<ammazzare>|<uccidere>)<DET><A><N>: avevo ammazzato le mie amiche;
- <DET><A><pezzo>: l'altro pezzo; gli altri pezzi;
- <V>(<A>|<DET>)<pezzo>: tolsi un pezzo, diventato in pezzi.

bollito

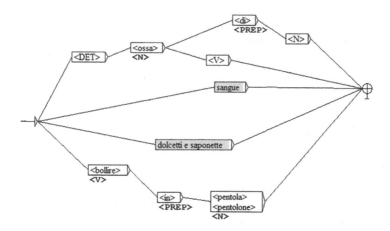

Fig. 4. Bollito graph

The last graph of :omicidi.nog grammar can retrieve expressions concerning post-murders phases, in which the woman, according to her statements, tried to prepare sweets and soaps with the victims' remains (Fig. 4).

- <V>(<E>|<DET>|<PREP>)<N>: fatto il dolce, fare dolci;
- <N>(<E>|<V>)<A>: torte dolci;
- <WF>soda caustica<WF>: la soda caustica allume, e soda caustica allume;
- <sangue>(<ADV>|<A>|<PRON>|<CONG>)<V>: sangue che colava;
- <N><di><sangue>: sbocchi di sangue, tracce di sangue.

4.3   Results

Omicidi.nog grammar has returned nearly 150 occurrences from the manuscript, through which it was possible to reconstruct the murder scenes.

According to the analysis, Leonarda's modus operandi consisted mainly of three phases:

- to hit the victims unexpectedly;

  "The martyr was sipping the coffee I raised the hammer - Ermelinda Setti -
  I think I worked like a thunderbolt, I think my forces tripled otherwise I could not
  do what I did" [3].

- to dissect their corpses;

  "I cut the head I had laid on the sink but no blood came out; later I cut all nine
  pieces into the sink" [3].

- to collect their blood and bones with the purpose of preparing sweets and dissolve their remains with caustic soda to make soaps;

  "With regret I observed that the soap was not perfect, also because I had put
  ash" [3].
  "At the top I put the caustic soda and rosin powder after almost 4 L of water" [3].
  "I gathered blood like if it was jam" [3].

Details about the dissection of corpses and the process of soap-making are given in all the corpora we have processed.

The sacrifice of the three women perfectly reflects the typical attitude of magical thinking, in which it is possible to trade something or someone in order to gain favors by means of supernatural forces.

5   Detecting Deceptions

5.1   Introduction

The linguistic investigation has proceeded with the creation of automata aimed at comparing specific features and information, within the three corpora. This strategy was designed to detect any possible discordant statements and favor the recognition of lies or alterations of the truth [5].

5.2   It is a Matter of Style

The linguistic transcription of the letters made it possible to identify the specificities of Cianciulli's writing style, with particular reference to the most used formulas, the spelling errors and the abbreviations [6], which were used for the construction of Comparazione_stile.nog grammar (Fig. 5).

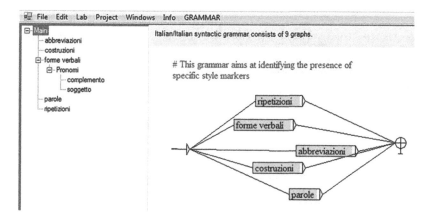

Fig. 5. Structure of Comparazione_stile.nog syntactic grammar

The results confirm that both the manuscript and the letters exhibit the same alterations and linguistic specificities:

- repetitions;

  a poco a poco, piccina piccina, Iddio Iddio, e pregava e pregava, buona tanto buona, baci e baci, orrore e orrore.

- Spelling errors in writing the verb to Have;

  non a'(creduto), che ai (detto), ne ai (voglia).

- Graphic signs on monosyllables that should never be accented;

  non so', chi sa', Dio sa'.

- Peculiar syntactic combinations;

  (quanti regali) ci avevo dati, (tutto ciò che) ci avevo dato, ci avevo data (la vita), (ciò che) ti bisogna, (quel perdono che) mi bisogna.

- Abbreviations;

  S. Antonio, S. Rita.

The comparative analysis of the style markers has revealed a great equivalence in Leonarda's specificities and aberrations, whose large presence is due to an inadequate linguistic competence and an attitude to exaggerate her emotions.

5.3   Analysis of Syntactic Complexity

A specific grammar was realized in order to measure the complexity of the propositions employed by Leonarda in the manuscript. The results were then compared to the concordances of the interrogatories and the letters. Complessità_sintassi.nog consists of five graphs, designed according to the type of proposition they are meant to extract: adversative, hypothetical, concessive, final, causal (Fig. 6).

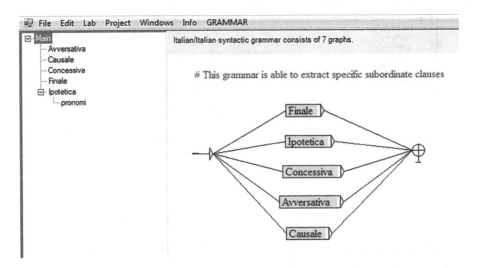

Fig. 6. Structure of complessità_sintassi.nog syntactic grammar

In the manuscript it was possible to notice the prevalence of final and causal propositions; however, although with some errors and in a small number, all the subordinate clauses included in the above-mentioned grammar were found in the text.

Since also the other corpora showed mainly the same results, no great discrepancies were found in the choice of sentence structures and syntactic aberrations. The presence of more complex sentences in the manuscript could depend on different factors, also because the act of writing demands greater attention, and not necessarily be proof of some content alteration.

5.4   Content Discrepancies

The last syntactic grammar was created to catch significant details in Cianciulli's declarations about experiences and facts, in order to notice possible variations or manipulations. "Comparazione_contenuto.nog" includes 4 graphs (Fig. 7):

- :figlio focuses on the information provided by the woman on the loss of her babies, with particular reference to the exact number of the deceased children and the circumstances that let them to death.

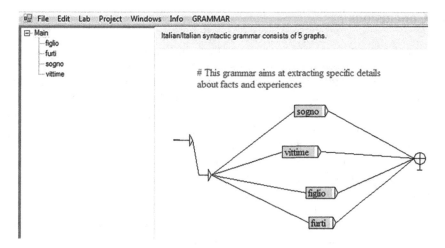

Fig. 7. Structure of comparazione_contenuto.nog syntactic grammar

- :furti is able to retrieve concordances dealing with the charges of theft levelled against Leonarda.
- :sogno was built to clarify the results of a previous interrogation, where the woman attributed the cause of her sacrifices to a nightmare.
- :vittime selects very specific details on the homicides.

Most data provided by Leonarda in the three documents is coincident. With particular reference to the three homicides, below you can see the convergences that emerged comparing the corpora:

- the corpses of Setti and Soavi were cut in nine parts;
- she tried to resurrect her victims;
- she affirmed that Soavi wanted to become her second victim;
- since some specialists asserted that she killed her friends just to steal their money and assets, Leonarda tried to demonstrate that their hypothesis was false revealing that Soavi was poor.

However, some discrepancies about the victims' belongings were found. In the concordances that follow, for example, we can see how Leonarda provides different versions in her manuscript and during the trial about Cacioppo's clothes:

"Not all the clothes were Cacioppo's - the furs were mine" [4].
"I had Cacioppo's fur, the paltò coat and two dresses, so I thought how to do it" [3].

Moreover, during the trial Cianciulli recalled some episodes, related to the appropriation of the assets of the victims, which are not mentioned in the manuscript:

"When I undressed Setti, I found 30 thousand lire in a handkerchief" [4].
"Soavi gave the key of her house to Marta Ferrari, and told her to give it to me because she would leave" [4].

6 Conclusions

The use of computational and linguistic methods in Forensic Sciences has brought to the emergence of a new field of study, where NLP techniques and tools are used to investigate judicial and jurisprudential contexts [2]. In the current study, the employment of computational linguistic techniques has aimed at extracting information that could be considered relevant within the scope of a criminal investigation. Through the comparison of the manuscript, the interrogatories and the letters, the analysis has achieved three significant objectives: the definition of a stylometric profile of the woman, the revelation of the most significant traits and contents of her thinking, the detection of discrepancies and contradictions in her declarations. As for the first aspect, the study has confirmed and enhanced the observations of those researchers who found in Leonarda Cianciulli's behavior a strong suggestibility, theatricality, and a particularly developed magical thinking. Thanks to the transcription of the correspondence, we were able to identify her writing style, syntactic and orthographic aberrations that allowed us to develop a stylometric profile and verify its equivalence compared to her manuscript. Basically, more specific grammars were ultimately built in order to compare Leonarda's statements and language within the documents. Although the analysis has revealed the presence of some discrepancies in the form and contents, we could not find any significant sign of deception in her declarations. We must also point out that Cianciulli's modus operandi is not particularly widespread among women, who only in rare cases adopt dissection practices aimed at hiding their victims'corpses[1].

The results of this analysis make us think that Cianciulli personally wrote her memoirs, although we cannot safely say whether and to what extent they were revised by someone else. The mythological figure of Leonarda Cianciulli is still very controversial, her story keeps on raising numerous questions among scholars, that remain unsolved even today.

References

1. Balloni, A., Bisi, R., Monti, C.: Soda caustica, allume di rocca e pece greca. Il caso Cianciulli, Bologna, Minerva edizioni (2010)
2. Calzolari, N., e Lenci, A.: Linguistica Computazionale: strumenti e risorse per il TAL, Forensics Group, 23 settembre 2016. https://forensicsgroup.wordpress.com/2016/09/23/71/
3. Cianciulli, L.: Confessioni di un'anima amareggiata, in Fascicoli processuali delle Corti d'Assise del distretto, Corte d'Appello di Bologna
4. Corte di Assise di Reggio Emilia, Sentenza – Procedimento penale contro Cianciulli Leonarda e Pansardi Giuseppe, N. 14/46 Reg. Gen. – 133 – vol. XX

---

[1] Cf Accorsi A., Centini M., I grandi delitti italiani risolti o irrisolti, Roma, Newton, 2013.

5. Coulthard, M.: Author identification, idiolect, and linguistic uniqueness. Appl. Linguist. J. **25**(4), 431–447 (2004)
6. McMenamin, G.: Forensic Linguistics – Advances in Forensic Stylistics. CRC Press, Boca Raton (2002)
7. Silberztein, M.: La formalisation des langues: l'approche de NooJ. ISTE Editions, London (2015)

Improvement of Arabic NooJ Parser with Disambiguation Rules

Nadia Ghezaiel Hammouda[1(✉)] and Kais Haddar[2]

[1] Miracl Laboratory, Higher Institute of Computer and Communication
Technologies of Hammam Sousse, Sousse, Tunisia
ghezaielnadia.ing@gmail.com
[2] Miracl Laboratory, Faculty of Sciences of Sfax,
University of Sfax, Sfax, Tunisia
kais.haddar@yahoo.fr

Abstract. Annotating sentences is important to exploit the different features of
Arabic corpora. This annotation can be successful thanks to a robust analyzer.
That is why in this paper we propose to mention the improvement of our
previous analyzer. To do this, we propose a description of our previous analyzer,
which presents advantages and gaps. Then, we choose a method of improvement, which is inspired by the former one. Finally, we put forward an idea about
the implementation and experimentation of our new cascade of transducers in
NooJ platform. The obtained results appear satisfactory.

Keywords: Arabic analyzer · Disambiguation rules · Disambiguation process
Cascade of transducers · NooJ platform

1 Introduction

The parsing of Arabic corpora remains a challenge on account of the richness of the
Arabic language. Due to its morphological, syntactic, phonetic and phonological
characteristics, Arabic is considered one of the most difficult languages to analyze in
NLP. Therefore, the use of computers and new visions can shed new light on the study
of this language. Indeed, with the parsing process, syntactic information becomes
clearer and this helps in such areas as the construction of stochastic parsers, automatic
translators, and the automatic recognizer of named entities.

Despite all the work to date, having a good syntactic representation (i.e. annotation)
of Arabic texts presents a challenge. Existing works suffer from several problems such
as ambiguity and non-robustness. Then, automation, optimization and disambiguation
are always desired and useful to improve a number of processes. In addition, the
enrichment of the system of rules by various linguistic phenomena increases the quality
of the annotation. The essential part in the annotation of a corpus is the constructed
grammar. Furthermore, the tags attributed to Arabic words and phrases must be
expressive to help in the understanding of syntactic information. All these proposed
solutions are feasible by means of a cascade of finite transducers.

In previous work, we have already built a parser based on a cascade of transducers
essentially processing the Arabic nominal sentences. The obtained results appear

© Springer Nature Switzerland AG 2019
I. Mauro Mirto et al. (Eds.): NooJ 2018, CCIS 987, pp. 204–216, 2019.
https://doi.org/10.1007/978-3-030-10868-7_18

satisfactory, but we have detected some problems in the annotation, especially in complex and embedded structures. To solve these problems we first added disambiguation and lexical rules allowing the complete annotation and secondly completed the cascade by the appropriate transducers. To improve the values of evaluation measures, we have also added other syntactic rules concerning linguistic phenomena untreated so far and dealing especially with the verbal sentence.

Therefore, the main objective of this paper is to improve an Arabic NooJ parser based on a transducer cascade with several disambiguation rules. To do this, we added a set of transducers treating Arabic linguistic phenomena by relying on a symbolic approach and based on linguistic studies. Linguistic resources will be constructed using finite transducers that are formalized in the NooJ linguistic platform. We use a corpus to test the effectiveness of our improved transducer cascade. The obtained results, evaluated on a large corpus, are ambitious.

In this paper, we begin by a state of the art presenting some existing works that are involved in the parsing and annotation of the Arabic language. Next, we perform a description about our previous analyzer to present advantages and disadvantages. Then, we present our proposed method to improve the Arabic analyzer and our experimentation. Finally, a conclusion and some perspectives conclude our paper.

2   Previous Work

Syntactic analysis is the result of a formalization of various lexical and syntactic rules. This formalization consists in the representation of various syntactic phenomena. Among the first systems created in syntactic analysis, we find Cass system (Cascaded Analysis of Syntactic Structure) for the parsing of English and German texts [1]. This system is based on a set of finite state automata applied in iterative order. In addition, the work of [9] presented the FSPar annotation system. The author proposed a cascade of transducers for the parsing of the German language. This work is based on a list of recursive transducers treating each group independently of the other forms. This cascade enriched the output text with the various syntactical features for each word. Also, in [4], the authors presented a tool for parsing Arabic text using recursive graphs. The used approach is based cascade of transducers implemented in NooJ platform. This tool is based on three steps: the segmentation phase, the preprocessing phase, and the annotation. Concerning the search for information, we mention the work of [7] which presented the ASRextractor system. The latter is a system for extracting and annotating semantic relations between Arabic named entities using the TEI formalism. ASRextractor is based on a transducer cascade for extraction and annotation.

Also, [2] ensured an analysis of the Arabic language, in particular the phenomenon of coordination. In this work, the author has developed a HPSG grammar based on a hierarchy of types in order to classify the different linguistic units for the Arabic language, essentially the coordinated forms. Besides, there are different researches linked to parsing Arabic language. In [6], the authors proposed a generator of TEI (Text Encoding Initiative) lexicons based on an Arabic word hierarchy.

Among disambiguation systems, we cite MADA, which is a tool providing multiple applications like POS tagging, diacritization, lemmatization, stemming and glossing.

This tool is based on a statistical approach by exploring SVM models (Support Vector Machines). The AMIRA toolkit improves the performance of both platforms. As a result, the MADAAMIRA [8] system explored Arabic and the Egyptian language. In addition to these systems, we find the Stanford parser, which is a system, developed at Stanford University. This parser and the used pos-tagger are based essentially on the Maximum Entropy Model (MEM) called Conditional Markov Model (CMM). The tagger used by the Stanford parser was inspired by the Arabic Penn Treebank (ATB), which provides a large set of tags.

All the cited works show that the parsing of the Arabic language is a difficult task and several issues remain unsolved because the full formalization is always a challenge.

3   Description of Our Previous Parser

In our first version of the parser, we focused on the annotation of Arabic nominal sentences. Indeed, the automatic annotation of Arabic nominal sentences is not an easy task. In fact, the disambiguation process becomes more difficult due to the specific typology of nominal sentences. In the previous work, we proposed an approach to disambiguation. This approach consists of three main phases: the segmentation, the preprocessing and the disambiguation. The segmentation phase consists of the iden- tification of sentences based on punctuation signs. An XML tag delimits each identified sentence. The second phase consists of the agglutination's resolution by using mor- phological grammars. The last phase aims to identify the adequate lexical category of each word in a given sentence and to construct different sentence phrases. This iden- tification is based on several syntactic grammars specified with NooJ transducers. Transducer's applications respect a certain priority, from the most evident and intuitive transducer to the least one. Also, a high level of granularity is used for lexical cate- gories which help to distinguish between nominative, accusative and genitive cases for nouns and can resolve the absence of vocalization.

After that, we implement our Arabic analyzer for the case of nominal sentence in the NooJ platform using a transducer cascade. The implemented parser also permits the automatic annotation of sentences. In addition, to experiment our implemented pro- totype, we used an Arabic corpus that contains 200 meaningful nominal sentences mainly from stories. Also, we used dictionaries containing 24732 nouns, 10375 verbs and 1234 particles. Besides, in our experimentation we used a list of morphological grammars containing 113 inflected verb patterns, 10 broken plural patterns and one agglutination grammar with 40 subgraphs. In addition, we used 70 graphs representing lexical rules, and a set of 10 constraints describing the execution of the rule's appli- cation. Then, we calculate the precision, the recall and the F-measure. As a result, we obtained, in case of precision, the measure of 60%, in case of recall, we obtained 80%, and for the F-measure, we obtained 72%. Those results are ambitious but not satis- factory. In fact, the automation, optimization and disambiguation are needed. Also, the enrichment of the system of rules by the various linguistic phenomena existed increases the quality. The essential part in the annotation is the improvement of the constructed cascade. Furthermore, the tags attributed to Arabic words and phrases must be more expressive in order to facilitate the understanding of syntactic information. All these proposed solutions are feasible to perform our analyzer and to generalize annotations in case of nominal and verbal sentence. To improve our analyzer, we need to know the different issues in the previous version. In fact, we recognize those issues especially thanks to the disambiguation process of our parser.

In the following, we present our proposed method that is based on a previous work, new disambiguation rules and the method of optimization.

4   Proposed Method for the Improvement of Arabic NooJ Parser

To improve our syntactical analyzer, we need to know the different problems in the previous version. In fact, we have recognized some problems especially in the disambiguation process of our parser.

As we have already indicated, the proposed method is based on previous work, that is presented in Fig. 1.

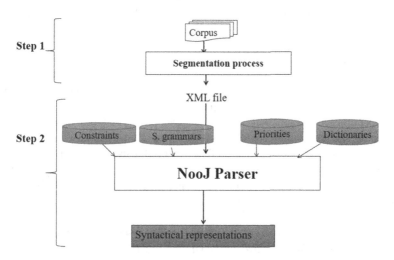

Fig. 1. Proposed method

The improvement of the parsing method is proportional to the improvement of the four entries. Those entries are constraints, syntactic grammars, priorities and dictionaries.

In fact, we elaborate new disambiguation rules and constraints. These rules and constraints are designed in form of transducers and are executed in a cascade with appropriate priorities. To do that, we firstly identify all structures of the Arabic sentences; we then make a study through a corpus for verbal and nominal sentences because a close relationship between these two forms exists. From this study, we achieve a system of syntactical rules allowing the annotation of Arabic sentences. A similar effort was given for the formalization step. In fact, the formalization of elaborated rules requires much effort to guarantee several qualities (i.e., optimization, recursion, without rule's explosion and ambiguities). Secondly, we study the nature of each sub-graph to add new syntactic graphs in the adequate location compared previous cascade. Note that each graph is based on the graph's complexity, the number of sub-graphs and their depth. After this study, we classify graphs by levels: from low complex one to high complex one. Thirdly, we studied the relation between graphs: elementary, embedded and recursive graphs. Finally, we created the transducer cascade, which respects the extracted graph hierarchy. In fact, the cascade executes the established transducers in an adequate ranking. This ranking is identified thanks to multiple experimentations. In the following, we will present some disambiguation rules and their transducers in the new cascade for Arabic sentences starting from specific phrases to entire sentences.

5 Linguistic Studies Allowing the Improvement

To improve the quality of our parser, we have studied several linguistic phenomena, e.g. relative clauses, coordination and ellipsis. In what follows, we will focus on these matters.

5.1 Elliptical Forms

By definition, elliptical forms are characterized by the absence of one or more words in a sentence. By referring to a part of the previous discourse, the general meaning of the sentence becomes understandable. There are two principal types of elliptical forms: nominal elliptical forms and verbal elliptical forms. The nominal elliptical form can exist in a nominal or verbal sentence. In this type of ellipsis, the noun phrase is omitted and can be found in the previous part of the sentence. Therefore, a sentence containing an incomplete nominal phrase contains a nominal ellipsis form. The words in brackets are the omitted words.

كان الثعلب يذهب إلى كروم القرية، ويقطف (الثعلب) العناقيد الحمراء والصفراء والسوداء

The fox went to the vineyards of the village, and the (fox) gather the red, yellow,
and black clusters

In the example, the elliptical form is a single word representing the subject in the elliptical sentence. This is an example of interaction between the ellipsis phenomenon and the coordination phenomenon in one sentence.

Verbal ellipsis exists generally in verbal sentences. In this type of ellipsis, the verbal phrase is omitted and can be identified in the previous part of the sentence.

أكل الثعلب الكروم الحمراء ثم (أكل الثعلب الكروم) السوداء

The fox eats the red clusters then (the fox eats the clusters) black

In the example, the elliptical form is a single word representing the subject in the elliptical sentence. This is an example of interaction between the ellipsis phenomenon and the coordination phenomenon in one sentence.

5.2 Relative Clauses

Relative clauses are the second of the most frequent phenomena in Arabic language. This phenomenon represents a subordinated phrase and it appears in any component of the sentence: either the subject or the object. The relative phrase is introduced by a relative particle, which can be followed by a verbal sentence, a nominal sentence or simple phrases. We illustrate this phenomenon with the following example:

إشترى الرجل الدار[التي تقع على الربوة]

'ishtara alrajulu aldaara allati taka'u 'ala alrabwati
The man bought the house which is located on the hill

The example presents a verbal sentence and the relative form appears in the component الدار (*Al daara*), which is an accusative noun phrase.

5.3 Coordination Phenomena

The coordination phenomenon aims to bring together of at least two linguistic units. The coordinated units can be simple words, phrases, clauses or even sentences. This phenomenon appears in a sentence in form of deleted verb, deleted subject or deleted the object.

[مريم و منال] أختان جميلتان

Maryamu wa manaalu 'ukhtaani jamiilataani
Mariam and Manel are two beautiful sisters

[نسمة فرحانة] ف [اليوم عطلة نهاية الأسبوع] و [جدّها ينتظر زيارتها]

NismatN farhaanatN falyawma àuTlatu nihaayati al'usbuài wa jadduhaa yantathiru ziyaaratahaa
Nesma is happy, the weekend begins today and her grand-father is waiting for her visit

The two previous examples mention two types of coordination: the first one exists inside the phrase, whilst the second connects three nominal sentences.

6 Disambiguation Rules

We carried out a linguistic study which allows us to identify lexical rules resolving several forms of ambiguity. The identified rules are classified with the mechanism of subcategorization.

6.1   Rules for Ellipsis

Elliptical forms can appear in two different sentence types in the text. The first type is the verbal sentence, it depends on the transitivity criteria of the verb, and the second one is the nominal sentence. Several particles connect the original sentence to elliptical forms especially particles of coordination:

الواو ، الفاء ، ثم ، حتى ، أم ، أو ، لا ، بل ، ولكن

Table 1. Table summarizing rules for elliptical phenomena

Type of the sentence	Verb valency	Followed structures
Verbal	Intransitive	VP (NPNOM) (adverb) (PP)*
	Transitive	VP NPACC NPACC (adverb) (PP)*
	Double transitive	VP NPACC NPACC NPACC (adverb) (PP)*
	Triple transitive	VP NPACC NPACC NPACC NPACC (adverb) (PP)*
Nominal	–	TopicNom AttNom

Table 1 shows rules for the ellipsis phenomenon. As we see, there is a dependency between the transitivity criteria and the number of the constituents in the followed structure. We formalize and optimize those rules to obtain a transducer recognizing verbal elliptical sentence (Fig. 2) and nominal elliptical sentence (Fig. 3).

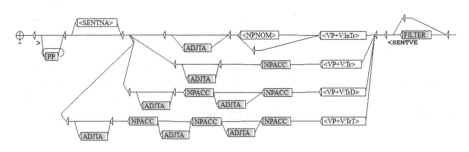

Fig. 2. Transducer for verbal elliptical sentence

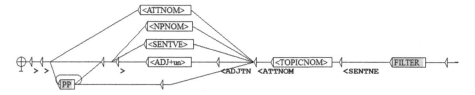

Fig. 3. Transducer for nominal elliptical sentences

6.2   Rules for Relative Clauses

Relative clauses are always introduced by elliptical particles. Those particles can be classified into two parts: particles followed by a verbal structure and particle followed by a nominal structure.

Table 2 displays rules for relative clauses. There are rules acting on verbal sentences and other acting on nominal sentences. We implement those rules through transducers which are illustrated by Figs. 4 and 5.

Table 2. Table summarizing rules for relative phenomenon

List of particles	Followed structures
اللَّذَانِ الَّتِي الَّذِي الَّذِينَ اللَّتَانِ اللَّوَاتِي اللَّاتِي اللَّائِي	Elliptical verbal sentence
مَنْ, مَا, أيّ	Elliptical verbal or nominal sentence

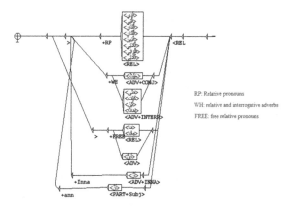

RP: Relative pronouns
WH: relative and interrogative adverbs
FREE: free relative pronouns

Fig. 4. Transducer for relative particles

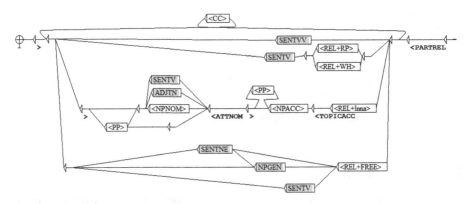

Fig. 5. Transducer for relative forms

6.3   Rules for the Coordination Phenomenon

The coordination phenomenon can link between different units or sentences. And generally the second part of the coordination is an elliptical clause. It can be introduced by the particles of coordination (Table 3).

Table 3. Table summarizing rules for coordination phenomena

List of coordination	Linked structures
Inside units	(NP)*
	(PP)*
	NP CONJ NP
	PP CONJ PP
Inside sentences	SENTV CONJ SENTV
	SENTN CONJ SENTN
	SENTV CONJ SENTN
	SENTN CONJ SENTV

Note that the coordinated forms can appear once or several times and it can be multiple to the same phrase. That is why the conjunction appears in all transducers, especially in filters.

7   Experimentation and Evaluation

To experiment our transducer cascade parser on the test corpus, we have used firstly our segmentation tool presented in [4]. Secondly, we have used our proper tagset inspired by Stanford's tagset (Table 4), a set of morphological grammars (113 infected verb patterns, 10 broken plural patterns and one agglutination transducer) and dictionaries that already exist in the NooJ linguistic platform (24732 nouns, 10375 verbs and 1234 particles). However, the resources that exist in NooJ are not complete and sufficient. For this raison, we have added two other dictionaries. The first dictionary named "verbeintr.nod" contains 91 entries (intransitive, double transitive and triple transitive verbs). The second one named "prenom.nod" for proper nouns contains 105 entries. This dictionary recognizes the missing proper nouns. Thus, all these resources have the same priority except the "verbeintr.nod"; it has a high priority of a single level "H1" compared to others. All lexical resources are presented in Fig. 6.

Table 4. Syntactic resources

NN	Indefinite Nominative Noun u
NTN	Indefinite Nominative Noun un
NND	Definite Nominative Noun u
NA	Indefinite Accusative Noun a
NTA	Indefinite Accusative Noun an
NAD	Definite Accusative Noun a
NG	Indefinite Genitive Noun i
NTG	Indefinite Genitive Noun in
NGD	Definite Genitive Noun i

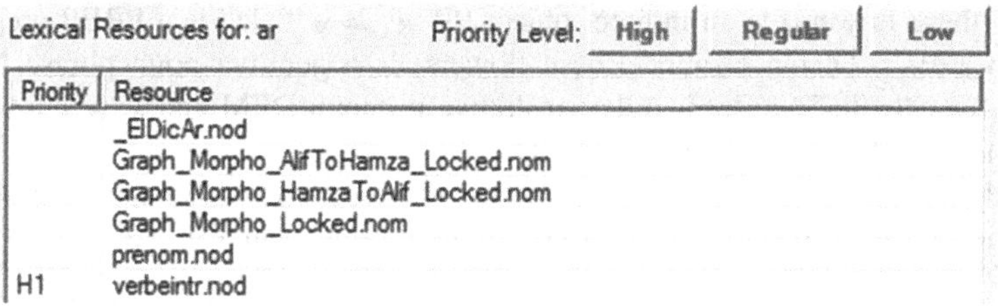

Fig. 6. Lexical resources

Thirdly, the proposed cascade executes 23 transducers including 100 sub-graphs. The transducers that are edited in NooJ linguistic platform called in a fixed ranking. Figure 6 illustrates the chosen order.

Fourthly, we tested our parser on two corpora. The first corpus is extracted from the Arabic Treebank (ATB) containing 836 sentences and the second is extracted from Arabic stories containing 5900 sentences. Concerning the ATB corpus, we deleted the sentence annotations in order to obtain a raw corpus or the test. In addition, the number of words in the sentences of the two corpora varies between 4 and 83 words. These sentences have different forms of verb phrases (with and without tools) with different tenses and modes. Also they have several noun phrase structures (one word, adjectival compound, annexation compound, relative compound, conjunctive compound and adjectival annexation compound).

The test result is a set of XML annotated sentences. As example of a sentence annotation after applying our parser on the following sentence:

لن تريد الطفلة أن تسلم على هذا الزهر

Lan turida altuflatu 'an tussalima 'ala hatha alzahri

The girl would not want to greet these flowers

```
|<SENTV><VP><TOOLSUB>لن</TOOLSUB> <VSUB>تريد</VSUB></VP>
|<NPNOM><NPDNOM><NND>الطفلة</NND></NPDNOM></NPNOM> <NPACC><PARTREL><VP><REL>أن</REL>
|<VSUB>تسلم</VSUB></VP> <PP><PREP>على</PREP> <NPGEN><NPIGEN><DEM>هذا</DEM>
<NGD>الزهر</NGD></NPIGEN></NPGEN></PP></PARTREL></NPACC></SENTV>
```

Fig. 7. Sentence annotation example

Figure 7 presents the annotation result of this sentence. The treated verbal sentence SENTV has « لن تريد » "lan turida" (would not want) which is a verbal phrase VP where « لن » "lan" (would not) is a subjunctive verbal tool TOOLSUB and « تريد » "turida" (want) is a subjunctive verb VSUB. « الطفلة » "altuflatu" (the girl) is a subject that is a nominative noun phrase NPNOM and more specifically, it is a definite nominative noun NND. Whereas « أن تسلم على هذا الزهر » "altuflatu 'an tussalima 'ala hatha alzahri" (to greet these flowers) is an accusative noun phrase NPACC and more precisely it is a relative part PARTREL where « أن » "'an" is a relative REL and « تسلم » "tussalima" (to greet) is a subjunctive verb VSUB and « على هذا الزهر » "'ala hatha alzahri" (these flowers) is an indirect object PP. « على » "'ala" is a PREP preposition and « هذا الزهر » "hatha alzahri" (these flowers) is a genitive noun phrase NPGEN where « هذا » "hatha" (these) is a demonstrative pronoun DEM and « الزهر » "alzahri" (flowers) is a definite genitive noun NGD.

For the evaluation, we used the known metrics: recall, precision and f-measure. We obtain the following results for the ATB corpus presented in Table 5.

Table 5. Table summarizing the metrics obtained for ATB corpus

	ATB corpus	Recall	Precision	F-measure
Cascade parser	836 sentences	0.9	0.94	0.91

The major advantage of the new parser compared with Stanford parser is the great reduction of the execution time (parsing 836 sentences in 59.2 s). However, there is no improvement in the measure values. Concerning the stories corpus, we obtained the following evaluation metric values illustrated in Table 6.

Table 6. Table summarizing the metrics obtained for stories corpus

	Stories corpus	Recall	Precision	F-measure
Cascade parser	5900 sentences	0.74	0.82	0.77
Previous parser	5900 sentences	0,6	0,8	0,72

The measure values of Table 6 show the efficiency of the cascade parser compared to the previous parser. But some parsing problems are detected especially in complex and embedded structures. To solve these problems, we must add some constraints. Also to improve the measure values, we must add other syntactical rules concerning untreated linguistic phenomena and specific to Arabic language.

8 Conclusion

In the present paper, we have improved an Arabic NooJ parser. This improvement is made on a transducer cascade by using several disambiguation rules. This tool is based on an improved method inspired by our previous method. We focused especially in lexical resource and the priorities criteria of each one. In addition, we have shown the efficiency of our new transducer cascade when compared with the previous one. Thus, the evaluation is performed on a set of sentences belonging to two corpora. The results obtained are ambitious and show that our parser can efficiently treat different sentence forms. As for perspectives, we would like to increase the coverage of our designed dictionaries. We will also improve our parser by adding other syntactic rules recognizing frozen forms of sentences.

References

1. Abney, S.: Partial parsing via finite-state cascades. Nat. Lang. Eng. **2**(4), 337–344 (1996)
2. Boukedi, S., Haddar, K.: HPSG grammar for Arabic coordination experimented with LKB system. In: Proceedings of the Twenty-Seventh International Florida Artificial Intelligence Research Society Conference, FLAIRS 2014, Pensacola Beach, Florida, 21–23 May 2014, pp. 166–169 (2014)
3. Hammouda, N.G., Haddar, K.: Parsing Arabic nominal sentences with transducers to annotate corpora. Computación y Sistemas, vol. 21, no. 4: Advances in Human Language Technologies (Guest Editor: A. Gelbukh), pp. 647–656 (2017)
4. Hammouda, N.G., Haddar, K.: Integration of a segmentation tool for Arabic corpora in NooJ Platform to build an automatic annotation tool. In: Barone, L., Monteleone, M., Silberztein, M. (eds.) NooJ 2016. CCIS, vol. 667, pp. 89–100. Springer, Cham (2016). https://doi.org/10.1007/978-3-319-55002-2_8
5. Hammouda, N.G., Haddar, K.: Arabic NooJ parser: nominal sentence case. In: Mbarki, S., Mourchid, M., Silberztein, M. (eds.) NooJ 2017. CCIS, vol. 811, pp. 69–80. Springer, Cham (2018). https://doi.org/10.1007/978-3-319-73420-0_6
6. Maamouri, M., Bies, A., Buckwalter, T., Mekki, W.: The Penn Arabic Treebank: building a large-scale annotated Arabic corpus. In: NEMLAR Conference on Arabic Language Resources and Tools, vol. 27, pp. 466–467 (2004)
7. Mesmia, F.B., Zid, F., Haddar, K., Maurel, D.: ASRextractor: a tool extracting semantic relations between Arabic named entities. In: 3rd International Conference on Arabic Computational Linguistics, ACLing 2017, 5–6 November 2017, Dubai (2017)
8. Pasha, A., et al.: MADAMIRA: a fast, comprehensive tool for morphological analysis and disambiguation of Arabic. In: Proceedings of LREC, Reykjavik, vol. 14, pp. 1094–1101 (2014)

9. Schiehlen, M.: A cascaded finite-state parser for German. In: Proceedings of EACL 2003, vol. 2, pp. 163–166 (2003)

10. Silberztein, M.: A new linguistic engine for NooJ: parsing context-sensitive grammars with finite-state machines. In: Mbarki, S., Mourchid, M., Silberztein, M. (eds.) NooJ 2017. CCIS, vol. 811, pp. 240–250. Springer, Cham (2018). https://doi.org/10.1007/978-3-319-73420-0_20

NooJ App Optimization

Zineb Gotti[✉], Samir Mbarki, Naziha Laaz, and Sara Gotti

MISC Laboratory, Faculty of Science, Ibn Tofail University, Kenitra, Morocco
twinz.gotti@gmail.com, mbarkisamir@hotmail.com,
laaznaziha@gmail.com, gotti.sara1990@gmail.com

Abstract. Most present systems are never finished or completed. They often need to undergo some changes, concerning for instance user's requirements or data formats, or in order to fix bugs and problems, improve the system efficiency or change the operating environment. This set of procedures is called "software maintenance", which is an important phase in the life cycle of any system. However, it is more difficult to maintain a system than to develop it, but it is not difficult to maintain a maintainable system that is extensible and adaptable for any future changes. A model driven system can be considered as maintainable; it is a result of platform independent models transformation. In this work, we have focused on an approach to automate the process of software maintenance. It is a model-driven software evolution concept based on Architecture-Driven Modernization (ADM) approach in which models replace the source code as the key artifact. The objective of the entire process is building a NooJ web application without errors, easy to modify and apt to receive new features. This process contains three phases: the model-driven reengineering, the refinement and the model-driven migration.

Keywords: Architecture-Driven Modernization (ADM)
Model-driven evolution · Parsing · Model-driven engineering · Refinement
Migration · Xtext · Knowledge Discovery Model (KDM)
Abstract Syntax Tree Meta-model (ASTM) · NooJ application
Grammar graphical editor · HtMLM · JavaScriptM

1 Introduction

Actually, software continues to change and evolve not to be like human, that is to say getting older or becoming less immune [1]. This is due to the "software maintenance" applied to refresh any system.

It is necessary to ensure that in the maintenance phase the software continues to satisfy users' requirements and to apply improvements and extensions with the least possible effort. It takes between 70% and 90% of software life cycle.

The use of MDE can reduce the maintenance effort by working with models instead of codes. Besides, the model driven system is extensible and adaptable for any future changes. As well, models contain a separate description for each system artifact. Thus, the system optimization will not be a very complex technique and it will be easy to improve performance without increasing costs.

© Springer Nature Switzerland AG 2019
I. Mauro Mirto et al. (Eds.): NooJ 2018, CCIS 987, pp. 217–227, 2019.
https://doi.org/10.1007/978-3-030-10868-7_19

In general, to develop a new software, we need to construct a high level of abstraction presentation of requirements and designs, and then we transform them into source code [2]. As well as in the maintenance phase, we can just identify the abstractions to maintain in order to apply changes, that of what we call the abstraction method which represents a key role in development and maintenance.

To automate the process of software maintenance, we use an architecture driven modernization-based approach [3, 4]. This architecture is divided into three phases, as show in Fig. 1: the first phase is the model-driven reengineering, that starts by parsing the source code of the existing system and then generates abstract models presented by the KDM Meta model [5] after a number of transformation chains. In the second one, the refinement step is performed: it progressively optimizes the generated KDM models to integrate the desired changes. We proposed for that a refinement method of transformations based on requirements and source code analyses. In the third phase, which is the model-driven migration, we transform the refined KDM models to create the new web program code.

We present below the optimization of the NooJ application [6], in order to improve its performance.

The remaining part of this paper is organized as follows: Sect. 2 is dedicated to the background, Sect. 3 presents the approach and technologies used to optimize NooJ system, Sect. 4 illustrates the result of the approach and Sect. 5 covers the related works. Finally, Sect. 6 summarizes the work.

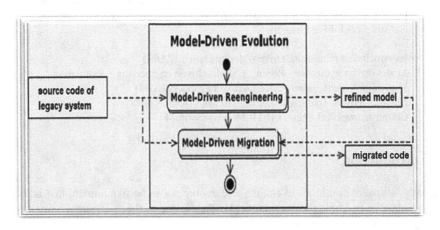

Fig. 1. Model-driven software evolution concept based on ADM approach

2   Background: Model Driven Evolution

In business terms, the software is being evolved because it is successful in the marketplace. The software evolution goal is to adapt system to the ever-changing user requirements and operating environment [1].

As well, lot of software systems become more and more complex over time. Thus, this complexity does not refer to computational aspects, but to the effort needed to understand the functionality of a given software system.

This effort depends on the structure of the software, namely on its components and the relations they set, an aspect that makes a software system more difficult to change.

In this paper, we use MDE techniques to support the software system evolution, namely considering that the software system evolution is pricey and risky.

Therefore, we will investigate the employment of the MDE methodology based on automation, which will be applied to the system evolution to provide cheaper and more reliable results.

We focus on MDE technologies based on a set of standards defined by the Object Management Group (OMG) under the name: Model Driven Architecture (MDA) and Architecture Driven Modernization (ADM) [7].

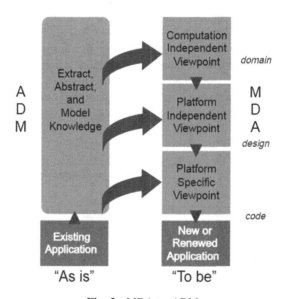

Fig. 2. MDA vs ADM

Within MDE, models are central units instead of codes. The concept of MDA is to develop a software by transforming abstract models, which are platform independent, (PIM) into more concrete Platform Specific Models (PSM) and finally into codes (see Fig. 2).

In addition to this approach, a model-driven framework should also address the way to integrate and modernize existing legacy systems according to new business needs. This approach is known as architecture-driven modernization (ADM) in the OMG. Basically, it includes three major steps. It starts from source-code to instance PSM models, then successive transformations are applied to build PIM model called Knowledge Discovery Meta-model (KDM).

Using this model, several modernization, optimization, and modification activities can be performed to solve legacy system problems. As a result, we transform the obtained PIM model into a PSM one, then to a modernized version of the target system source code.

Furthermore, MDE is based on a basic abstraction idea, i.e. the development of software by separating functional specifications from the technical details of a specific platform.

The support of the automated model transformation and abstraction were the principal reasons for which we were interested in MDE technologies to handle software evolution tasks.

3   Approach and Technologies

In this work, we want to achieve software systems evolution using the model driven engineering approach that reduces the maintenance effort by working at the model instead of the code level.

During maintenance, we focus on identifying the abstractions of the existing software implementation in order to make modifications correctly.

The entire process is divided into three phases. Figure 3 shows the first phase, which is the model-driven reengineering. It starts with the source code of the existing systems, in order to reverse engineer it into KDM models as platform independent models.

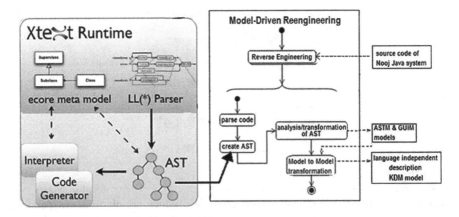

Fig. 3. The model-driven reengineering phase

In this phase, various tools are used to extract information from the source code. The existing source code is transferred, and thereby analyzed into a code-model. Clearly, the program code is parsed and converted into an Abstract Syntax Tree (AST) that will be subsequently parsed to generate the AST model. This model represents the code structure and the GUI model represents the presentation layer.

For it, we used the Xtext parser that leverages the powerful ANTLR parser which implements an LL(*) algorithm [8].

During the processing, these code-models are created and analyzed by various analysis tools, with the help of model slicing technique. The aim is to improve the maintenance engineer's understanding.

After that, we analyze all the information obtained and present it in a higher level of abstraction using a model-to-model transformation implemented by QVTo transformation language [9]. This abstraction is presented in KDM models.

In the second phase, in order to make modifications or apply changes to satisfy users' requirements, and for improvements and extensions of software systems, we used a refinement method to add these changes in the generated KDM model through PIM-to-PIM transformation. The new refined KDM model contains all modification needed.

In the third phase, the model-driven migration step is performed. It integrates the existing functionality and creates new or modified program code, according to the new platform. It gradually remodels an application within the model level from a higher to a lower level of abstraction. It integrates the existing functionality and creates new or modified program code. Clearly, the obtained refined KDM models are then migrated to other models with web components, as for instance javaScriptM and HtMLM models.

Finally, we generate the target source code in the web platform by keeping the same appearance of the legacy system interfaces. For that, a model-to-text transformation is defined, and it is based on Acceleo technology [10], in order to generate the code with web interfaces (see Fig. 4).

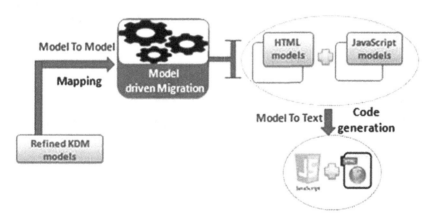

Fig. 4. Model driven migration phase

In this work, we focused on the NooJ graphical editor as a case study to implement the process. The equivalent web editor will be based on the Konva.js [11]. The criteria listed in the table below favor the choice of Konva over the other existing frameworks in the market as the framework adopted for the creation of the NooJ web editor (Table 1).

Table 1. Comparative table for why we use Konva.js

Features	Konva.js	fabric.js
Documentation	Well	Well
Flexibility	Flexible	Little flexible
Learning	Easy	Not easy
Layering system	Considered	Not considered
Object transforming tool	Manually implemented	Easily implemented

Konva extends the 2d context by enabling canvas interactivity for desktop and mobile applications. It supports the features figured in Fig. 5:

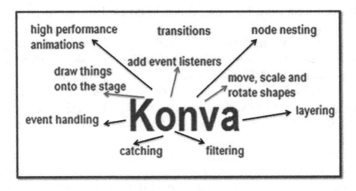

Fig. 5. Konva features

To control and ensure the quality of our approach, we analyze the most important part responsible for graphs editor. Figure 6 shows the amount of analyzed data.

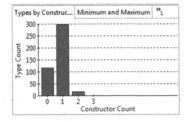
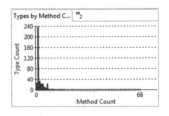
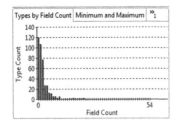
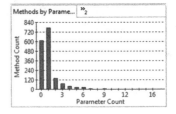

Fig. 6. NooJ source code analysis

Our work considers all these necessary elements for the graphical edition of the grammars, in order to generate modern NooJ UIs that respect the same appearance of the legacy ones.

4   Result and Discussion

The implementation of NooJ in java has a structural aspect and not oriented-object aspect. Thus, nodes properties are managed in separate tables and not in a node objects. Also, nodes are identified by an index which allows us to retrieve all their information.

This structure has facilitated the correspondence operation between the java and web-based systems. Figure 7 is an example of node creation mapping.

```
if (e.isControlDown() || e.isAltDown())
{
    // create a new node
    int rx = (int) (controller.mouseOX / controller.grf.scale) - controller.grf.epsilonWid / 2;
    int ry = (int) (controller.mouseOY / controller.grf.scale);
    int snode = controller.grf.addNode("<E>", rx, ry);
```

```
container.addEventListener("click", function (event) {
    graph.mouseX = event.clientX - document.getElementById('container').getBoundingClientRect().left;
    graph.mouseY = event.clientY - document.getElementById('container').getBoundingClientRect().top;
    if (event.ctrlKey) {
        createNode();
```

Fig. 7. Node creation

However, we encountered a problem with mapping event bubbling and layer event canceling: when we trigger a node event, the layer event gets triggered also in the target web system. To solve this problem, we created a box above the layer, which overrides the layer (see Fig. 8):

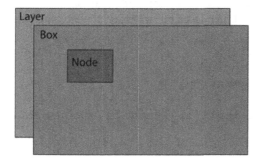

Fig. 8. NooJ layering system

This event treatment will lead us easily to the proper management of nodes selection. This is the equivalent algorithm for node creation:

```
//allowing the selected nodes to blink
If (nodes are selected())
For each node
   Get the node coordinates, width and height
   Draw four arcs in the top, left, bottom & right
   Increment a variable timer var each number of sec-
   ond
While (var has changed its value)
   Change the selected node flashing color
   Repaint() the graph by adding marks to the selected
   node
```

To improve the performance of sub-graph generation treatments, we apply our optimization algorithm that uses the refinement method, with the following refinement algorithm:

```
Add Main graph to the top of the tree.
Visit it nodes that start with ":"
If nodes are not in the tree and are not yet visited
   If they are graphs
      then call the method VisitEmbeddedGraphs() to
      visit its sub-graphs
   If not
      Add these nodes to the tree + "X" character
      ...
```

The above algorithm does not work when it comes to a graph with multiple levels of nesting. It raises a problem in editing a nested graph. To solve this problem, we proposed the following algorithm:

```
Add main graph to the top of the list.
Add it nodes that start with ":" in subGraphs object-
json
Foreach subgraph
   If it has cheldren
      CreateElement('ul')
   Else
      createElement('li') add "X" character
      ...
```

As stated before, we focused on the NooJ graphical editor that allows graphical manipulation of grammars. For this, several analyses have been applied in order to extract all the necessary elements. This automatic process reproduces user interfaces with modern representation. It retains data related to graphical components: properties, position and behavior.

Figure 9 represents the graph of the equivalent "_Date Translation en2fr" grammar in web platform:

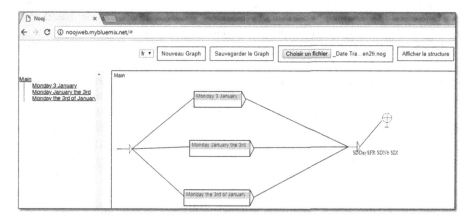

Fig. 9. "_Date Translation en2fr" graph structure

You can navigate in this grammar structure, by opening its sub-graphs. Figure 10 shows an example of "Monday the 3rd of January" sub-graph with the display of node selection:

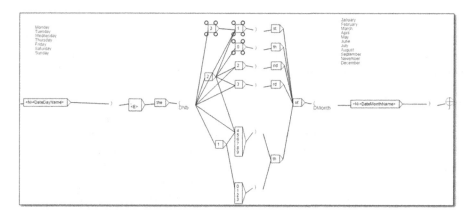

Fig. 10. The third sub-graph

5 Related Works

Here, we briefly discuss a selection of the most relevant works on model-driven evolution.

The authors in [12] argue that modeling environments did not treat software evolution problems, which leads to an emerging need to deal with software changes at the model level. They analyze the problems raised by the evolution of model-based software systems and identify challenges to be addressed by research in this area.

Thanks to [13], we have focused on the Architecture Driven Modernization ADM approach, as the best solution for the NooJ system evolution, in order to capture all knowledge needed for the construction of the future web NooJ system. The process affects both the structural and behavioral aspects of the NooJ user interfaces.

In [2] the authors propose an ADM-based approach that uses a static and dynamic analysis to obtain knowledge of the structure and behavior of source code. The approach gives a solution that generates three independent models (KDM, IFML and TaskModel) for good understanding and evolving the existing software artifacts. The models capture the aspects about tasks, presentation and dialog structures and behaviors of the design knowledge needed for the construction of the future user interface (UI). They use a static and dynamic analysis to obtain knowledge of the structure and behavior of source code.

In [14], authors have focused on the forward engineering phase of ADM by generating Platform-Specific Models (PSM) from KDM, which is an independent-language platform, and it is able to represent several aspects of a software system. They consider this phase as essential as it belongs to the final part of the horseshoe cycle of ADM that completes the reengineering process.

6 Conclusion

The main concern of this work was to investigate the techniques that reduce the risks and costs involved in the evolution of the NooJ system. To structure this procedure, we introduced a model-driven methodology to record, analyze and understand the NooJ system information. The approach relies on the ADM features. First, we started by presenting the extracted information in two models, which are ASTM and GUIM. Then, we transformed these models into a higher level of abstraction presented by KDM models. After that, we used the refinement method to add required system changes. Finally, we migrated the refined KDM models obtained into new specific platforms, which are the JavaScript and HTML, to benefit from the web technologies assets. The process generated just 30% of the desired result and we developed the 70% remaining code. This is due to the disparity between the two development environments.

References

1. Fürnweger, A., Auer, M., Biffl, S.: Software evolution of legacy systems - a case study of soft-migration. In: Proceedings of the 18th International Conference on Enterprise Information Systems (2016). https://doi.org/10.5220/0005771104130424
2. Gotti, Z., Mbarki, S.: Java swing modernization approach - complete abstract representation based on static and dynamic analysis. In: Proceedings of the 11th International Joint Conference on Software Technologies (2016). https://doi.org/10.5220/0005986002100219
3. Platform Level Task Force. In: ADM Platform Task Force|Object Management Group. http://adm.omg.org/
4. Wagner, C.: Model-driven software migration. Model-Driven Software Migration: A Methodology, pp. 67–105. Springer, Wiesbaden (2014). https://doi.org/10.1007/978-3-658-05270-6_3
5. Knowledge Discovery Metamodel (KDM). https://www.omg.org/technology/kdm/
6. Silberztein, M.: NooJ. In: Proceedings of HLT/EMNLP on Interactive Demonstrations (2005). https://doi.org/10.3115/1225733.1225739
7. Bézivin, J.: Model driven engineering: an emerging technical space. In: Lämmel, R., Saraiva, J., Visser, J. (eds.) GTTSE 2005. LNCS, vol. 4143, pp. 36–64. Springer, Heidelberg (2006). https://doi.org/10.1007/11877028_2
8. Efftinge, S., Spoenemann, M.: Why Xtext? In: Xtext - Language Engineering Made Easy! https://www.eclipse.org/Xtext/
9. About the MOF Query/View/Transformation Specification Version 1.3. https://www.omg.org/spec/QVT/About-QVT/
10. Obeo Acceleo. In: The Eclipse Foundation. https://www.eclipse.org/acceleo/
11. Konva.js - JavaScript 2d canvas library. In: Konva.js - JavaScript 2d canvas library. https://konvajs.github.io/
12. Van Deursen, A., Visser, E., Warmer, J.: Model-driven software evolution: a research agenda. Technical Report Series TUD-SERG-2007-006 (2007)
13. Gotti, Z., Mbarki, S., Gotti, S., Laaz, N.: Nooj graphical user interfaces modernization. In: Mbarki, S., Mourchid, M., Silberztein, M. (eds.) NooJ 2017. CCIS, vol. 811, pp. 227–239. Springer, Cham (2018). https://doi.org/10.1007/978-3-319-73420-0_19
14. Angulo, G., Martín, D.S., Santos, B., et al.: An approach for creating KDM2PSM transformation engines in ADM context. In: Proceedings of the VII Brazilian Symposium on Software Components, Architectures, and Reuse on - SBCARS 2018 (2018). https://doi.org/10.1145/3267183.3267193

Author Index

Printed in the United States
By Bookmasters